# IN MA HEAD, SON

*Also by George Sik*

**I Think I'll Manage:**
**Football Managers Reveal the Tricks of Their Trade**

# IN MA HEAD, SON

# SON

*The Footballer's Mind Revealed*

Pat Nevin and George Sik

**HEADLINE**

First published in 1997 by
HEADLINE BOOK PUBLISHING

10 9 8 7 6 5 4 3 2 1

British Library Cataloguing in Publication Data

Sik, George
In ma head, son!
1. Soccer – Great Britain
I. Title II. Nevin, Pat
796.3'34'0941

ISBN 0 7472 1978 8

Typeset by Avon Dataset Ltd, Bidford-on-Avon, Warks

Printed and bound in Great Britain by
Mackays of Chatham PLC, Chatham, Kent

HEADLINE BOOK PUBLISHING
A division of Hodder Headline PLC
338 Euston Road
London NW1 3BH

For my Dad, Mum and Annabel
**Pat Nevin**

For my family and friends
**George Sik**

# Contents

# Acknowledgements

George of course and all those he mentioned.

My family for laid-back support.

Friends for their help, indulgence and consideration.

Fans of Chelsea, Clyde, Everton, Tranmere and Scotland for their encouragement.

Players for not hounding me out.

The PFA for the incalculable good they do for me and every other footballer.

Good coaches and managers. From schools and boys' clubs all the way to the international teams, the best ones do it for the love of the game and for the selfless joy of helping kids make it in football and in life.

Pat Nevin

I suppose my biggest thanks should go to Pat for being so easy to work with, however sickeningly corny that may sound. I'd also like to thank our literary agent, Jonathan Harris, along with Ian Marshall, Lindsay Symons and all the team at Headline for letting us do our own thing, revealing very little of what we were up to until the eleventh hour. I appreciate what this must have done for their blood pressure.

Further thanks go to Mum, Dad, Joan and my new brother-in-law Steve for their encouragement and support when computers crashed and discs went pear-shaped, as they tend to. The enthusiasm of my friends, as always, means everything to me. I won't name them or they'll want free copies, but I couldn't do this sort of thing without their humour, their honesty and their drinks. They know who they are and how much I appreciate them.

Finally, thanks to Kevin Keegan and to all the staff and regulars at Scribes – gone, but not forgotten.

George Sik

# Preface: It Happens to the Best of Us

*So many changes have befallen football recently that there can be little left to surprise anyone who follows the game. When Pat Nevin was sent off, however, jaws fell and, as* loaded *magazine would say, bacon sandwiches were dropped. Pat Nevin and red cards went together like Mary Whitehouse and the* Sunday Sport. *Here was a player who was chairman of the Professional Footballers' Association, one of the game's respected elder pros, a player admired as much for his agile mind and his ability both to articulate and to record his views on the game as for his breathtaking ball-control and the speed at which he twisted and turned past defenders – and there was an early bath waiting for him. How did it feel to receive the only red card in your career? This was just one of many fascinating areas we were to discuss over a turbulent season, a season nearer the end of his career than the beginning, enabling him to look back on what he'd learned and on the changes he'd seen in the game. In a season where injury plagued him, his manager's faith in him seemed at times to be nonexistent and commitment to his union came very close to him leading footballers out on strike, Pat never brushed a single issue under the carpet. It was the first time he had bared his soul in this way, but the result was a very different kind of football book to that produced by many players in his position . . .*

George:   It was your first red card ever. What was the build-up to this moment of destiny?

Pat:      It was really annoying. It happened on one of those nights where you knew that things weren't going to go right from the very start. I'd been back from injury, playing in the previous six games and things were really going quite well. Then I was told by the manager that he didn't want to play me against Charlton, because on the previous occasion when Tranmere had played them, we hammered them 4–0 and he was keen to put out exactly the same side again. I could see the logic behind that, so I didn't grumble.

Things didn't go well and with us trailing 2–1, he brought me on for about half an hour. As I came on, one of our defenders, Gary Stevens, came off, having broken his arm in the course of a tackle, so the situation was looking a bit tricky as it was.

I was actually quite pleased with my performance. I had created a few chances and helped make a few more. We kept hassling and hassling and it looked as though we were going to get the equaliser, even with two minutes to go. I received the ball and tried to pass it back to our centre-back, who was standing on the centre-circle, but it stuck in the mud. There was that horrible moment when both your centre-halves look at it, but the opposing centre-forward manages to nip between the two and intercept that short pass. Although the goal is 50 yards away and there are three players between them and the goal, you just know at that point that he's going to score! You've seen it before. When the ball ricochets in a certain way, you know it may not happen for about 10 seconds, but it's *definitely going in that goal*!

George:   The fans feel those moments, too. I've seen the ball bounce in a particular way and *known* it was going to result in a goal.

Pat:   There is a sense of inevitability about it all. Anyway, Carl Leaburn, the Charlton centre-forward, had the ball and I knew that I had to try and catch him, so I threw everything into it. It was the fastest I had run this season over 60 yards. He flicked it around our keeper, and was brought down by our keeper in the process. I was hurtling towards him at full speed, unable to stop, so I jumped over the top of him, falling over as I did so. Their left-winger got to the ball and slotted it in.

George:   And then came the red card. How did it feel at the moment you saw it?

Pat:   The referee must have been absolutely desperate to send me off. I don't think my knees had touched the ground before he had whipped that red card out. There's a new rule at the moment which states that if there is the possibility that the other team can obtain an advantage from what's happened, the ref can allow the play to go on for a few seconds. If the referee had done that, Charlton's goal would have stood, they would have been 3–1 up and the game would have been over. Instead, he felt it was much more sensible to stop the game, send me off and award a penalty.

Well, Charlton scored anyway, but there was a lot of furore over my sending-off, which resulted in a fracas with 30 seconds of the game left to go. What could have been a sweet victory for Charlton ended on a sour note. It almost ended in major disgrace.

On seeing the evidence, the referee admitted he'd sent the wrong man off. He had also accused me of diving in the penalty area at the other end earlier on in the match, and the video evidence showed that I *had* been fouled and it *had* been a penalty. So it could easily have been 2–2, rather than 3–1 with a player sent off. With a player sent off in each of the two previous matches we'd played – under equally dubious circumstances – benevolence towards the refereeing position isn't exactly running high at Tranmere.

George: But what did it feel like at the actual moment you saw that red card? Did it have the same devastating effect that Gazza's second yellow card did against Germany in the semi-finals of Italia 90?

Pat: Everyone wants to know how I felt the moment he brandished it. To be honest, I can't really remember it. I remember it through pictures I've seen subsequently. There was one in the *Daily Mail* the following day. I didn't get it, but I saw it over someone's shoulder.

George: And they'd caught your facial expression?

Pat: Yes, they had – and it was wonderful! I looked totally shell-shocked and devastated at the unfairness of it all. It wasn't a case of: 'Oh! There goes my record of 750 games without being sent off.' I don't really give a monkey's about that – perhaps I should! It's not something I'm hugely proud of, it actually means very little to me. I was just stunned by the unfairness of that particular moment. It was more the fact that the game was finished, we'd lost and I'd directly contributed to it. That was the most upsetting thing.

We appealed, but the FA said they couldn't even look at the video because it wasn't mistaken identity, it was simply a refereeing error, which is what we submitted in the appeal. They added that even if it was mistaken identity, then our keeper was the one who brought Carl down and he'd have to serve the punishment instead. As a result, I said that I'd drop my appeal. Having done that, and told all the newspapers that I'd take the rap, a week later I heard that my punishment had been quashed. It was farcical. Who knows if they'll change their mind again!

The hilariousness of it all certainly impacted on other people. For it to happen to the chairman of the PFA must have led to a lot of sly giggling. It's like when a vicar is caught with his pants down. My wife was listening to the match on the radio, while driving up to Scotland with the kids. When she heard the news, the car nearly veered off the A7. At first she thought they must have mixed me up with Kenny Irons or someone. Then Kenny Burns, who was commentating, said: 'Oh no! Not Nevin *again*? The man's an animal!' Deep irony, I think. Especially as it was coming from Kenny Burns, of all people. Actually, I found Kenny's remarks rather funny. Anyway, my wife found it hilarious and so did everyone at the PFA. Gordon Taylor actually tried to console me, asking: 'Was it just a moment of madness?' He of little faith! I'll try not to gloat too much about getting off. Or maybe I will!

Everyone was very concerned that I'd be much more upset over the red card than the result, but I'm really not sufficiently self-absorbed for it to mean that much to me. It happens to centre-backs in our team with monotonous regularity. If it has to be my turn, it has to be my turn. Any shock, as suggested by the photo, must have been very momentary. That just gave way to disappointment. However, it did strike me that although I'd played really well during the game, the sending-off was all that people would recall.

Of course, people tend to remember things like that, the freak incidents. I've played in 750 games, scored about 150 goals and represented my country, yet people still ask me about that penalty miss against Man City. I guess that's part of our culture.

*George*: It's the same with Paul Gascoigne. The first thing people remember is the tackle in the 1991 FA Cup final that led to his knee injury.

*Pat*: Yes. They remember that over a million pieces of wonderful skill. It's the same with Chrissy Waddle – it's the penalty miss in that same World Cup semi-final that Gazza got his second yellow card. Now the same is true of Gareth Southgate and Gary McAllister. People award these single incidents disproportionate significance. Football is very unfair that way. And what about yourself? You've done all that studying as a psychologist, trained all those people, written all those papers and articles, and the first thing people ask you about is when you were a contestant on *Blind Date* 10 years ago! Is there no justice in the world?

*George*: I fear not. They'll probably end up putting this right at the front of the book.

*Pat*: They wouldn't dare!

*George*: Yes, they would. Publishers are like that.

*Pat*: By the way, what *was* it like on *Blind Date* . . . ?

# INTRODUCTION:
# How This Book Came to Be

*George*:
*The footballer's mind revealed?* That's going to be a very short book,
isn't it? You might as well do one on Jeremy Beadle's sex appeal
and knock out Chris Evans' guide to etiquette while you're about
it. It'll take you about an hour.'

It's a reaction I had been expecting. The tabloid stereotype of
the footballer (thick as two short planks, mock-Tudor dwelling,
married to or knocking about with a model, likes Tina Turner,
Phil Collins, Oasis, *Only Fools and Horses*, chicken and beans)
is still evoked readily, even by publications that should know
better. When you're a psychologist, the paraphernalia is
different but the caricature is just as strongly drawn (beard,
glasses, couch, Rorschach inkblots, word association, funny
tie). It's the stuff of cartoons in the *New Yorker*, and of course,
*Punch*, which has always nicked ideas for its cartoons from the
*New Yorker*, giving people in this country the misleading
impression that psychoanalysis is as popular on these shores
as it is in Manhattan.

Pat and I were aware of these stereotypes when we set out to
write this book, and we were determined to have a bit of a
laugh with them (hence the slightly surreal photo on the cover).
He's not a stereotype footballer, and I very much hope for
my own mental health that I'm not a stereotype psychologist
(in America, the suicide rate among psychologists and
psychiatrists is twice as high as that among psychiatric
patients). It was fortunate indeed that Pat agreed to do this
book with me, though to be honest, I was a little surprised. 'He
could write it perfectly well himself. He doesn't need a ghost-
writer!' I told my publishers. 'Lovely idea, but we'd never get
him.'

Imagine my delight, then, when my agent Jonathan Harris

phoned me to say that he'd spoken to Pat and that actually he
was very keen. He was not, of course, keen on having a ghost-
writer, something quite unnecessary for a player who writes with
his imagination and honesty. What he did fancy, however, was
doing something that would be a bit different. Something which
hadn't been done before in a book written by a footballer.

A collaboration between a player and a psychologist is certainly
new. Nevertheless, there have already been some fine books
looking at the psychology (with a small 'p') of being a player, an
excellent recent example being *Left Foot Forward* by Garry Nelson.
The great appeal of that book was that Garry was just an ordinary
footballer (not *that* ordinary – let's not kid ourselves that anyone
could play for Charlton – but certainly not a big-name star). It is
rare that books – certainly successful ones – are written from this
point of view. The fans want to read about *stars*. The trouble is that
stars generally don't want to write the book themselves, so they
bring someone else in, generally a journalist but sometimes their
agent or solicitor, to write it with them (the cynical would say *for*
them). It amused me  to see that the audio-book of Ian Wright's
ghosted autobiography, *Mr Wright*, was actually read not by the
player himself but by Shane Ritchie. It's come to something when
a player not only doesn't write his own autobiography but doesn't
even read it out.

I wanted something else, and Pat, whose first book this
represents, agreed. When John Cleese paired up with family
therapist Robin Skynner to produce *Families and How to Survive
Them*, and the sequel, *Life and How to Survive It*, the result was
something unique. A comedian had never written a book with a
psychotherapist before. The result was an insight into the world
of the family and the frequently strained relationships within it,
but it was also very funny. The same principle was then applied
to look more generally at the human condition.

I wanted to be involved in writing something that revealed
more about how it really feels to be a footballer than ever before
– not an easy task. I didn't want this to be what a novelist or a
journalist – or, come to that, a psychologist – *thinks* it is really like
to be a footballer. I wanted the genuine article. Like one of my
heroes, Dr Anthony Clare, I then wanted to find out as much as
I possibly could by careful probing.

I was very fortunate that Pat was quite happy to be carefully probed.

# George on Pat

Pat isn't a typical player. But then, who is? Is Gazza a typical player? No. No player attracts more publicity, so he can't be. Is Alan Shearer a typical player? No. No player (to date) was ever transferred for a larger amount of money, so he can't be. All right, then – is Garry Nelson a typical player? Not at all. He has a unique set of interests, a special outlook on life and a set of aspirations, hopes, dreams and so on that are different from anybody else's. And so it goes on. Somewhere out there *is* the typical player. This player's ability, level of interest in various things, preferred way of behaving and so on is 100 per cent typical for footballers in general. He draws a wage that represents the arithmetic mean of all the wages earned by different players, he is of average height and weight, scores an average number of goals (although he's a midfielder or a defender, rather than a forward or a goalkeeper, because there are fewer of the latter about) and eats average food (the old chickens and beans, more than likely).

But would you want to read a book about him?

One of the reasons I became a psychologist rather than a sociologist is that I think the uniqueness of people is very important. Lumping everyone together and saying 'This is what footballers do' or 'This is what Tory politicians do' or 'This is what members of the working class do' is fraught with complications, because it ignores the fact that each of those groups is comprised of individuals. Tory politicians are not all alike. If they were, then Michael Heseltine, Teresa Gorman, Kenneth Clarke and Michael Portillo would probably get on like a house on fire, assuming that birds of a feather flock together. As it is, all they can hope for is that there might be something in the attraction of opposites. May Day 1997 revealed this to be a bit of a far-fetched hope.

An argument peddled by the likes of Jimmy Boyle, viz. 'I was a violent criminal largely because I was brought up in the Gorbals', strikes me as very offensive to the many people who were born in the Gorbals and didn't grow up to be violent criminals. Treating groups as though they consist of identical individuals leads to stereotyping, intolerance and any number of -isms. Whenever I hear fellow psychologists utter a line like 'Footballers are thick' or 'Footballers are greedy' or even 'Footballers do this or that' the hairs on the back of my neck stand on end. I don't actually punch them, of course. That way lies Cantona. But I want to.

Having said that, Pat is probably about as far from the cliché as you can get. Walk into his house and you won't see a single thing connected with football (apart from the telly, on which a match might be showing). You'll see Penguin classics, Jane Austen videos, paintings, CDs – but not a shirt, not a signed match-ball, not even a photo of Pat playing is displayed. Ironically, my own front-room has considerably more in the way of football memorabilia displayed, while his has more books by the celebrated neurologist Oliver Sacks than mine does.

All this is perhaps as it should be. He's interested in psychology, I'm interested in football – terrific! There's also a danger that it might make me feel a bit redundant. After all, as a shrewd observer of the game, Pat is a fine amateur psychologist himself, whose views I find more valuable than many expressed by my professional colleagues. What can I do? I suppose I'll have to ask questions others wouldn't, explore avenues that have never been explored before, give you, the reader, a different insight into one remarkable footballer and into the game of football as a whole. Originally, we thought about calling it *Football and How to Survive It*, in homage to the Cleese and Skynner collaborations. That may yet turn out to be a fairly accurate representation of its content.

I first met Pat as the 1996–97 football season was getting started. Perhaps that's not quite true. When I was in Sweden in 1992 for the European Championships, I went to all of Scotland's games with my friend and colleague, Stephen Smith. At the match with the CIS, formerly the USSR, Stephen wore a plastic Viking helmet, which he remembers Pat complimenting, after his cry of 'Go on yersel'!' had prompted the player to turn around. Pat was sensational in a match which finished with a score of 3–0 to Scotland.

So the *second* time I met Pat at the house where he lives with his wife Annabel and their children, Simon and Lucy. We talked about the book and threw around ideas. I found him charming, unnecessarily modest, highly committed and a possessor of the kind of sense of humour that is always sharp without ever being cruel. Yet he is also a man of paradoxes. While his popular reputation makes much of his love of art and his keen sense of aesthetic, the kits he picked for the football team he had assembled were voted the worst of all time, narrowly beating Dulwich Hamlet's fetching pink-and-blue ensembles. And what can you say of a man who chooses a hairdresser who is himself completely bald?

I knew that evening that the relationship would work and that, in a sense, this would be an easy book to write. We were both determined to give it our best shots. We spent the rest of the evening trying to work out whether theatre director Sir Peter Hall was *really* the brother of Eric Hall, the agent, as one radio programme had claimed. As it turned out, he wasn't.

I live and work in a Chelsea-supporting area of London, where news that I was working on a book with Pat Nevin caused many of my friends and associates to comment: 'You lucky, lucky bastard.' They were right.

# Pat on George

I have been asked many times before to write a football book of sorts. After reading the Cleese/Skynner collaborations, I thought this seemed a pretty good and unusual way to write about football. As the idea was formulating in my mind, the literary agent Jonathan Harris called. He was in the right place at the right time for me. When he mentioned George and his profession, I felt it was too good a chance to pass up, so I agreed to meet him.

We immediately got on well and although we had many ideas in common, we had enough different and indeed opposite attitudes for intriguing and passionate discussions to develop. So even though George had shown fairly poor judgement in appearing on *Blind Date*, spends a little too much time in Scribes wine bar (at least, he did when Terry Venables owned it) and has actually *changed* the team he supports – sacrilege! – I was happy to get to work right away and the original germ of an idea quickly took shape.

Although I have always felt a bit of an outsider within football, I couldn't have worked with someone who didn't understand the passions involved in the game. George not only understands the passions but feels them acutely, because he is a real football-lover. Whether it is Newcastle, Spurs, Scotland, Celtic or whoever, he is always interesting and knowledgeable. Combining that with the expertise of his field and my inside information, I hope we fulfil the original aim of this book: to make footballers more understandable and understood.

# SESSION 1
# True Faith

*It was a crisp, sunny morning in Chester when we began our explorations. The season was just starting. Pat was at Tranmere Rovers, with another two years of his contract to run. At the end of those two years he would be 35 and, he felt, it was likely that he would hang up his boots.*

George: We hear all the time that a professional footballer's life is one seething cauldron of pressure and stress. How much would you say this is true from your own experience?

Pat: Right from the start, I didn't feel any pressure being a professional footballer, mainly because I didn't particularly want to be one. I didn't choose to be a footballer, it was kind of chosen for me.

George: Was there any football in your family at all?

Pat: Yes, we were all very keen. My brothers all played and my Dad coached. But there were no professionals, so there was never any thought of becoming a professional player – certainly not from me! My Dad thought I could be a professional, but at no point did I ever consider it a possibility. I started playing professionally with Clyde, part-time, while studying for a BA Commerce at Glasgow Tech. By the time I moved to Chelsea, my mentality was that if I succeeded, I succeeded, and if I didn't, then I didn't mind. I could always go back to my studies.

But I was very, very dedicated to it, so there was a strange dichotomy there. It's not that I didn't care, it was just that I didn't mind if I didn't make it. Eventually, though, I felt some pressure. I suppose being married with children creates it, simply because you're providing for them. But that was the only *real* pressure I had felt in the first 11 or 12 years of my career. I think I was a better player when I felt no pressure, when I was totally carefree and doing whatever I liked on the field. The pressure of a cup final does not affect me, I feel no pressure in that situation. I don't get nervous, I have never let football take over my life to the degree that I would get nervous about it. This attitude rather upset a few people over the years. On one occasion, the late, great Jock Stein heard one of my more chilled-out interviews. He let me know, via Andy Roxburgh, that he didn't look kindly on these airy-fairy 'continental' attitudes.

George: An excellent example of that, if I may dredge it up, is when you made a complete dog's dinner of that penalty against Manchester City when you were a Chelsea player. You turned away laughing, rather than the accepted reaction which is to walk away and shoot yourself. (Some fans are still not prepared to forgive Gareth Southgate for being insufficiently racked with guilt over his vital Euro 96 miss in the semi-final against the Germans. Why, he was even able to joke about it afterwards in that Pizza Hut advert!)

Pat: Well, we were actually 4–0 up and there was a minute to go in that match. I'd had a very good game that day. I had made two or three goals and was Man of the Match. I just laughed my head off. I thought it was hilarious, but I was trying to hide it so that the manager didn't see me. Well, he found out, so I got in trouble anyway. But in those days, I genuinely felt no pressure at all. Recently though, that's been changing a bit and I have started to feel it more. Certainly, during my years at Everton I began to feel it. As with many players, it is the stress of having to play well in order to secure another contract in order to provide for your family that is the biggest fear. So there was a bit more of that, which meant I was a bit less relaxed and perhaps I wasn't the same player for that reason. I was and am aware that this is my problem, my weakness, and not my family's.

But the other things you would expect to stress a footballer in the job didn't worry me at all.

Then last year, I signed a three-year extension to my contract with Tranmere Rovers, which takes me to the end of my career, the *official* end anyway – it might go on a bit longer, it might not – so you'd think I should now be totally relaxed. I expected to be totally relaxed, the fears over family security having been sorted out, but, alas, it didn't actually work that way. All the way through last season, I played a huge amount of games – more than 60 – and played more than half of them with injuries, which I wouldn't have done – *shouldn't* have done – but the pressure was on to be part of the Scotland squad, pressure I had put on myself. It meant a great deal to me to continue to be part of the squad which, on and off, I'd been part of for 10 years. As the European Championships came nearer and nearer, I began to feel that if I missed any games for Tranmere at all, it would be an excuse for Craig Brown to leave me out of the national team squad. I knew that, at 32, if I was left out, I would never get back in again. So I kept on playing through my injuries, and finally, in the last qualifying game for Scotland against San Marino, I started, scored one, made three and I *half-relaxed*, thinking: 'I'm in the squad.' So I just played my normal game and thought, 'If I need to rest an injury, I'll rest it.' The injuries had been building up and had begun to slow me down and to affect me quite badly. I knew that with a couple of weeks' rest, I'd be in mint condition again.

George:  Has your commitment to the Scotland cause increased with age?

Pat:  Not at all. It's exactly the same. The ideology is very, very simple – if I'm not picked, I'm not picked. But it's wonderful to be chosen to represent your country. I don't get offended at being left out of the squad, I don't get angry with the manager. But I *really* wanted to be part of this Euro 96 championship. I had been the first reserve for two World Cups, I had played in the games just before those championships only to be dropped at the last minute. Then I played in the first games *after* these World Cups – I think, on both occasions, I started those games. So Euro 96 became very important to me. When I was disappointed in the '86 and '90 World Cups, I had just shrugged my shoulders, as it hadn't really mattered that much to me. This time, however, for whatever reason, I really wanted to play in the finals of the European Championships. Maybe this was because it was being played in England, but it was probably more to do with the fact that I sensed this would be my last chance. The one major finals I had played in – in Sweden in '92 – I had played with a broken ankle! I had never really had the chance to shine on the international stage and I realised I badly wanted to.

George:   Why now? Was it just a sense of missed opportunity and of time running out?

Pat:      It was mainly the fact that I have realised that international football suits my style, probably more than the domestic game.

George:   What is it about your game that you think would particularly shine on the international stage?

Pat:      The big attraction about playing international football is that foreign defenders, however good they are, don't play against you on a regular basis and are therefore unfamiliar with your style and your tricks. They might have seen you on video, but there's a lot they won't know about. I've certainly had fun playing against international teams for Scotland – even some of the best German defenders could be surprised – and then coming back and facing some tiny little domestic team who were much more familiar with my repertoire would cause me huge problems.

          You can be more creative in international football, more adventurous. If I tried some of my more extreme moves that I use in international football in British games, I would never get away with it. They know me too well.

George:   Familiarity breeds contempt?

Pat: To some extent, yes. Of course, the worst kind of international fixture from that point of view is against someone like the Republic of Ireland, which is full of players who you're playing against week in, week out. Against sides like that, the usual attractions of international football don't apply.

George: Those tournaments in which you didn't play – did you follow them very avidly on television?

Pat: No. During one of them, I travelled around the north of Scotland vaguely following it. I watched the odd game. I certainly watched all the Scotland games keenly – after all, those were my old pals playing. To be honest, to start with, in the early days, the feeling within the squad was none too great, but as the years have progressed, the squad feeling in the Scotland camp became fantastic. It was largely down to a very deliberate effort by Andy Roxburgh and Craig Brown.

George: I think you once said that 1992 in Sweden was perhaps the pinnacle, that it was the best team spirit that you have ever experienced within the Scotland squad on that occasion . . .

Pat: It was just incredible to see us taking the Dutch to the limit, bullying the Germans and then annihilating the Russian (CIS) side, all down to the closeness of the group of players there and an amazing support from the Tartan Army. People talk about Wimbledon's 'Crazy Gang' spirit and about the closeness of the players at Rangers Football Club. I've always been intrigued by these great team spirits. They are not easy to manufacture, and each has its own special dynamic. At Rangers, it's all wrapped up in humour. That kind of spirit is probably worth 10 points over a season, often enough to make the difference between winners and runners-up.

George: I remember Walter Smith telling me that that was one of the main deciding factors that convinced Paul Gascoigne to come to Rangers.

Pat: That's good, because I've just written an article in *Arena* about him and that's what I said.

I've watched the team spirit develop in the Scotland camp – as usual, slightly as an outsider – and I really wanted to be part of it. As a result of my performance against San Marino, I felt I had probably got there. After that, there was a friendly against Australia and with injuries still niggling, I declared myself fit. I came on as a sub and played quite well, so for a moment I allowed myself to relax. I should never have done that. The next game, I was shocked to find myself in the 'B' squad and I knew then that it didn't matter what happened next – I was out! The 'B' team got hammered in Sweden, as did the 'A' team, but that confirmed things: I was finished, I was out of it.

So after that, I decided to take a rest. I knew that if I carried on playing the way I had been, living on pain-killers and anti-inflammatory pills, I would end up doing myself some long-term damage. In 15 years of professional football, I have had *relatively* few serious injuries, so I can't complain. I missed the last six games of the season for Tranmere, and of course missed the European Championships, which I knew was going to happen. It had happened exactly the same way the last time I'd been dropped by Scotland, which was before World Cup 90 in Italy. I got shipped out to the 'B' squad. I was bitterly disappointed, but I wasn't angry with anyone. I'd done my best, it had meant a lot to me, I'd taken chances with my health, I had given everything, but I just couldn't manage it. There's no bitterness, though. I don't have any bitterness towards anyone in this job, because it's a brilliant job to have and there's no room in my personality for that sort of bitterness.

I see a lot of people in football who seem embittered by the way it has gone for them. First and foremost, they seem unhappy men, and secondly, it is a negative feeling that rubs off on those around them. It isn't a good emotion to infest a group who continually have to work near and for each other. Quite obviously, team spirit and morale are affected by it.

What it led to was a lot of writing, some radio and

television work, but more particularly the writing, which I really have enjoyed. I learned a lot about myself through thinking about these articles and I realised the real reasons why I wanted to do this, which we'll no doubt talk much more about.

So I came back this season with the usual determination to have a great year. My pre-pre-season preparation was very much as usual: lots of middle-distance running which, to the amazement of my team-mates, I rather perversely enjoy. My last run before joining them for pre-season proper was four miles up a hill on the island of Arran, round Loch Tanna at the top, before embarking on the four-mile descent. I love this type of run – the colours, the dramatic views, even the total silence is amplified by the adrenaline pumping through your body. You seem to be able to glide effortlessly along, hardly touching the ground . . . that is, unless a huge boulder gives way under you as you start the descent! By the time I had stopped rolling, 20 feet later, I realised I had badly damaged my ankle. I was four miles up in the wilderness at eight in the evening, unable to walk, the darkness and the weather closing in. Worse still, it was only two days before the season's training started.

So I started off the pre-season with an injury, though I succeeded in doing all the sand-dunes and so on. Then I managed to get another rather strange injury, *Plantar Fasciitis*, a wear-and-tear injury that has kept me out of the first-team action right up until now. So I haven't played football since six games before the end of last season. This, of course, would normally have me tearing my hair out. I *need* to play, I *love* playing. I feel I should be worrying about my next contract, about letting my team-mates down and about getting into the Scotland squad. Well, of course, the Scotland squad is no longer a concern and Tranmere are playing quite well, so there is no worry about letting them down. It is good to see the lads doing so well. It really means a lot to me to see them succeed. I am not like some players, who want to see the team do badly when they're out, thereby highlighting their indispensability. As for the contract, that's in place until the end of next season, so the pressure has been limited. I've felt really, really good. I've had this lovely, totally confident feeling of wanting to get better, do a few sand-dunes, get myself to an extraordinary peak of fitness and, as soon as my second injury has cleared up, walk back in there and I'll be flying!

I'm physically fitter now than I have been for a year or two, because I have had such a good rest. Old injuries which have niggled me for months on end have had the chance to be rested. Last night the physio gave me the green light and is happy my injury is totally healed and I'll be able to walk normally again – although probably not today because out of sheer frustration, I ran about 20 miles last night! I feel a tremendous sense of *release*. It's a release of all sorts of pent-up things, but this time it hasn't been tension or aggression. It just feels as though I've been shot out of a gun.

George:  One of the clubs I looked at in my previous book was Dulwich Hamlet, and they had a player there called Dave Coppin who was out with a very serious long-term injury – cruciate ligaments, I think – and he would come along to almost every match and training session, because he was so keen to remain part of it all. Even though he couldn't contribute directly, he'd be there contributing to the team spirit. It must be very difficult, though, when you're out with injury, to continue to feel involved.

Pat:  This is a theme I will come back to again and again, and I hope it doesn't get boring. I began at Celtic Boys' Club and you learn things there – not, I hasten to add, the things we've been reading about in the papers, regarding suspicions and allegations about some leaders' relationships with some of the boys! You learn about the right way to treat people, particularly your team-mates. It's a philosophy that's sort of Socialist or Christian, catholic with a small 'c', about the oneness of the team, about the importance of the team cause over and above the wants of the individual, about wanting the group to do well whatever your own personal circumstances. It is totally bred into you. If there was any antagonism towards the team, such as anyone saying, 'Well, I'm not playing today, I hope we get beat,' they would be *slaughtered*. Everyone else in the team would be quick to let them know how much they were letting 'the cause' down.

I was amazed, on turning professional, to discover that not everyone always has the same feelings towards the team. Of course, that is all wrapped up in insecurity, but there was no room for that within the Celtic Boys' Club indoctrination. It was almost Jesuitical and they were very good at it. I've learned about indoctrination from other areas, and this *was* indoctrination, but with a real social attitude. It was so bred into you to be a consummate, 'right-thinking' professional with the good of the team always uppermost in your heart. That has never left me for a second. If you look at some of the players who have come through Celtic Boys' Club – Tommy Burns, Roy Aitken, Paul McStay and Billy McKinlay, who is now with Blackburn – they have all got that attitude and it is wonderful. Watch the current Celtic team before each match even today – they get into a huddle and cement the team spirit before each game. It's no surprise to me, because ex-Celtic Boys' Club player Tommy Burns is the manager.

This attitude has stood me in good stead, and like many indoctrinations, in religion or whatever, it answers some questions when you don't necessarily know the right answer for sure yourself, because of either uncertainty or inexperience.

On occasion, I have felt a bit of peer pressure if I have been out of the team for a while and three or four teammates are sniping. It would be easy to join in, but my answer is ingrained in me. You have to confront that negative attitude, even if it makes you unpopular. After all, if I get back in the team, the sniping will almost certainly be aimed at me. I've always carried that attitude with me and, as I have become an older pro, it has become part of my image. My image has changed over the years – not just my self-image, but the image other people, especially team-mates, have of me. That's definitely changed.

At Chelsea, one of my nicknames was 'Weirdo', because I was such an outsider and had interests that must have seemed strange to some of the other players. Nowadays, team-mates see the older pro, the PFA chairman, a seasoned international . . . there may even be a slight element of respect creeping in there – perish the thought! But I find I'm using those lessons learned early in life more and more, so, to return to the original point, I can happily walk into the dressing-room, even if I'm not part of the team, and encourage the other players without any embarrassment. I will sit beside them and chat to them – more often than not, the player I will talk to is the player in my position or a similar one. I am not sure what the manager makes of it – I hope he thinks positively of it – but each of these six or seven games I've been out for, I've watched the match from really high-up in the stands to get a better overview, and I've gone down at half-time and said things, in a very positive way, to the players in these positions. I would say: 'Maybe you could try such and such and it might help you a wee bit.' Now, it may seem strange that I'm helping the guy who has got my place in the team, but I still feel underneath that he's my team-mate – though, just as importantly, I'm also still better! I have the self-confidence that once I recover from injury, I'll get him out on merit.

*George*:   The analogy with the workplace more generally is an interesting one here. If you think of the office environment, say, a sales team, and you've got a dynamic, effective young performer, often the more established rep who is most suspicious, and therefore most potentially antagonistic, is the one who recognises he's really not at all that good himself. Whereas those reps who know that they are good at their jobs too might go out of their way to help the young and talented one. The fear of failure is much stronger in those who feel they are not as good and this young whippersnapper is chasing their position.

What would happen, though, if you felt that one of these younger players in your position actually *was* better than you? Would that alter the approach you took?

Pat:    It's a funny one. I just don't think like that – as soon as I step onto the pitch, I feel I am good enough. I'm not arrogant about it in any way. When I say I'm a better player, I wouldn't say it to a team-mate. I think a lot of players feel this way. I believe you really need to have that feeling, and I'm lucky I have it. Without it, the self-doubt would destroy me as a performer.

Another thing I have inherited from Celtic Boys' Club is the concept of the importance of the fans and the debt you owe to them. I am still very much a fan myself, I am a Celtic fan, and even though I've never played for them at senior level, I am still a supporter. When I stop playing, I will go and watch Celtic, getting a season ticket if I can afford it. Because of this, I feel I still have a fan's mentality as much as a player's. I still feel that players should consider that the fans pay their wages via the turnstiles – even if, increasingly, the money comes from TV deals and the sale of merchandise. So it is important to me that the fans of any club I play for are aware that I would never have the attitude that would allow me to envy someone in my own team to the extent that it would have a negative effect on him, and thus the team.

If I were ever to forget the effort of the fans, all I have to do is think of the lengths my father has gone to in order to see me play. Apart from the fact that, more often than not, he makes the journey to Tranmere – and made it to Everton, before I moved across the Mersey – he used to travel all the way from Glasgow to London and back in the same day, by train, to watch me play for

Chelsea every week. He would also tell me of the efforts
and expense many Chelsea fans would go to, when he
chatted to them on the trains. There has always been a
sense of my debt to the fans, and, of course, a good old-
fashioned dollop of guilt when the team or I played
badly.

*George*:  But to what extent have you encountered the opposite –
players who are *very* insecure about others getting their
place in the team?

*Pat*:  I've certainly come across that attitude and naturally,
it's understandable. I wouldn't be nasty to a player who
felt that way, but I'd have to say: 'It's disgraceful showing such a negative attitude towards a team-mate. I
know the old argument: you have got to feed your
family; you're very competitive and determined to do
well, but you've got to have the right attitude for the
team because, as well as all the other reasons I've
mentioned already, eventually the two of you will probably have to play together. You wouldn't want to have
bad feelings towards each other still lingering because,
on a previous occasion, you were both fighting for the
same place.'

I often think, when I am giving advice to youngsters
who play in the positions I generally play, that it's
natural that they should be wary. Of course, they might
think: 'He's at it. He's up to something. He's sneakily
trying to undermine my confidence by telling me about
my faults.' Because I have this reputation for being an
intelligent player – something I have neither encouraged nor condoned, by the way – then their suspicions
are likely to be aroused. There was one particular player
who, after knowing me and being given helpful hints
by me, finally came round to believing I was doing it
for purely altruistic reasons – but only after three whole
years. It took that long because people can be very
cynical. I had tremendous respect for this player and
rated him among the most skilful I have ever played
with.

I am frequently asked: 'Why are you working with

me? Why are you helping me? Why do you work with the union when you aren't paid for it? What's in it for *you*? Well, nothing really. Actually, it gets bloody annoying after a while. I just want to give something back into the game. I think if you keep on acting the same way, keep on helping, keep on showing a good attitude, then people come round in the end. They think: 'Yeah, he's all right. He's trying to be helpful. He isn't being a religious freak about it, it's just the way he is.'

George: Can football have room for altruism, though? Of course it's a team game, but in my research with my colleague Stephen Smith, I found that while footballers tended to be just like everyone else with regard to most aspects of personality – running the whole gamut of preferences for each particular area – they were, as a group, intensely competitive, much more so than the British population as a whole. Now, that's unsurprising, but competition is *inevitably* selfish, isn't it? And with agents and the media focusing more and more on high-profile *individuals* within the game, surely that serves to encourage a rather self-centred attitude, one which can be the enemy of good teamwork?

Pat: Over the years, I have seen it go over the top, if you'll pardon the phrase, when a player has kicked another in training just to get that player's place. But although it has happened, it is incredibly unusual. Other players can spot it a mile away, and words are quickly exchanged to stress that you simply can't go round doing that. There are players capable of that kind of mentality, but then there are Mafiosi who wouldn't think twice about shooting someone in order to take their place. Human nature has a broad spectrum.

There are obviously individuals who are far more concerned with themselves and their own position than that of the team. I guess that is the popular image of certain players – usually the centre-forwards! They can get labelled selfish or greedy or whatever. But it's like the old Paul Gascoigne theory: if you get rid of the madness, you risk getting rid of the genius. Similarly,

with centre-forwards, if you lose the greed, you might
lose the instinct to kill and they'll stop scoring as many
goals for you. So you really need to balance that positive
greed with an element of team spirit. I wouldn't necessarily agree with the premise that competitiveness
must always have a direct correlation with acute
selfishness. It isn't that simple. If you look around, Alan
Shearer, who is the best in the business, is the perfect
example of a player who *doesn't* fit that stereotype. He
is competitive, selfish in front of goal, but still the
perfect team player. There are others – Stan Collymore
is often mentioned – who it is suggested aren't such
team players.

Young men tend to be very competitive and you'll
get this syndrome in any environment where a lot of
young men are working closely together, whether it's
sales reps or dealers in the City. Some of those City
dealers form a fairly good analogy for what it is like to
be in a football team. It is a comparison I've considered
more and more recently: young; highly paid; high-
profile; high-pressure jobs, etc. You will come across
some very selfish people working in that type of
environment. They just want to do better and make
more money than anyone else – that is their primary
goal. Everyone has their primary goal. I won't allow
what should be secondary goals, such as headline-
grabbing and selfish personal glory, to interfere with
the primary goal, which is the team's good. There are
plenty of players with the breadth of vision to look at it
this way, no matter what some people may say.

*George*:  I suppose you're in a fortunate position, in a sense,
because you have other strings to your bow. There is
your writing, your experience as chairman of the PFA
and so on. If *all* you have in life is football, however –
and I've come across the odd player who wasn't even
able to read – that must increase the selfishness,
increase the wish to grab as much as possible from the
game before that very early retirement that all players
face . . .

Pat: That attitude definitely exists and I totally understand it. It is one of the important arguments for footballers being paid the relatively large sums of money that many of them are. I also feel that the fact that I didn't have that attitude was a major reason I made it in professional football. With a panicked and rushed approach towards a football career, I would have struggled. As a kid, I played for Celtic FC as a schoolboy and they told me that I wouldn't make it, that I'd never make it as a pro . . . I was too small.

George: I think that Rangers concluded the same about Kenny Dalglish!

Pat: That's right! So I concentrated on my education, as they suggested. I enrolled at Glasgow Tech (as it was then) for BA Commerce. After two years, I left to do what was supposed to be a two-year sabbatical at Chelsea FC. I always stress to those journalists who continually get it wrong that I haven't got a degree . . . yet! But being in the fortunate position that I had something to fall back on totally relaxed me, at least until the commitments involved with having a family came along. For that, a degree doesn't always help you – you need money! I had that safety net, if you like, and as I've got older, I've tried to come up with alternative safety nets for what I hope will be the long years after my retirement from the game. There's the writing and three or four other possibilities from which I hope to make enough money to get by. The main reason, however, is that if I feel my whole life doesn't depend on my football, I will relax a bit during the game – and I am a better player when I'm relaxed. A tense, uptight player will have the ball bounce off his tensed-up, rigid foot. Being relaxed and supple – just the way Ruud Gullit appears all the time, being the extreme – I will be able to control a ball far better, with a softer, almost caressing touch.

I realised five or six years ago that there were some young lads with similar personalities to me who weren't playing as well as they could be. The reason? They were worried, panicking about their futures. One youngster, who is 18, asked me earnestly: 'What on earth am I going to do when I'm 35?' I thought: 'Steady on, mate! Look to the future but don't let it totally ruin the present.' He will be OK – he is easily good enough and will make it anyway, but I could all too easily understand his agitation. He has no safety net. Others in his position who have no other strings to their bows and aren't assured of success, aren't so lucky.

As I realised how many youngsters were in this position, I began to talk to them about what they could do when they were no longer playing. In football, there is often a good deal of free time, plenty of time to do a bit of studying – and it's worth it in the short *and* long run. That's one of the things that drew me towards working for the union, the Professional Footballers' Association.

*George*: That's one of the big commitments of the PFA, isn't it – to help players find jobs after their playing days are over?

*Pat*: Yes, it's a huge commitment. Last year we gave out over a quarter of a million in grants for players to go on courses. These may be for coaching licences – there was even one who did Church Ministry last year! There is deep-sea diving . . . anything, as long as it can lead towards a job. There are scores of players now doing computer courses – the list is bordering on endless.

*George*: Is this also true of some of the game's big stars?

*Pat*: Yes, but less so, understandably.

*George*: Because they've already got an enormous amount of money?

*Pat*: To a degree, yes. Some argue that we shouldn't be paying grants to the wealthier Premier League stars at all. The FA, the Football League and the Premier League contribute to the Education Society too, and some feel that 'We shouldn't be subsidising the most wealthy, as they can afford to educate themselves.' However, it does tend to be the lower league players who use the education grants, along with ex-players. We have worked hard for it to become the established norm for players to start to plan for their futures in this way.

It is beneficial firstly for the reasons I've mentioned already. Also, they become better players, as they're more relaxed about the future and they have less to worry about if they don't do so well in the game, or if – and this is a big fear for all players – an injury like a snapped cruciate finishes their playing career. I've had a torn cruciate, but fortunately it didn't snap. If it snaps, you might be finished there and then. Any player who has only been injured for *two weeks*, say with a pulled hamstring, begins to think: 'My God! I might be finished!' You can see the fear etched on their faces when they are alone. I've been injured for eight weeks now and I have looked around at my injured colleagues. They disappear inside themselves in a trance-like state and have no idea that they are staring silently into space.

Players are so desperately keen to get back that 90 per cent of them come back to play long before they have made a full recovery – I'm no different. That is the attitude in this country, there is desperation to show that you're keen. It's the culture. It has been interesting to watch Ivano Bonetti at Tranmere this year. An experienced Italian player, he retains the culture of his days in Italy. His attitude is that there is no point in even trying to play unless you are 100 per cent fit. It is an alien attitude to us, bordering on being a bit soft, but in actual fact it is simply being very professional.

In the first week back, players walk about not talking to anyone. They habitually have a glazed, vacant look on their faces. They are constantly questioning whether they are really quite ready to come back, if the injury has cleared enough to last the game. On the coach the other week, while everyone else was sitting playing cards, chatting, having a laugh, there was one lad just sitting there on his own. He didn't know it, but he was just sitting there silently, looking ahead. In the past, he was often the most gregarious person on that coach. Of course, this was to be his first game back after injury!

Just the other day, I walked up to another player who was in the same position, wandering around aimlessly in the corridor, lost in thought, and I said: 'I bet you're thinking about your injury.' Immediately, out it all came: 'Yeah, it was on my mind. You have your whole body and you're just concentrating on that tiny little spot on your leg the whole time.' And on he went, happy to be able to get it off his chest for a moment. People in other jobs could probably forget about it if it wasn't giving them immediate pain, but because you're a footballer and your fitness is your livelihood, it gets lodged inside your head permanently.

I chatted to the lad for a while and explained that every single player feels this way, urging him not to get downhearted or depressed about it. It passes. In the wider scheme of things and in the long term, over the length of a season, it isn't that important.

*George*: The physical vulnerability of players must give some of them a lot to worry about, I'd guess. If someone's working in the office, physical injury, unless it's very, very serious, isn't going to stop them. Obviously a serious head injury could affect their cognitive functioning and some of this may decline a bit as they get a lot older, but generally they're not in a very vulnerable position. A player, on the other hand, could be crippled in any game he plays through no fault of his own, and psychologists might argue that this encourages a mentality that puts what happens to you in life firmly in the hands of others (this is sometimes called having an External Locus of Control). People are generally much happier if they feel in control of their own destiny and don't let too much happen that's outside their control (having an Internal Locus of Control), but in football that must be very difficult. Realistically, your fate might indeed lie in the hands of others. The minute you start to believe that other people are behind what happens to you (managers, agents, chairmen, partners, luck, chance, Mystic Meg and so on), in other words adopting an External Locus of Control, it suddenly becomes much harder to stay calm. Generally, people with an Internal Locus of Control cope much better, unless they encounter something totally outside their control, like the death of a loved one. That can be exceptionally painful to someone who has grown to believe that his destiny lies in his hands. But for the most part, it is those with an External Locus of Control who find it hardest to cope with day-to-day living, and it could be argued that the culture of football perhaps encourages such a mentality. I remember seeing a television programme about players' wives, and one made the comment that basically, players have almost everything done for them, from sorting out travel arrangements to being told exactly what to do in training. Is that a realistic picture of football's culture? Does it encourage others to take responsibility for what happens in your life?

*Pat*:     In fact, my wife was interviewed for that programme but they cut her bit – she was talking too much sense . . .

*George*:  Yes, that tends not to make very good television!

*Pat*:     No, it's a great exaggeration, but I do find it very interesting that a lot of people think footballers have that complete lack of control over their lives. From the injury point of view, it's true that you have no control over that. Usually, you have total control of your body, much more than most people. Then an injury comes along and you've lost control, not only of your body but of your career as well. Right away, there is stress and, if you think the injury might be serious, immediate and fairly extreme fear.

It is the contrast that makes it particularly difficult to deal with. When not injured, professional sportsmen usually have a unique and uncanny control of their bodies. For example, before a game, your mind will automatically start preparing your body for the 90 minutes it is about to endure, before you even consciously think about it. You start sweating, but it isn't nervousness, it is your body preparing, getting its temperature adapted. The blood starts pumping more through the muscles and limbs and less to the organs, in preparing for the hard 'shift' ahead. It's called a cardiovascular shunt.

Everyone has these abilities, but athletes learn how to use them and get to know instinctively how much help they will get from adrenaline, how well damaged or tired muscle-groups can improve with specific preparation and so on. I've tried to explain to people in the past that an athlete will have an unusual control over his or her body that is hard to prove. The body can be put through incredible strains, but the strength remains until you 'switch off'. At the end of every season, I am ill within a week of the last game – you psychologically relax and your body can no longer fight, but somehow you have managed to 'put the illness off' until it is less important for you to be well.

As for players allowing clubs or agents to take over the control of certain parts of their lives – well, they allow it, but only to a certain degree. It's hard to generalise, but I know one player who was very bad at taking control of his own life. He is still, sadly, trying to play football in his forties, he's living in a caravan, yet in his heyday, he made all sorts of moves to clubs which are now in the Premier Division. But he didn't know how to control his life and he let other people do it – people who shouldn't have been allowed to do it.

*George*:  You only have to look at some of the ex-pros and you can see that they've thrown all they made out of the game away, and are now struggling to get by . . .

*Pat*:  You're right. You do see some of that, but I think that's far too much of a generalisation, or more accurately a cliché. Most ex-pros are quite capable of looking after themselves very nicely, thank you. When it comes to things like the club sorting out all your travel arrangements for you, it's true that you tend not to bother about things if someone else is determined to do it for you. I remember encountering one very difficult situation: when I was 17 and playing for Clyde, I was supposed to do an A-Licence coaching course. I had been voted Young Player of the Year or something and the course was part of the prize. I told Craig Brown, who was manager of Clyde at the time and has, of course, since gone on to bigger things, 'I'm sorry, but I'll be backpacking around Europe on the Interrail thing.' I think he was totally staggered at first. Thankfully, Craig is a learned and worldly type of chap and although he tried to argue, I was stubborn and said: 'Look, I just want to go on holiday. I'll be all right.' He agreed, but told me to be careful, in an almost fatherly way. In fact, I managed to pick up a gastric infection and was very ill, so I wasn't all right at all! But at least I had learned to travel by myself.

Within a few years, I was playing professional football full-time and soon realised that when you're travelling with a club, the first thing you do is hand in your passport and you don't see it again until it's given back to you at the airport on the way home. I was shocked! I felt naked without my passport – but everyone else was incredibly relaxed about it. I wasn't. I just couldn't feel right, losing that control.

*George*: It would be exaggerating to say it just applies to footballers, though. I know consultants who are so used to having their secretaries sort out their flights, hotels and so on, that when, for whatever reason, something has gone wrong with the booking, they act completely lost too!

*Pat*: A lot of people say footballers aren't capable of running their own lives, but I don't see it. When push comes to shove, they know what to do. A culture has developed in the game for as much to be done for players as possible when they travel. It is reasoned that players are under a lot of pressure and they have already got enough to think about. When they're travelling abroad, with changing circumstances, different food and so on, all the club is doing is decreasing the number of things the players have to worry about, so that they can be totally focused on the match. Every athlete is the same. In this respect, footballers are no different from Linford Christie: they want to be totally focused on the task at hand. So that is simply why clubs do it, not because they think the players are too thick to look after themselves. This is a mistake often made by the public and a piece of information regularly peddled by some journalists, who should have a little more insight and knowledge.

I interviewed Stuart Pearce for *goal* magazine, and I can't remember if this bit made the finished article or not, but he told me he wanted to go and see a show in London but didn't know how to do it, because he had not booked something like that for that many years. Now, Stuart's a sharp bloke, he's an intelligent lad who has a life outside football [*a few months after this session, he became Nottingham Forest's manager*] – he used to go to a lot of punk gigs, keeps horses and so on. Eventually, it took an Icelandic player at the club, Toddy Orlygsson, to sort out the tickets for the show. Stuart was so embarrassed that he didn't know how to organise something that basic, yet a foreign lad could with ease. However, in the next sentence, he was telling me about his holidays. He goes everywhere, on the most adventurous trips all over the world, to places that aren't necessarily tourist-friendly, always away from football and football people – and of course, he and his wife organise it themselves.

I think you'll find that with a number of footballers. Initially, they might think: 'Hey! That's usually organised for me.' But then they just deal with it. It's like anything you haven't done for 10 years and then someone asks you to do it. It takes a wee while for your brain to click into gear. I think some of the people who have cast aspersions on footballers' travelling abilities have been those who have been travelling on the same flights, having perhaps sorted out their own travel arrangements – though not necessarily. Maybe they see these 20 shell-suits all standing together like sheep, and from that get the idea that footballers can't think for themselves. Some journalists, often on the same flights, share that view, even though they tend not to have sorted out their own flights either. I think that the journalists who write those dodgy pieces about players being unable to travel without having their hands held, or being unable to sort out their lives, are poor writers. They are either blatantly lying or haven't bothered to walk 30 feet up the aisle to do some real research.

*George*: And of course, nobody writes about what journalists get up to when they go abroad!

*Pat*: Well, that's maybe partly the reason why I want to do a bit of writing. I've read things written by journalists that are basically untrue. They're poorly researched and show a serious lack of insight. So even if I'm a poor writer, if I can put some of these points about footballers across honestly, that would be worthwhile. It isn't always directly from a footballer's point of view, because I always felt – and still feel – a bit of an outsider in the football world. I'm always in this kind of grey area between participant and interested observer. Most importantly, I have lived and worked with footballers, so I hope that I've gleaned some understanding of them.

*George*: That's a theme to which we'll no doubt return many times.

*Pat*: Apart from watching footballers and their behaviour, I like to watch the journalists, too. It is particularly informative on international trips when the two species collide.

*George*: I remember discussing the 'Cathay Pacific incident' with Terry Venables. I think one of the reasons that there were so many conflicting stories about it was that there were so few journalists there to witness it – they had all stayed over drinking in Hong Kong for a few more days!

*Pat*: So few were sober enough to give a reasonable report on it. Twist my arm and I could believe that. I shouldn't be too harsh. I understand the press have their pressures too. After a big game, they have to file their reports very quickly and I can see that a few may be in need of alcoholic relief when it's over. The flights home from international matches are usually fairly boisterous affairs throughout, with the exception of the cockpit ... *usually*.

*George*:   And of course, the great unwritten rule is that
          journalists don't write about the escapades of other
          journalists – *Private Eye* excepted. But there must be
          some journalists who really love the game, really love
          football, and others who you suspect are only sports
          journalists because their papers wouldn't trust them
          with any other kind of journalism. They wouldn't
          dream of letting them loose on the foreign news or the
          features desk, so they end up doing sport because
          they're not good enough to do anything else.

*Pat*:    I do see a lot of journalists, and at the risk of generali-
          sing in a way that I get infuriated about when it's
          applied to players, there are certain types. From read-
          ing the lines, but more often from reading between
          them, it is obvious that there are some that still love the
          game, one or two who are still in awe of football. There
          are a few who want real insight into the game and its
          players, and they probe a long time. Many, however,
          just want an easy story. It's lazy. I understand laziness,
          but not at the expense of truth and the embarrassment
          of the interviewee. It is quite easy to see the ones who
          just want to knock out x thousand words and get it to
          their editors in time, truthful or not.

          I can remember what really attracted me to
          journalism. One of the first people to interview me was
          a chap called Jim Traynor. He was working for the
          *Glasgow Herald* and I realised quickly that he didn't
          seem like some of the others. He wanted much more
          depth, and as well as being a talented interviewer, he
          was also a very good writer. He wanted to know *why* I
          did things, *how* I thought as well as *what* I thought. It
          wasn't just the painful 'What makes you tick?' – that
          question means nothing, and I've been asked it time
          and time again. If footballers have the lunar-hopping
          cliché, this is the journalistic equivalent. Traynor went
          into considerable depth, and it was obvious that he was
          good at it. I began to think: 'I would like to be able to do
          that, and if I had the inside knowledge too, it would be
          a new direction.' So even before the age of 18, I had

formulated a plan, if I managed to get past the con-
siderable hurdle of making it in the game.

George: It certainly puts you in quite a unique position. There
are so few players who really want to write . . .

Pat: . . . In depth! As I say, I've been aware of this niche for a
long time. The plan was to go into it when I stopped
playing, but I got asked by the *Sunday Times* to do a few
articles. They seemed to quite like them and ever since
then, I've been writing for various publications. I don't
do it for the money at the moment. I just want people to
understand footballers a little better and, happily, it fits
rather snugly alongside the union work. Footballers
deserve a better press, or rather, a more *honest* press. I
remember a book by Hunter Davies about Spurs
entitled *My Life in Football*. I found it quite laughable –
and I like some of the other stuff Hunter has done. But
that book I found almost funny. I can see how the
players would have reacted towards him. He didn't get
*inside* the game or the club at all, though I could see
what he was trying to do.

There are the journalists who want to get the stuff
done, get the words out and get away, and there are
some who, after watching football for 25 years, think
they know football inside out. They are the ones who
are the most risible of the lot, to be honest. They are
simply hilarious. Players read what they have written
and laugh out loud. They're so caught up in their own
self-importance . . .

George: Not Harry Harris, *surely*?

Pat: I wasn't thinking of Harry! But a number of journalists
I know fall into this category, and the reason that they
are so laughable is that they haven't learned anything –
or very, very little – yet they've managed to catch hold
of every cliché that every other football writer has
written. They start to believe what they're writing, treating as gospel and insight ideas that are just recycled
versions of some vague idea someone else had about a
decade ago. There is, of course, another group who
have been doing it for a number of years and actually

|         |                                                                      |
|---------|----------------------------------------------------------------------|
|         | do know quite a lot about the game, and are very keen to learn more . . . |
| *George*: | Like Patrick Barclay, perhaps?                                     |
| *Pat*:  | Yes. Paddy's a great example, as is Phil Shaw, as is Chris Lightbown. Although they already understand the game very well, they are eager to learn more. Chris doesn't start off with an idea – he is very inquisitive, sometimes painfully so. Actually, I think he must have been a Spanish Catholic in a previous life: he is dedicated to finding out more, to prising out information – his is a tortuous method, but it gets the desired result. |
| *George*: | A lot of journalists nowadays seem to start off with the sub-editor's headline. |
| *Pat*:  | That's true, but in fact I'm not talking about the tabloid writers when I talk about these categories, because I consider tabloid journalism to be an entirely different job. Readers aren't stupid. They know how the tabloids have to behave and most people have a healthy scepticism about what they read in these papers. I'm not sneering at this kind of journalism as a profession, because I think it is in fact an incredibly difficult job. It takes a great deal of skill to communicate ideas while only being allowed to use very limited space and vocabulary. I've tried it myself and found it all but impossible. |

You've got another group of journalists – and there is obviously a certain amount of intermingling of these groups, it's not always nice and clear-cut – who are potentially the ones who annoy me most of all. These are the ones who identify with maverick seventies players. In every other article, they are at pains to point out that 'the game's gone'. Apparently, it's not what it was – the skill has gone, as has the invention, as have the characters, etc, etc.

|         |                                                                      |
|---------|----------------------------------------------------------------------|
| *George*: | The 'Fings Ain't What They Used To Be' school?                    |
| *Pat*:  | Precisely. And they try to build an argument around their blinkered views and prejudices, and they are more laughable than all the others put together. A lot of it is built around *huge* amounts of jealousy. These hacks first |

got into the business when they were 25-year-olds. They grew up with these mercurial seventies stars and kind of admired them, which is fair enough, and they've been in the business long enough to watch them grow up and watch these kids come in. Now they think: 'Hang on! They're just a bunch of weans and they're earning millions of pounds.' So there's enormous envy. They're absolutely convinced that they know more about the game than anyone else, and they don't – you can watch a hundred games and learn nowt! On the other hand, some people can watch one game and learn a huge amount. But these people spend all their time harking back to some mythical golden era of yesteryear – it isn't always the seventies, there are those who go on about the fifties or sixties, too, depending on the age of the journalist. There is a sub-group within this lot as well. Theirs isn't an obsession with a particular era, but a fixation with a certain foreign league – generally Serie A or the Bundesliga. What they should really be doing is looking more closely at our own leagues, at players who are right under their noses. There is a parallel here with some footballers. The ageing process sometimes produces a very similar effect. These guys originally wanted to do well at the game and they did, because of the sharp learning-curve in their early career. Then they reached a certain level and eventually started to decline again, and instead of applauding and helping the new generation, they become bloody bitter towards these 'upstarts'. There is no need to single people out, is there? We all know who they are!

The point is that whatever era you played in, the people who came after you will always earn more than you out of the game. In 10 years' time, players will probably be on higher wages than we're on at the moment. It doesn't matter if the player of the future is average and you are just as good as Kenny Dalglish, he'll still take home a fatter pay-packet. That's the way the game goes and the way it has always gone. Within the game, I find this one of the most saddening aspects.

This bitterness and jealousy towards young players is dreadfully unhealthy. How can you help and give positive advice to the game's future heritage while you have such negative feelings underneath? They have to let it go and accept that it's just the way life is . . . even if you were a better player than he will ever be.

# Brass in Pocket

*I knew that we would be returning to many of the themes from our first session later, elaborating on them and examining other aspects. As we continued, however, I could see that we were going down deeper and more unexpected avenues. It has always been my instinct that if the conversation appears to be going off at a tangent, you should run with it. You never know where it might lead . . .*

George:  One of the things which makes football a bit unusual as a profession is that it has all the trappings of a traditional working-class trade, in that players serve an apprenticeship, just as they might if they wanted to be carpenters or electricians, yet by the time they are in their thirties, those at the top of the game can earn amounts of money that are difficult to match – certainly per amount of time worked – in almost *any* other kind of job, except perhaps after-dinner speaking or heavy-weight boxing.

Pat:  Many thousands of people in this country play football and it is only a tiny amount of them who make an incredible amount of money from it. It's a minute wee band at the very, very top. Talk about any major industry in the world and there will be a huge amount of people involved in it. It's like a pyramid: only at the top of that pyramid do you get the Bill Gateses of Microsoft and so on, who earn the silly money. It's getting like that in every industry and in many sports now – those that are like an industry, anyway: golf; tennis; motor racing and boxing, in particular. As every-one knows, football has become increasingly openly business-minded. It is a huge business and, at the top of the football pyramid, you are as such going to get the phenomenally high earners – it would be very strange if that wasn't the case.

But people do get it slightly wrong. They hear what Stan Collymore earns and they assume that that's the average wage. In reality, the average wage is absolutely nowhere near that. It's nothing like 15 or 20 grand a week. It's not even anywhere near the five grand a week that a lot of people assume must be about par for the course. Nothing like it! That said, it *is* increasing and it's getting to quite a high level. Various people have commented that the money in the game has gone mad of late – Gary Lineker was talking about it just this week – but sheer market forces should eventually pull everything together.

*George*:   Are you concerned that just as the bottom fell out of the City at the end of the eighties and the earnings of yuppie high-fliers crashed, so the same may happen in football?

*Pat*:   I hope not. I hope there will be a bit of sense from chairmen and they will not make a habit of paying 40 grand a week for every Italian international. I was particularly heartened when Sheffield Wednesday refused to give in to Lombardo when he asked for an astronomical sum to come over. I hope it is the dawning of a new realism.

*George*:   Especially when they see that it's done Middlesbrough a fat lot of good [N.B. *This quip was sneakily inserted into the transcript with the benefit of hindsight.*]

*Pat*:   In the end, they'll agree that it's simply not worth it, that they would rather be chairmen of clubs that aren't always on the verge of bankruptcy. Instead of people whingeing on about players' demands ruining the game, they will realise that some players aren't actually demanding these wages at all, they are being *offered* those wages – and who is going to say no under those circumstances?

*George*:   Alan Sugar is a rather hilarious voice in this debate. He clearly feels that because he personally isn't prepared to pay his players huge wages, no-one else should be allowed to do so either! Here we see someone who's supposed to be one of the success stories of the free-market economy questioning the rationale of wages!

Pat:      Should players' wages be capped? Has Alan turned into a socialist all of a sudden? I mean, it's a difficult one to argue. People often say to me: 'How can a centre-forward earn 30 grand a week playing for Middles-brough when a nurse who does such a wonderful job with such long hours would be lucky to earn anywhere near that in a year?'

Well, it's a perfectly good argument and I for one wouldn't attempt a comparison, but then that nurse probably does as worthy a job as many MPs and look what they earn and the percentage wage increases they award themselves every year. Of course, it could be just the age-old economic truism of supply and demand. Robbie Fowlers are in very short supply at the moment. Demand certainly outstrips supply – hence his high value and cost.

George:   I suppose we'll always have these differentials in a capitalist society that, for whatever reason, values a lot of entertainers, MPs, sportspeople and whatever above nurses. I'm reminded of a time when I was translating a personality questionnaire into Czech with my father – actually, Dad was doing all the work! – and one of the questions, which was part of a group looking at career ambition, asked whether you would rather work in a secure job that paid a steady salary or in a less secure one that paid by results. Now this, at the time, seemed a bizarre question in a Central European country where the Iron Curtain had only just come down: 'What? You mean it's possible to be paid by *results*?' Now that quite a lot of Central and East European players are coming to play in Britain, they must be experiencing quite a culture-shock. Take Kanchelskis, for example. The sheer contrast between life in the Ukraine and life over here must be difficult to imagine . . .

Pat:      Certainly, if you look at the picture from 10 years ago, a number of players were coming across from these countries and just weren't coping. It was nightclubs and generally enjoying the 'good life'. The feeling appeared to be that after seeing out a year or two of a decent contract here, you could return and live like a king back home.

*George*:  Who was the Polish guy at Celtic a few years back? Dariusz Dziekanowski, was it?

*Pat*:  'Jackie' Dziekanowski, yeah! I was actually thinking about him, but he really was an excellent player! A lot of people will say that different nationalities will portray certain different traits, and it can lead to misunderstandings and unnecessary disagreements. It is considered by many, for example, that the Russians are prone to alcoholism – come to that, many say the same thing about the Scots!

*George*:  Well, the Czechs certainly seemed to enjoy a bevvy during the Euro 96 tournament – and it didn't seem to do them too much harm!

*Pat*:  When you arrive in England as a foreign player, the trick is to be able to deal with and adapt to certain cultural changes, not so much in everyday life but more so within football itself. Our attitudes can be very different and rather idiosyncratic on this little island of ours – try explaining to an intelligent foreign player that he really ought to play on with a gaping head-wound à la Terry Butcher, unless he wants to be thought of as a big girl's blouse. It might elicit an incredulous reaction!

Some of the players who have come over from East European countries have shown weaknesses and some have failed, but as time goes by, a lot of these players have probably travelled extensively on international duty, especially after the fall of the Iron Curtain. They will arrive on our shores with a wider view of the world and of life. They do tend to cope a lot better these days. Some of them cope very well. There are, however, some who still think that all their Christmases have come at once and they just love living the 'mythical' footballer's life. These lads sometimes don't produce because they lose the incredible hunger they once had. The *need* to succeed has been taken away overnight with that big contract. Harry Redknapp at West Ham claims he has suffered from this problem during the season. They'd maybe retain some of that hunger if we paid them a lot less, and they'd probably still come, but we're not in the business of being a centre for cheap foreign labour. That would, of course, be disastrous for the development of our own young players.

*George*: Of course, it's not just foreign players who can lose that hunger. Dave Bassett has talked about players getting into 'comfort zones': they're earning enough to be going along with; they're happy where they are – what does it matter if they're not banging in that many goals?

*Pat*: I think that, increasingly, it could creep in, but I still believe it will be a very small minority. There will be some players who, if they get a four-year contract, will not want to move on even if they are not in the team, because nobody will pay them equivalent wages. So yes, they will carry on playing in their own little 'comfort zone', thinking: 'If I get in, I get in; if I don't, I don't.' Big shrug of shoulders. It is, of course, sad and I believe you have to question the clubs as well. I think that if you're going to pay x million pounds for a player, you really have to question whether you've looked into his character enough, whether you have spent some time considering the psyche as well as the physique. Is it really acceptable to spend millions of pounds on a chance purchase without 'studying the form' in depth? Even a racehorse owner wants to know about the 'character' of each horse he intends to invest in.

*George*: Some of us have been saying this for years. In many businesses, psychometric testing is adopted, using personality questionnaires to give a better picture of the person you are about to take on – and of course, the amounts involved in salaries and training are generally a fraction of what you'd spend on a top player. I think Stan Collymore said himself in a widely quoted interview with *FourFourTwo* that in no other industry would someone spend £8.5 million on a purchase they knew so little about. Just how much investigation of your psychological make-up will a manager generally make before signing a player like you?

Pat:       A lot of it is done at the time when the manager meets you, while you're ostensibly talking about contracts and the money involved. You'll have a chat, and a lot of managers try to use that opportunity to figure out something about your personality. Sadly, in an hour or two's chat, you can be a great liar – or deliberately put across a totally incorrect impression. If I was a manager, you wouldn't believe the depths I'd go into! Really serious depths! I'd have a lot of long discussions, I'd take them out for dinner and I'd want to find out a lot about their real personality, their hopes and wishes, to cut through the clichés and the telly-speak that many of us have learned to perfect over the years.

George:   This is something I often wonder about, as a fan. When, say, Kevin Keegan decides to spend £15 million on Alan Shearer, *has* he taken him out and quizzed him at great length about his philosophy of the game and so on?

Pat:       I think certain people are easier to read. Shearer is an easy one. You *know* his attitude to the game. Five years ago it was the same attitude. I think if you get to that level, you have to be very channelled, to have tunnel-vision, if you like, and most of the players who have got to that level do have a very professional attitude. They want to succeed very much and won't give it up lightly. Players like Shearer will never fall into that comfort zone. But there are players who do, and that angers most managers. To be honest, if I was a manager, it would infuriate me.

I hate it if I see it, because of all the attitudes I was brought up with. When you're out of the team, you should play so well in the reserves, and in every training game, that you're constantly applying pressure to get back in.

Of course, it gets more complicated when the manager simply doesn't rate you, doesn't like you – or worse still – is jealous of you. I've come across that more than once. So through no fault of your own, whatever you do will not be good enough. There was one fellow international player in the Scotland squad who suffered from his club manager's jealousy. He was very popular and the new manager came in and wouldn't play him, buying all sorts to replace him. I am sure it was down to the fact that the player in question was more popular with the fans than the manager was.

George: You talked about having that attitude drummed into you – even indoctrinated – at Celtic Boys' Club. I'm sure that the other big clubs, Manchester United and so on, try to instil similar values in young players. Do all clubs do this equally well, or are some much better at it than others?

Pat: Oh, some are definitely better at it than others. Some hardly do it at all. But it all comes down to the way those clubs are managed. I mean, how do you become a manager? You play 700 games, a few internationals and – hey presto! – apparently you're a manager! Has anyone bothered to look at some reference books to find out what a manager is supposed to be and do?

You just have to look at the ones who are successful and see what they do. Alex Ferguson studies character. The true greats in management have been wise men with an ability or gift for being able to read people's true characters. From that, they have to be able to know how to manage and manipulate them to get the very best out of them. Alex Ferguson is the obvious modern successor to Stein, Shankly and Busby in this area.

Cynics would, of course, suggest that a bunch of footballers is a fairly untaxing group to be able to read. They are, in fact, a very broad group and it only takes a quick comparison of such characters as Eric Cantona and Vinnie Jones to see the breadth of variation. It may well be that getting the best out of Cantona has been Fergie's greatest single piece of management. A difficult and complex guy on a number of levels, he has blossomed under Ferguson in a way that would have been unimaginable in his earlier career.

*George*:  Yes, I'm afraid I have to admit that he does that very well. He knows 'which buttons to push', which players must be handled sensitively, which ones he can shout at and it will lead to an improved performance, and so on.

*Pat*:  It's one of the greatest skills a manager needs, and if you talk to anyone in the game they'll tell you he's got it. But not all managers have it, by any means. Some of them never will.

*George*:  It's said that he was very influenced by the approach of Jock Stein, who liked to get to know players inside-out. He liked to find out everything he could about a player, even to the extent of visiting the pubs where he drank and asking the regulars what he was like. It's said he compiled dossiers on players, containing everything he knew about them.

*Pat*:  I had the honour of talking to Jock a few times when he was alive and I certainly felt that. There was a really deliberate determination to find out all he could about you. He was a hero to me and my family, as he was to every Celtic supporter, a god-like figure. I played in an Under-21s international in Spain, and Jock was there. I had always been very fit and very sharp. I looked a wee, wimpy guy, but I could comfortably go for a seven-mile run every day – I'm still very good at long-distance running, often leaving my team-mates far behind. Jock knew I had this stamina. He's read the reports about me. On this occasion, though, I was marked out of the game by a young Spanish player.

I ran and I ran for 45 minutes and this player was marking me. There was no expression in his eyes – they were like a shark's eyes. It's occurred to me since that he might have been on drugs! But I couldn't get by him. I tried everything. It was one of the only times in my career that I actually hit a player to slow him down. It had no effect. He just thumped me back, twice as hard.

So I came off at half-time knowing this boy was beating me, but thinking that there was no way that Jock would have a go at me, because I'd done everything, everything that was humanly possible. Jock wasn't the manager – it was Andy Roxburgh – but Jock stood in front of me, a huge man, a hero, and he blasted me for about 10 minutes solid! He bawled at me, completely slaughtered me. He questioned my commitment, my drive, my motivation. I always answer back when I believe I'm right, but for the first time ever I sat there in blind panic. I simply couldn't understand it, especially not from him, the manager I had most respect for in the world – indeed, one of the men I had most respect for in the world!

I went out and played a fairly decent second-half, and there was never another word said on the matter. For weeks afterwards, I thought: 'What a big galoot!' – as you would. 'He's a swine! He's not what I thought he was!' But it wasn't true. He just wanted to see how I'd handle it, wanted to check if I could hack it. He'd seen and heard various things, and he wanted to know something else about my character.

Afterwards, I went out and carried on doing exactly the same things I'd done before, and I think I got better, but it wasn't because he'd given me advice or told me what to do or anything. I just kept doing the same things, and although I was shocked by what had happened, it didn't crack me in any way. I get the feeling, years on, that he just did it to find out about my resilience, my strength of character – and I hope he found out something good. If anything, it had the positive effect of strengthening my resolve. It helped me in the end, but it was a tough lesson to learn from a hero and a legend!

Of course, it more than crossed my mind then and since that he simply thought I was useless. It does say something of people who command his level of respect in the game that whatever they do or say, you try somehow to gain something positive out of it.

*George*: Just how much shouting and bawling do you get from managers nowadays? Do they still like to give players a good old-fashioned bollocking – or, as Jim Smith mentioned in my previous book, have times changed in that players won't accept that any more?

Pat: Most – not all, but most – of the managers that I've worked under have done it once or twice a season. It's frequently done for effect, and it's deliberately kept to that. If you do it too often, it loses its effectiveness. It can come from having a real passion from the game – but perhaps being *too* passionate. But managers learn quite quickly and adapt. I think a lot of them shout things in the heat of the moment to a crowded dressing-room, which they then think about four hours later and regret. They realise that they've said the wrong thing, particularly if they watch the video of the game more closely. A brilliant example of this is Alex Ferguson, who used to be the biggest shouter and bawler in the world, apparently! I talk to Brian McClair a lot, who plays for him at Manchester United, and it seems that he's all but stopped doing it. It's now very, very rare. But it still goes on with certain other individuals.

I was taught a lesson while I was at Celtic Boys' Club – a lesson that went on for a whole year. The manager at the time was Frank Cairney. For a whole year, I was convinced he hated me. He shouted and bawled, he slaughtered me nearly every game for a whole season. He is a tall guy, and he stood three inches from my face and bellowed at me. I really struggled to handle it at first, but then eventually I managed to deal with it. I realised that the only thing to do was to take on board what was right and ignore the rest of it. It was hard to understand at the time why he and certain other individuals take such an aggressive approach.

George: Could it be because they themselves were brought up in that tradition, with their own managers screaming abuse at *them*?

Pat: No, not at all! I don't think Frank had ever played football to a high level. I just thought the guy didn't like me. My attitude was: 'I'll never play for Celtic now – he has too much say in whether Celtic FC sign players from the Boys' Club.' I went along to the end-of-season awards ceremony – at first I wasn't going to go, because I was still angry, but I was the season's top scorer again so I thought I ought at least to show my face. At the end of the evening, they announced the top award for the whole club from the under-11s to the under-16s, and I got it! I can remember to this day how stunned and confused I was. It didn't make sense. As I walked by Big Frank, he whispered: 'I only shout at the good players. You've learned a wee lesson, I hope. Now no-one will be able to get through to you, upset you and put you off your game.'

I said: 'Er ... OK, but did you have to do it for a whole year?' And he said: 'Yes. You'll never, ever be affected by it again.' It was true. Ever since then, absolutely nothing fazes me at all. Nothing has ever been worse than what I got off him – it could only be worse if someone walked up and punched me in the face! It was merely a lesson.

Celtic Boys' Club was almost a school in that respect. It was an academy and it was very professionally run – to be honest, more so in certain respects than some professional football clubs! A lot of good learning came out of it for me. There were other people, away from the football side of things, you could chat to about any other problems, even psychological, you might have; in particular, one fine gentleman called Hugh Birt. If I complained to him that Frank was giving me hell, he would say: 'Don't worry, I'm here to make sure that everything is alright.' If everyone had been aware of that, the eventual problems that surfaced in the club could have been nipped in the bud. In the end, I have to say I learned lessons at the club that have stayed with me all my life.

*George*: Was there something almost amusing about the extremity of it all? I remember Jon Pertwee told a story about a sergeant-major whom, despite all the bluster and barking orders at everyone, he found impossible to take seriously. On one occasion, this man bawled at him: 'What do you find so funny?'

'You, sir!' Pertwee replied.

'Aren't you scared of me?'

'No, sir!'

To which the sergeant-major pleaded, 'Well, for Christ's sake *try*, could you?' I wonder whether some of the fiercest people in the game are actually seen that way?

Pat:    Early on in my career it did amuse me a great deal, but now I find it interesting because I want to know why people do it. I wonder: 'Is he doing it because he has lost control, is he doing it for effect or is he doing it for some other reason?' Once again, I usually feel in this situation that I am an outsider, looking in, observing the scene . . . even if it is directed at me.

George:    Just as a behavioural psychologist might . . .

Pat:    If you say so! I think about the effect it's having on the others present, and if there's a young lad who doesn't seem to be coping with it well, I'll go and talk to him and reassure him. People in authority like football managers *are* trying to control certain things. They're not entirely uncontrolled ranters. They're trying to move people in a certain way. I must admit that now and again, I've had somebody bawl something at me and it's affected me. The bawling hasn't affected me, but the words have. I would be just as responsive if the words were said quietly as if they were shouted, and I tell people that. I won't take offence because they've shouted at me, but I tell them that they don't need to do so, I listen to the information whatever the decibel level. Of course, some shout to engender fear. I've certainly never felt that as a pro, not even a young pro, thanks once again to Frank Cairney.

George:    To what extent do players like authority figures who get very emotional? After all, if the manager shows very little emotion, it's difficult to get much empathy going. An apparently emotionless manager might be seen as a cold fish or a bit of a politician. The fans certainly like players like Gazza or Ian Wright who show their emotions very openly. They see that they have passion, that it's more than just a job for them.

Pat:    Certainly, different players may have attitudes very different to my own. To me, it doesn't matter much what's said and when. What's important is what *comes* of it. But players vary a lot. Some are impressed by shouting, others are impressed by words of wisdom, still others by a manager who can stand back and see an overall picture. You find quite a lot of guys who, if they're in the team will listen and will be positive, but if they're out of the team will despise the manager! One manager said – I think it might have been Ron Atkinson – that the trick in management is keeping the six players who hate you away from the five who aren't sure yet. There's definitely an element of that. The manager is set apart from you as players. Even if he was your best pal, someone you've played alongside for five years, he is apart now, he is no longer really part of the group.

    A manager has to accept that he will, inevitably, have players turn on him and be antagonistic towards him. He has to learn to stand off a bit, find ways of dealing with that – and learn how to control them. Different managers have their own ways of dealing with it, and they can never really convince everyone. The players will always either say 'He shouts too much' or 'He doesn't shout enough' – depending on whether you have a good relationship with the manager or not, or, more accurately, whether he rates you or not!

George:    At Tranmere you have John Aldridge, one of the player-managers who, following the success of Kenny Dalglish, now seem to be springing up all over the place. It isn't always as easy as Kenny made it look though, as Kevin Keegan and Bryan Robson – to name but two – have been finding out. How hard a transition is it to make from being 'one of the lads' to being the gaffer? It must be hard not only for the individual, but also for the players to re-adjust their view of him . . .

Pat:    For the first six games when John Aldridge took over, it was just such a novelty that he remained one of the lads in our eyes and we all worked together. He's now in a more difficult position, as every player-manager will tell you – and he'll tell you himself! – that you can't be one of the lads any more. He couldn't go to the races with the boys. He felt he had to stay away. It's not really possible to be one of them any more: he's going to be responsible for dropping some of these players; eventually he's even going to have to release some from the club. He has already begun to stand back, and will do so more in the future. If he were able to learn the job overnight, he'd be a genius. He isn't. He's learning it. He's learning it quickly though, because basically, he has to.

*George*:  I remember having a conversation once with Tommy Burns at Celtic who, although he no longer plays, is a young manager. He certainly sees it as a continual learning-process in that he actually goes off to other clubs like Ajax to see how they work, and tries to incorporate some of their ideas into his own thinking.

*Pat*:  Tommy's like that. I think he's a bit of a scholar anyway. If it was me, that's what I would do. I'd go about it in exactly the same way as Tommy Burns. But getting back to the player-manager 'syndrome', if there's anybody in football that everyone has a huge amount of respect for, it's Dalglish. He's scored more than a hundred goals in Scotland and the same in England, won the European Cup, scoring winning goals in that competition, a hundred games for Scotland, winning the Championship as a player then as manager with Liverpool, winning it again as manager with Blackburn . . . The list just goes on and on. You name it, he's done it, and he's done it brilliantly. He's incredibly popular with players, though not with the media. Journalists mean nothing to him. As far as he is concerned, it is the *people* – the players and the fans – that are important. It's a Celtic attitude, but when he joined Liverpool he would have found that they have the same attitude. The old Liverpool, anyway.

But even he struggled. You remember that weird

night when he made his decision to leave Liverpool? It came after that incredible match, the 4–4 draw with Everton. Well, I was in the Everton team, sitting in the dressing-room next door, and after the match, Kenny and the team were bawling at one another, shouting at the tops of their voices. We could all hear it from our dressing-room – it was mayhem! Now, Kenny has since said that it was already in his mind to chuck in the job before, but whatever the reality of the situation, managing Liverpool was obviously not plain sailing, even for someone of Kenny's stature. He was no longer 'one of the lads', he wasn't part of that group any more, because they never would have shouted and bawled at him when he was just a player. So even Kenny found it difficult to make the transformation from player to manager.

Well, he took a bit of a break from it, and then his next job was manager at Blackburn. I think it's significant that during his time as manager there, he didn't buy a single player from his previous club. I don't think he bought any. Now that is *incredibly* unusual. Normally, the first thing that managers do after moving into a new job is start plundering their old club for players. My view – and I might be wrong – is that Kenny thought to himself: 'Right! It's a bloody difficult job, this management! I'm going to do it differently this time.' The dilemma of having to drop mates, or to try and offload them as they get older, was something he could do without.

*George*:   So he didn't want any links with the past?

*Pat*:   Absolutely. Though even in that situation, when he first started as player-manager at Liverpool, they did very well. They won the League – beating Chelsea, in fact, in their final game. I played for Chelsea that day and I remember Kenny himself scoring the winning goal in a 1–0 win. At that time, needless to say, things were great for Liverpool. But as time went on, it got harder and harder for him.

*George*:   It starts off well, but then it's downhill all the way?

*Pat*:      More or less. As you begin to back away from the
            players, it gets harder. Kenny learned it, but it took a lot
            of pain to learn. I think every player-manager finds out
            that there's a lot of pain involved. John Aldridge will
            find it, too. That's nothing against John, it's just the
            nature of the beast.

*George*:   An interesting contrast with Kenny is his friend Alan
            Hansen, who made it very clear that wild horses
            wouldn't drag him into football management. On the
            other hand, it must look a tempting career-choice for
            many footballers coming to the end of their playing
            days. Now you even have the more successful – and
            presumably more comfortably-off – players going
            straight into management, missing out the traditional
            intermediate step of coaching – Kevin Keegan, Bryan
            Robson, Tommy Burns, Glenn Hoddle – with varying
            degrees of success.

*Pat*:      Some walk straight into management, but that's a very,
            very small number. Most players who now aspire to be
            managers are pursuing their coaching badges while
            they're players. It's one of the things that the union, the
            PFA, can contribute money towards through a grant.
            You can do the FA coaching badge, which is much better
            than it used to be and I would argue that is largely due
            to pressure from the PFA. The union got them to
            improve it. I'm not saying the old badge was crap . . .
            well, yes I am! It was rubbish when compared with
            European coaching badges. The Scottish FA one was
            much better, too! Miles ahead of it. However, the union
            did a study, sending people all round the world looking
            at coaching standards everywhere. We ploughed a lot
            of money into it and came back with a really convincing
            report, compiled by our man Paul Power. That pressure
            from us got the FA to improve the product. It is greatly
            improved now, and I hope that very soon we'll have
            something that's on a par with the European
            classification.
                It's great that it's happened, because along with the
            European ban following Heysel, it was one of the main

reasons why football in this country was held back. When people complained about the standard of football in England and why we had fallen behind Europe, a lot of the explanation lay in the quality of coaching here, because coaches had done the FA badge and nothing else. They should have done what Tommy Burns did, travelling around Europe checking out how they coach over there. Tommy was one of the first people to do that, despite the fact that the Scottish FA's coaching badge was superior to the English one – it looked to Holland and to Italy. That wasn't good enough for Tommy, he wanted to see things for himself.

But with the improvements, it's really taken off. You wouldn't believe how many coaches we have playing for Tranmere at the moment! They're fully qualified and as time goes on, you'll see them moving into coaching – or even into management. They'll have the backing of the badge, but even that's not everything. They could probably do with a spot of management studies, too. That's my personal opinion, that a wee management course wouldn't go amiss for football managers. If I was going into management, that's what I'd do – and I must stress in the strongest terms that I'm *not* going to go into management! I fully agree with Alan Hansen on that one!

I've done a little bit of coaching before. I've touched on it and learned a little, and when you do that, you see just how much you still have left to learn! That's the problem, really. We've had some people go into management who have not been well enough prepared for it, and although they've been great players with great experience, they haven't done well. Some people are just not cut out for it. With Dalglish, well . . . some people are just brilliant, no matter what they do. His experience certainly equipped him for some aspects of the job, but not all. He is the classic exception to prove any rule.

If I was going to go into coaching at all, the areas that would interest me are coaching kids up until the age of

18 or else taking some kind of background role, looking at the overall picture and liaising with a manager in some way.

That's another problem with trying to combine management with playing: as a player, you're generally too close to the action, and you can get too close to football. You can be *physically* too close if you're watching the game from the bench, which you should never do. You should always try and watch it from the stand, maybe phoning down to the bench, where you've got someone positioned to relay the information for you.

For the past three years solid, I've hardly missed a game. Then, as I said, I was out injured for six games at the end of last season. During that period, somewhere vaguely at the back of my mind a wee voice was saying: 'Get out, get upstairs and watch the team play! If you've got injuries, don't fight against that – go upstairs and watch, because you might learn something up there!' There's definitely something outside that you don't see while you're playing on the pitch, and over time you begin to get caught up in areas you were never caught up in before. If the opportunity arises, take a step back – and what looked like an abstract picture can start to take shape from a distance.

*George*:   So as to avoid not being able to see the wood for the trees?

*Pat*:   Precisely. I used to study videos, especially at Everton. That was brilliant, because Colin Harvey, the manager there, was intelligent enough to suss that it's no use watching videos of the type you get on *Match of the Day*, with close-ups of the action, players' facial expressions and the rest of it. He got a camcorder and placed it right at the top, at the back of the stand, where it showed the whole pitch. He recorded whole matches from that angle. I would borrow the videos and watch how I played in matches shot in that way, seeing how my performance contributed to the whole picture.

Colin Harvey was ahead of his time from that point of view. I rated him very highly, considering Everton sacked him, but I'm glad to see that he's now back doing the job he's best at – he's coaching again. Other aspects of the manager's job didn't suit him so well, but he was an excellent coach. He did the same in the reserve games, taking an identical approach. It looked the most ridiculous thing in the world, but he'd be there at Bellefield, the training ground, sitting on a chair on the roof, watching the match! Many other managers wouldn't have the bottle to do that. He used to climb up around the back, through a little window and up onto the roof, put a chair up there and sit watching what was going on. He would then be in a position to make small changes to the overall pattern of the team and the shape of play, as well as to individual players' styles.

Anyway, I recalled those days at Everton and in the back of my mind, I knew that I needed to stand back again. I thought about going to see another team play, but it's not the same thing. You've got to watch your own team play, even if it's without you.

*George*: Just like the player I mentioned at Dulwich Hamlet, Dave Coppin.

*Pat*: Yes. And as a result of being up there watching matches for those final six games of last season, and for the first few matches of this season when I've still been injured, I feel I've learned far more than I would have done had I been playing in those games. By standing back, I've thought of a couple of things I can do to improve my game. The break also relaxed me all over again. It's as though it *needed* to happen to me. Some companies in the 'real' world suggest a sabbatical for their employees, so they can come back afterwards invigorated, re-charged and with a clearer overview of the company's direction, as well as their own. That's what it was like for me.

# SESSION 3
## Fear and Loathing in the Hotel

*Travel abroad and spending time in hotels form an integral part of an international footballer's life. Catching up with Pat, appropriately enough in a hotel, it was time to find out what it was really like to share a room with a player you'd cheerfully have strangled prior to the experience . . .*

George:  They say that travel broadens the mind. You mentioned earlier that Stuart Pearce likes to travel to exotic parts of the world and that you yourself had been Interrailing. What have you learned on your travels with the various football teams you've played for?

Pat:  When I was at Chelsea, we went to Baghdad. It was a chance to play an international team, but also an opportunity for Ken Bates to meet up with his old soul-mate, Saddam Hussein – only kidding, Ken! Don't sue . . . please! It was probably the weirdest trip I've ever been on. We played in front of a huge crowd. The game was delayed a couple of hours because yer man didn't turn up – he was busy. Maybe it was his brother, now I come to think of it. Either Saddam or his brother didn't turn up for a couple of hours, so we were kept waiting. There we were in the middle of the park, all kitted out, just hanging around. We couldn't do any warming-up – it was much too hot for that. The crowd were all assembled, but we couldn't start. So we waited and waited and waited. Then suddenly it was prayer time, so they all got into position, facing Mecca. I mean, what do you do? It was very embarrassing moment. Do you get down and join them or what? I've never been sure of the correct etiquette in this particular situation!

So we were all a bit unsure what to do. I mean, you

don't start kicking the ball around when everyone
around you is praying, do you? Suddenly, it was less of
a football stadium and more like an outdoor mosque.

Well, eventually, everybody got up again and the
game started. We won. At the time, Saddam Hussein
was just a name to us. We wouldn't have recognised
him. It was only later that he was to achieve such notor-
iety. We went up, shook hands with him and received
our little medals, before applauding our opponents.
Then the Iraqi national side went up and got their
runners-up trophy, and it was massive! You wouldn't
believe the size of the thing. It was bigger than their
centre-half. You can bet that in the following day's
papers, there would have been a picture of the Iraq
team, holding this trophy aloft, accompanied by a
report saying they'd beaten us 5–1 or something!

The following day, I decided to forgo those papers,
and the exotic pleasures of getting bevvied with the lads
in the Baghdad Hilton's plush downstairs bar, instead
plumping for an early-morning stroll through the
ancient and slightly dangerous bazaar. John Millar, who
then went to Hearts, was with me, and we both dressed
scruffily in order to blend into the background, before
hopping casually into the back of the complimentary
white limousine.

We eventually talked the chauffeur into dropping us
at the edge of the bazaar. After he sped off and the dust
settled, mostly on us, we turned around to be greeted
by a semi-circle of locals, staring at us menacingly. Our
arrival had all the inconspicuous subtlety of a third-
world video-shoot for Duran Duran, and for the next
five hours, we made our way through a maze of alleys
and stalls, closely followed by a host of shady-looking
characters.

As we walked, we got more and more tired, hungry,
thirsty and, finally, hopelessly lost. Every other corner
had a machine-gun-toting macho man in combat gear
and regulation reflective sunglasses. The spectre of war
hung in the air even then, though it was still years

before Saddam became a frightening face on our television screens. Even Indiana Jones would have been shaken! Suddenly, the controlled atmosphere of the hotel bar with a bunch of Chelsea players knocking back the pints seemed much more civilised.

*George*: So, curiosity nearly killed wee Pat.

*Pat*: It seemed that way at the time. Before this incident, I would always travel to our destination with the team, and as soon as we got there, I'd go off by myself and explore. That made me a little bit more wary, though! All the same, I still like to go off and explore – usually the art gallery. But I can see why players are sometimes scared of doing so, because that incident *was* scary. Normally, people would fear that sort of experience – it's so removed from everything you're familiar with.

That bizarre story – that *bazaar* story – was only part of it. I missed the team bus to the match. I had been listening to Teardrop Explodes on my headphones, a track called *Thief of Baghdad* as I recall, and just totally lost track of the time, which is typical of me. I went downstairs, the coach had gone and there were all these guys in dark glasses hanging around. I pleaded with them to get me some kind of transport to the ground, and they said they'd take me personally.

They told me it was about 25 minutes to the ground, and the coach had left five minutes ago. I thought we might be able to catch it up. Unfortunately, they were quite ungripped by any sense of urgency. Twenty minutes later, we still hadn't left. Being a bit of a control freak, I was going crazy.

When we did set off, however, there was no stopping us. We went through red lights, ignored policemen . . . they say that the Italians are mad drivers, but this was a million times worse! We were bumping cows to get them out of the way, mounting pavements, just missing kids. I was saying, 'It's only a football match – calm down, chaps!' as the sweat was pouring off me. Then it occurred to me that I had no idea where they were taking me. Here I was in this car, in a strange land, with people who were obviously secret-police types who I didn't know from Adam, and they could have been taking me anywhere. I'm rarely fazed by anything, but this felt really hairy.

Anyway, we arrived before the coach did! That was one weird trip from start to finish.

George:  Football must have given you real opportunities to travel all around the world . . .

Pat:  Yes. I have to say I took it a little bit for granted at first, because I've always been a really keen traveller and had done a bit outside football. I love travel writing, too. However, once I was in the Scotland squad, all of a sudden the travelling really began. I've played in wonderful places like China, and the great thing about being part of an internationally organised football squad is that they take you to places where tourists wouldn't normally be allowed to go. Most players, I have to say, were uninterested and said: 'Ach, we're staying in.' I took every opportunity to see everything. I thought it was wonderful.

I know that the idea of pre-season tours is to bond with the other players, and keeping together is part of the Scotland set-up as well to some extent, but when I'm abroad, I just think: 'For God's sake! You're in Sofia or you're in Belgrade! You may never see these places again! Go out there and look around!' On the other hand, players are professionals, they have a job of work to do, and they have to be focused. Exploring exotic places is, admittedly, a distraction, so from that angle, they might be right. Staying in the hotel, focusing on the game and your pre-match diet is important. I know that the papers take the mickey out of people like Gazza, missing out on the opportunity to see the Great Wall of China, but if that would be a distraction for him, if it helps him to be focused *not* to go, then I can understand that. *I'd* go, though. I think I can still be focused, even if I explore places.

I remember playing in Bulgaria, staying in Sofia. I had got very keen on Bulgarian folk music, which I

think is absolutely beautiful – particularly the voices.
John Peel had played some of it on his show and I was
very enthusiastic about it before I'd even set foot in
Bulgaria. I had written to one of the bands and they
had sent me some tapes, which Peely loved – he'd never
seen the originals before. One of the musicians was very
keen on football, and when he was in London, I took
him to a match. He promised that if I was ever in
Bulgaria, we would meet up.

Anyway, two years later, there I was in Bulgaria and
sure enough, my friend was waiting outside the hotel
for me. He knew the city and he showed me round. We
went to the museums and galleries, but we also went to
places that I never would have seen if I hadn't been
with a local who knew Sofia like the back of his hand.

I remember being shown a shop down one of the
backstreets and being asked to guess what sort of shop
it was. It was a bit weird, because all you could see was
a valve here, a leg there, a bit of box over there ... I
looked at it and they watched me looking at it, but I just
couldn't figure it out. It was a television shop! There
were no televisions in it, because people couldn't afford
a whole television, so they'd buy it, bit by bit, and
assemble it themselves. I said: 'You're kidding!' Being
Czech, you'll have seen that part of the world, but for
me, it was a revelation. I couldn't believe it and neither
could the lads.

*George*:  I know what you're saying. When my parents travel
back to the Czech Republic and stay with relatives or
friends, they're almost embarrassed to buy too much,
in case it reveals how affluent they are compared to the
average Czech. Even now, things like yoghurt, which
they wouldn't think twice about buying over here, are
much more expensive, relative to the average Czech's
salary. I don't want to exaggerate, but it's still very
apparent. Naturally, it makes it an incredibly cheap
place to visit for British or American tourists. Unfortunately, although Czechs are now free to travel wherever
they like abroad, they would find prices over here

incredibly expensive. I've noticed that on the official exchange-rate, the maximum fine for travelling without a ticket on the Prague Metro is less than the price of a ticket on the London Underground!

Pat:    What got me in Bulgaria were the attitudes that people had. The things in shops were different and unusual, too, but it was the attitude to work in particular. That took me ages to get my head round. I had been walking around with these Bulgarians for half a day, and then it occurred to me that they were supposed to have been working that day. 'Oh, don't worry about that,' they said. 'In fact, if you want to see some more tomorrow...'

'But what about your boss?' I asked. 'You could lose your job.'

'Oh, we'll find another one,' was the reply. 'The regime guarantees us a job.'

That really opened my eyes. I still have firm socialist beliefs but I was really quite a strong lefty then, and I began to wonder whether this kind of system could ever really work. I could see hundreds of people around me, but it was three in the afternoon and all of them should have been at work. None of them were, and nobody seemed the slightest bit concerned. There seemed no reason for them to be dedicated to their jobs ... hence, I suspect, one of the reasons their economy was in ruins. It certainly affected my politics a bit, and my view of the world as a whole. When that happens to you, you want to share it with the other players.

But it's hard to get players to come along with me. Some are lazy, some don't care, some just want to focus their mind on the match. I remember Stuart Pearce telling me he was once in Sydney and the whole team could have had free tickets for a big show at the Sydney Opera House. In the end, only two of them bothered to go to see one of the modern architectural wonders of the world.

But to some extent, I had missed the point. Certainly,

if it's a pre-season tour, sightseeing and culture aren't the idea at all. The idea is to build team spirit and camaraderie, away from home, away from the family – wives are never invited. Playing a few matches, getting a bit of sun by the pool and having a drink together in the bar is a good way to achieve that. I just think that my sense of team spirit is so ingrained, so indoctrinated maybe, from my time at Celtic Boys' Club, that it's as good as anyone's. Howard Kendall didn't recognise that in me. He thought I was an outsider and that I was sneering. He didn't see beyond my surface behaviour.

Some football people may see me as an outsider, a maverick and a loner. Though there are elements of all three in me, more than any of these I am very much a team player. I can sit next to anyone on the team coach and have a good conversation with them. At a certain level, I have no problem mixing at all.

Having said that, I've always been wary of large groups, ever since I was a child. I've often despised the 'mob mentality' which you can find in large groups who pick on the weakest individuals in those groups. The roots of hooliganism and much deeper social problems lie there. When I was very young at school, I was top of my classes and the best football player. Even so, I tended to steer clear of groups, being suspicious of their functioning. If I ever saw someone picking on anyone outside of the group, generally someone who was weak, victimising them unfairly, I'd come down on them very hard. In that sense, I must have seemed quite influential in the playground.

By secondary school, we'd moved house and I was much more drawn to groups, but I'd always spend my time with the weaker, the weirder, the more unusual members of that group. Looking back, I guess I was probably seen as a bit of a nice, 'establishment' boy, well-groomed, did well in exams and so on. Yet I liked the slightly unusual, slightly eccentric, more interesting people, if you like. They were always my friends. They were often ones who everyone else hated or were scared of. It wasn't just the boys – a lot of my friends were girls in those days. I was always attracted to these pariahs.

If I ever saw one of them victimised by the group as a whole, I took great pleasure in taking every one of the group to one side and confronting them about it. There's a nasty side of me that enjoyed watching the group's members squirm when individualised and they couldn't justify what they'd done, confronted one-to-one. Even if they were much taller than me, I'd look them straight in the eye and challenge them about what they'd been doing. I always had that confidence and I've always despised the way a group can turn on an individual.

My experience has always been that if you target three or four of the group on an individual basis, especially if it's the ringleaders, then it stops happening. They no longer pick on weaker members of the group. All these traits occur with any group of boys, even if those boys are no longer at school, but watching or playing professional football. I'm not saying players are just big schoolkids, but that sort of victimisation can and does occur in clubs. There are psychological bully boys, and I am still always happy to challenge them . . . especially when I can isolate them, they appear different creatures on their own.

Now, I'm happy to play the role of an outsider, but others who are less confident than me and are more keen to be a central part of the group, sometimes desperately so, haven't got my arrogance, confidence, call it what you will, and deep down, not being able to be part of the group hurts them. There was an 'article' in *Viz* recently, entitled *The Agony of the Egghead Footballers*. It was very funny but also, as is the case with the best comedy, dangerously close to the truth. The outsiders in the group can suffer, even when it is because they are perceived to be too clever or, more precisely, too educated.

*George*:  Perhaps that's true of a player like Graeme Le Saux?

*Pat*:  Players like that can suffer a wee bit. They may worry why they're not fully accepted, whether there's something wrong with them. Certainly, Graeme should be confident enough in himself, his ability and his intelligence to rise above it.

I'm still drawn to people like that, players who are less typical of the group and may feel unhappy that they're not a greater part of it. Graeme Le Saux came to Chelsea when he was 15 or 16, and I asked if any of the kids wanted to stay behind after training to work on their skills. Not one of them did, except for Graeme. He was very dedicated and willing to learn. So Graeme stayed back and I worked with him to help improve his technique as a left-back – he was a very good player to start with, of course – every afternoon. He was bored in the evenings, so I encouraged him in his interests in the theatre, in music, in books and in art.

We even tried out one another's roles in training sessions, with him attacking and me defending for a change. After all, you never know what's going to happen in your career. I'm not saying I made him the player he is, but I like to think I helped him, just as he was starting out. Of course, he helped me a great deal, too. He was a tough opponent. In fact, I used to worry sometimes when I couldn't beat this 'kid'. How was I to know he was soon to be England's left-back?

The trouble is that if you're not a strong personality, being the outsider can be a tough role to play in the team. I don't think that's true of footballers alone, it's a more general group characteristic. Maybe Graeme isn't as headstrong as me, so I think he got upset about the stuff people said about him for a little while.

*George*: We saw a bit of that last season when he had that clash with his team-mate, David Batty. [*Later in the season, Le Saux was to fight back from his injuries and end up in the England team alongside Batty, their altercation apparently forgotten.*] I read an interview with Graeme in which he said that he tends to prefer his own room when he's on England duty. How do room-mates get decided at club level – or international level, come to that?

*Pat*:     Obviously, they try to arrange it so that you're sharing a
           hotel room with someone you like and get on with, but
           it doesn't always work out that way. You can end up
           sharing a room with someone who you despise! But it
           doesn't necessarily work out badly, even when that
           happens. It can ruin your night and leave you angry
           before the game, but it can lead to a much better under-
           standing and perhaps a thawing of hostility.

           On international duty, they tend to put me in with
           another 'Anglo', a Scot playing in England, as if this is
           some guarantee that we'll be like two peas in a pod. I've
           often shared with Brian McClair and we've become great
           friends. I think the basis for that was that we both started
           higher education courses and we read the *Guardian*, the
           *Independent* and the music press! One of my unlikely
           pairings was with David Speedie. David and I had an
           almost telepathic understanding on the field, but off it
           we had a psychopathic abhorrence of one another! We
           were total opposites in personality and didn't under-
           stand where the other was coming from at all.

           We went up to Scotland together and it was David's
           first time in the Scotland squad, after some fine per-
           formances for Chelsea. It hadn't even occurred to me
           that a blissfully unaware Andy Roxburgh would think:
           'Aha! Two Chelsea boys. We'll put them in the same
           room!' I saw this period of four whole days stretching
           out in front of me. Four whole days! There was so much
           antagonism between us that it could have led to murder
           – and I didn't fancy my chances.

           Boredom is always the biggest thing you have to beat
           if you're in a hotel, miles from anywhere. One night in
           a hotel is bad enough, but four nights, without being
           able to drink or wander too far outside, was going to be
           hell – and with David Speedie in my room, it was going
           to be even worse! We can all endure the odd embar-
           rassing silence, but there was no way it could last four
           days and four nights. I came very close to withdrawing
           from the squad through injury! I think I was mentally
           bruised.

*George*: Did you find anything to talk about?

*Pat*: We did. We owned up that we hated each other and then we tried to understand one another's point of view. By the end of the four days, the hatred was gone. It's like many things in life – the fear springs from not understanding. The hatred was really a fear, a fear of not having a clue about the other guy's personality. I'm very glad that this breakthrough didn't simultaneously kill the understanding we had on the field. But that was one of those wonderful situations where you had people who were polar opposites stuck in a hotel room together and something good came of it.

*George*: Like one of those disaster movies with people stuck together in a lift or a cable car?

*Pat*: Very much like that, though without the music. We had some very long conversations. I don't know whether it's because I'm incredibly nosey or I just like understanding people, but I began to appreciate where he was coming from. I learned that this fire within him, which I couldn't understand because I was very laid-back, this anger and hatred and nastiness was actually tempered with a lot of humour and he was capable of snapping out of it when he felt like it. Spending that time with him, I was very curious to find out where this anger came from. Part of it, it turned out, was just this chip on his shoulder – maybe a number of chips on each shoulder – that a lot of players possess . . .

*George*: The sort you acquire if you're a Scotsman growing up in Yorkshire?

*Pat*: And you're short and balding, yes! So there were a few chips – enough for a sausage supper. But there was also something else I learned – and this is true of a number of other players I've seen since – and that was that this anger, this nastiness, this 'I'll do anything to get my way' was actually rooted in a rather beautiful thing. The fierce determination, fire and abrasive iron-will came from the noblest of sources: the desire to get the best for his family. That was at the heart of it all. Behind all that anger was the drive to get the very best for his wife and kids. That was the craving. You get this cliché that a player is 'a bit nasty on the field but he's a lovely family man', yet it really holds true. A lot of love on one side causes a lot of apparent hate or aggression on the other. He would have fought anyone or anything for his family.

Julian Dicks is another example. When you face him as an opponent, you look into his eyes and they stare blankly at you. There is no soul, no apparent humanity there while he's on the field. When he hurts you, there's no emotion. With him and Stuart Pearce, in particular, I don't show any emotion back to them on the field, because I've learned that that's the way to deal with them as opponents. Julian portrays himself as a killing machine. His nickname is 'The Terminator'. Show fear or agitation and he has already won the psychological battle. Yet he's got a very apparent weakness, and that's his family. When his daughters got stick at school over that incident where John Spencer's head attacked his foot, that's what broke him, that's what made him so upset.

These are not evil people. There obviously are one or two people in the game who really do just enjoy hurting people and are complete nutters, utter psychopaths, but they're not normally the ones you immediately think of. A lot of it is driven by a desire to help others, their families especially. I remember going to Mexico to play their young national team and I was spending the evenings catching up on my PG Wodehouse collection. My attitude was very much 'I say! Steady on, chaps! Play the game, what?' while they spat and gouged and kicked us all over the park. But when you consider their poverty, their determination to fight their way out and, through football, get a better living for their families, you can see where that violence springs from. It doesn't last forever. Players tend to lose it as they get older and more secure.

*George*:  You see it in very aggressive sales reps, too. People say: 'Oh, they'll calm down now that they've got a family,' whereas, very frequently, reps become even more aggressive when they have a family to support, when they have more mouths to feed. If they started off ready to wound to get a deal, they'll be ready to kill by the time their kids come along!

Pat: There are some wonderful links between the two jobs. As a footballer, you're selling yourself, you're there waiting for a big club to buy you, so you will go to great lengths to do so. You *have* to compete, even against your friends. Even against your team-mates, when it comes down to it. There is a competition between all of you. In football it may be that little bit nastier, because every day you go to work in the morning with someone who quite obviously and transparently *wants your job!* They want your position. They want to take your livelihood away from you! So there isn't just the competition from your opponents, there's the competition from within your own team, too.

George: The other difficulty when it comes to sharing with players in hotels must be when you have a very hyper-active player like Paul Gascoigne, who sleeps very little, likes to talk and have a laugh continually, and runs the risk of tiring his fellow players out. Have you ever found yourself in that position?

Pat: Players like that are fairly rare. We had Mickey Thomas during my time at Chelsea. He needed very little sleep, was very, very active and couldn't sit still in one place for long at all. Like most of these hyperactive lads, though, he was wonderful fun to be around. The manager soon found, though, that whenever Mickey shared a room with a player, that player tended to have a very poor game the following day! As a result, he was given his own room, but that can have a detrimental effect on the hyperactive player because he needs the company of others, or he starts to feel down, to get too introspective.

George: How much choice do you get over who ends up where?

Pat: You might get 18 players down for an away match, nine double-rooms allocated, and at least eight or so will end

up swapping and changing their room-mates from the
ones they've been allocated. I'm usually the one who's
left at the end – like the kid who's always picked last in
school football games! I like to chop and change, to
spend time with different players, listen to them and
find out what their problems are, what's worrying
them, maybe try to help if I can. I can't always give the
best advice myself, but maybe I can pass them on to
someone else who can help them. I wouldn't betray
their secrets or anything like that. I think they know
they can trust me from that point of view.

So I don't have an automatic room-mate. I did have
one for about two years, and told him all my secrets. It
was the captain, John Aldridge. Now he's the manager
and he knows everything about me!

*George*:   Oh dear.

*Pat*:      On Scotland duty, it was very much a question of who
I got on with. I shared a lot with Billy McKinlay, who
used to be at Dundee United and is now at Blackburn
Rovers. His humour and my humour exactly fit each
other. He's a great player. He hasn't, to use a Scottish
phrase, set the heather alight down here yet, but I feel
sure he will. He's sort of in the mould of David Batty as
a player, but his humour is brilliant. We were together
for a match against Sweden, and we spent three days in
one another's company. I think I must have laughed
solidly for about six or seven hours on each of those
three days. It's a wonderful, relaxing feeling. Even if a
player like that isn't playing, his presence has such a
positive effect on the rest of the team. I would buy a
player like that and have him around whether he was
fit or not, just to keep team spirit sky-high. The uplift-
ing effect on the other players is very noticeable. You
need that joker, the guy who lifts the spirits of others.

*George*:   They say that of Paul Gascoigne too, of course.

*Pat*:      There is no more perfect example than Gazza. His
humour doesn't necessarily translate all that well to
television or to journalists, but if you spend time in a
room with him, I guarantee you'll fall about laughing.

A lot has been made of his injury and whether he'll ever be the same again, but unless they take away that humour, unless they drug him with haloperidol or something to calm him down, he'll always be a brilliant person to have around and always an integral part of the team. He would be worth investing in to promote team spirit, even if he never kicked a ball again in his life.

*George:*   Finally on this theme, is it true that Kenny Dalglish was once very suspicious about sharing a room with Graeme Souness, as he was extremely wary of any player who had his own hair-drier?

*Pat:*   Kenny is the one who actually tells this story. Souness in those days had a perm and a blow-drier, and Kenny thought he might be a bit 'light in the old Puma boots', as they say. But times have changed quickly, and Kenny with them. If you took the Kenny of those days into a dressing-room today, with all those players who double as male models wandering around, I think he'd run out screaming and shouting.

*George:*   No wonder he doesn't seem too sold on David Ginola!

# SESSION 4
# Everybody Hurts

*It had not been the best of starts to the season for Pat. When I next caught up with him, he had sustained an injury at the worst possible time. I had been intending to explore the feelings a player has about injuries in more detail anyway, but events had given this theme an unexpected salience . . .*

George: So tell me about this blow to your comeback. It sounds as though it's been 'out of the frying pan and into the fire', one injury after another . . .

Pat: Well, I was really fit at the beginning of the season. I'd worked really hard before getting this injury running down this mountain in Scotland. I managed to get over it and even managed to train through it, so as not to lose much fitness. However, I then managed to pick up a different injury, this very unusual one called *Plantar Fasciitis*, which affects the sole of the foot. It is particularly annoying because it is simply caused by the constant stress and strain of running on hard ground, not a more 'butch' reason like being kicked or twisting it after a tackle. I immediately had a cortisone jab from the doctor and . . . it didn't help at all.

After a week or so, I'd lost my chance of a place in the team, and even my chance to be first-choice reserve. It is frustrating, because after three years of playing first-team football constantly, it feels terrible to be out of it. I tried to be philosophical and told myself that I could probably do with a rest, that 60 games in a season would probably put a real strain on my ageing body this year.

Three weeks later, though, there was still no improvement, and by this time the worries had begun to surface and I was getting very concerned indeed over whether it was ever going to get better. So I did something which, for me, is a bit unusual: I decided to accept a second injection. Too much cortisone can have terrible effects in the longer term, but I reasoned that I hadn't had that many injections throughout my career, so it probably wouldn't do too much harm. It was probably only the third or fourth injection of this kind in my whole career. There was the added bonus that this jab wasn't into a joint, making it safer and less prone to long-term complications. Our physio, in common with most physios these days, is very wary of too many injections. The legacies of past mistakes are too apparent in the old pros hobbling about at the clubs.

I had realised I was miles out of the team and the reckoning, and although I had been working very hard, I knew I would continue to drift. This particular injury allowed me to do as much training as I liked on sand, I just couldn't run on hard surfaces. The pounding was the problem. I was going up and down sand-dunes constantly. I've got what I think must be something of a Scottish mentality – certainly, lots of Scottish people I know have this mentality: we really enjoy working until we are physically wrecked. The other injured players groan when I ask the physio if we can go to the dreaded dunes again. It may be something to do with wanting to show these Sassenachs how hard we are prepared to work, or a feeling of needing to work hard because we are getting paid a good wage when not being available for selection. The Protestant work ethic and good old-fashioned Catholic guilt together make a powerful cocktail.

So I was going in early for training and doing extra weights, over and above the hard shift with the physio, but it still didn't improve. All the ghosts began to haunt me – in despondent moments, I started to question whether it would ever be right. Would I ever be able to walk properly again? When I retire, I would like to do a lot of hill-walking. Would I be able to do it? For 17 years,

I've dreamed of taking time out at the end of my career to climb a few *Munroes*, and the dream was beginning to look questionable. Most of the time I was, of course, quite calm about it, but in my darkest moments, it had really begun to concern me.

Anyway, for the second injection I was sent to a specialist. He stuck the needle in for the injection and by the time he took it out of my foot, it was fully recovered. Torture and torment for weeks on end, and total relief in five seconds!

George: It was really that sudden?

Pat: Not a word of a lie! He put it in, I jumped down from the couch and it felt perfectly all right. The specialist had said: 'Jump down hard from the couch and if it doesn't hurt, it has worked and you will be fine.' It was the most incredible feeling. The specialist obviously knew exactly what he was doing – he hit the spot and it was back to full training the next day.

George: Let's talk in more depth about how it feels to be injured. It must be one of the worst possible feelings a professional footballer can experience . . .

Pat: Ironically enough, I was just talking to Gary Mabbutt today, who had that terrible facial injury after he got caught by John Fashanu's elbow. Well, obviously it's very frustrating getting an injury, but particularly so at the very start of the season, when you've just reached the peak of fitness and you are raring to go. Gary suffered this after the first game of this season, breaking his leg. It is infuriating, especially when you have got through all the horrors of pre-season training. I read in your previous book about some of the things that managers won't tell players about the extent of their injuries, often encouraging their physios to do the same.

George: Yes, Mark McGhee talked about that. He felt it would totally demoralise players sometimes if they knew the extent of their injuries. Better to give them hope and keep them optimistic, taking them up to one milestone on the road to recovery and then the next – rather than telling them how long the whole road is going to be.

*Pat*:      I've only ever had one injury that's been really long-term, but you kind of know it at the time and you're constantly chatting to the physiotherapist, trying to get information out of him, but the accepted wisdom is that they don't tell you too much. Some characters wouldn't be capable of working through their period of injury if they knew its extent. It upset me slightly when I had mine, which was while I was at Everton – it was a torn cruciate, before many people were aware exactly what this is and how serious it is, i.e. before Gazza got his – because I am sure that if they'd told me it would take a certain amount of time to heal, and were realistic with me, I would still have done the work. I wouldn't have got too disorientated personally. But not everyone can be like that, so the general rule is that you don't tell the player – you give him small, progressive targets to aim for.

*George*:  But from your personal point of view, you'd definitely prefer to have known, however bad it actually was?

*Pat*:      Oh, definitely! That would then allow me to aim in certain directions at certain times and attain the goals I needed. In the end, the biggest mistake I made – and I probably wouldn't have made it if I'd been aware of the full extent of my injury – was to come back far too early. It's one of the things about 'the English game', or certainly the British one, indeed the British psyche, that players *almost always* come back too early. There is certainly a pressure from the clubs and a pressure from the management for them to do so. Liverpool under Shankly was an excellent example of this. Shankly apparently wouldn't talk to you if you were injured – he'd take your injury as a personal affront! It's true, it was no joke. You'd be going through all these personal traumas and fears, and your manager or coach is just making it worse by making you feel like a 'shammer'. The physios might think a little, at the backs of their minds, about what you must be going through, but other people at the club, managers especially, seem to be simply offended by your being injured.

This has an effect on the player. Whether the feeling is the player's own paranoia or if it comes from the manager in a more calculated way, I don't know – it could be both – but you're made to feel a little bit of a cheat.

George:  That you're betraying your team-mates by being injured?

Pat:     Yes. That you're faking it slightly. Obviously, if it's a broken leg, it shows, but there are plenty of injuries – probably some 90 per cent of them – that don't show. If it's a torn cruciate, or if it's what I had this season, *Plantar Fasciitis*, there's nothing to see. It's just your word that you're suffering against everyone else's.

So you have to deal with all that. If the injury is a long-term one, you have to go on a kind of journey, and the road you're on has a lot of twists and turns in it. Your first reaction is: 'I'm going to fight it, I'm going to face it head-on, work hard and get through this injury quicker than anyone has ever got through it before!' Then a slight depression definitely settles in. That tends to come three or four weeks into the injury, when you realise that you have got a long slog ahead of you. But with many of these injuries, before they start to get better, there's a long time when nothing seems to be happening at all – and that's the worst time.

George:  Where there seems to be no progress at all?

Pat:     Yes, the progress is so unbelievably slow, you don't notice it at all and you begin to think it'll never end. I don't mean that in a flippant way – you really feel that this might always be with you. Then, towards the end of a period of injury, there is a period of two weeks or so in which you experience an almost exponential growth in fitness, and that's a wonderful feeling. However, you just don't know when that's going to happen and every little step-forward that you make, you think: 'This is it!' So you try and go out and run on it or do something with it, and that actually makes it much worse. You realise you can't do it, that forcing it is dangerous.

So all the players have this fear that they'll be seen as malingering. The manager is giving out signals that he

believes it, and if you've been bought by a club, particularly if it has been for a lot of money, you're worried
that the fans are gong to start thinking it too. You imagine you can hear them muttering that you have gone
soft, you've made your money and no longer care. I had
played only three games for Everton after a £925,000
move from Chelsea before my cruciate-ligament
damage. In other words, it's a hotbed of paranoias. But
on top of all that, way on top of everything else, whatever injury you've got – and it doesn't matter whether
it's something like a medial-ligament strain, which
everyone knows takes four weeks to heal, or something
more serious, which is less easy to attach a timescale to
– you always end up wondering whether you'll *ever* be
the same again. Even if, rationally, you don't think that,
you always *feel* it, emotionally at some point.

Deep down, that fear has been there with every
injury I've had, and I think most of the lads who have
been injured experience it too. Many footballers do not
think ahead to the days beyond their playing careers in
too much detail, so an injury stopping them playing
would take them into alien territory they've never really
given much thought to, and that becomes another fear
– the fear of the unknown. The fact that you're not
supposed to own up to being scared about it makes it
doubly hard. You are expected to have a cool, confident,
relaxed attitude in front of your team-mates. On the
other hand, you don't want to be seen as someone who
isn't fighting against his injury hard enough. So, with a
brave face, it all compounds inside. It's a very difficult
period to handle, understand and accept.

George:    It's a terrible position to be in. To what extent do you
think it's even worse for a younger player? Graeme Le
Saux is an example that spring to mind. He's just
coming back from a very long-term injury.

Pat:    I don't know what's worse. Clearly, if it happens at the
start of your career, it can ruin your chances totally. You
are judged at that point and the injury may just cause
your chances to slip away. Six months of injury might

slow your progress down by a couple of years in some instances, especially if it happens at a time when you are about to make a career jump. One player, Ian Snodin, who I played with at Everton, was on the brink of an England career when he was injured. Called up that week for the first time, a great career as England's right-back for many years beckoned. He was a fine player and still is, but he never managed to scale those heights again.

George:   I remember Danny Thomas, a Spurs player in the late eighties, who was very promising, but he was the victim of a damaging tackle by QPR's Gavin Maguire and that was the end of his career. He never played again after that.

Pat:   That's the one which everybody fears most, the injury that ends a career. If that happens, there are things that the union has in place to help players in that situation. If you have, in union-speak, PTD, which is a horrible abbreviation but stands for Permanent Total Disability, then we try to help. It's a shocking term, isn't it? We get about 20 or 30 players contacting us regarding this every quarter, every three months, which is quite a large number when you think about it. Every year, there's another 100 or so players coming to the union saying: 'Look, we really are incapable of playing anymore because of serious injury.' I think this just goes to show that while you may think that players are a little bit paranoid over injuries, that they are plagued with all these irrational fears, statistically speaking, the fears are not actually *all* that irrational!

George:   Absolutely not. Most players will know a colleague or a friend who has been through it, presumably?

Pat:   Oh, yes! It'll be a lot more than just one or two. The list is usually fairly long. But the culture in our country is still push and push and push to get back to playing. I remember coming back from my cruciate injury after three and a half, maybe four months. Paul Gascoigne, although he snapped his and I tore mine, was out for a year, which is a sensible time. He gave it the right kind of rest. But three and a half months, looking back now, was total and utter recklessness, bordering on stupidity. It made absolutely no sense at all. I had just been bought for £925,000 and there wasn't even any direct pressure from the club to get back to playing – the pressure I was feeling was self-imposed. I certainly felt pressure from the fans as well and from all around, so it wasn't just me! I would have to say, however, that the club themselves were very considerate.

I just remember playing at QPR, having just come back from this cruciate injury, running about on the field at Loftus Road and thinking: 'What on earth am I doing here? If someone touches my leg, I'll just crumple in a heap!' I was so close to being completely incapacitated again, yet I'd managed to make it to the first team. I know there's a genuine, normal but still irrational fear of that first tackle when you get back playing, but I knew realistically that I'd come back way too early, that I wasn't anything like ready yet. That's a mistake that an awful lot of players tend to make. Understandably, sometimes a club is having a tough time and it needs its players badly, so they apply pressure. But to be totally honest and totally fair about it, most of the time the players put it on themselves.

This is the opposite of the culture that you get on the continent, as a whole. I remember telling Ivano Bonetti, our Italian player at Tranmere, about my *Plantar Fasciitis* and he casually informed me: 'Oh yes! I had it for one whole year.' This rather upset me for a day or two. I admit that got me quite down for a little while. He was injured at the same time as me, and while we were working through our injuries with the physio – who works you incredibly hard – I noticed that Ivano's attitude wasn't the same as mine, the 'Right, it's nearly ready. I'll go and play through some pain and make the effort now' attitude was missing. His attitude was: 'I want to be 100 per cent right, or at least 100 per cent sure of not breaking down again, leading to another long lay-off, before I take a chance.'

Our physio has a useful simile for this situation. He said that recovery is like walking down a slope with an ever-decreasing gradient, and it's up to the player where he wants to jump off. An Italian player will probably jump off near the bottom at 90 or 95 per cent fitness when it is very safe, while a British player will dive off at 60 per cent, taking a bigger risk. It's just the culture of our country to do that. So which approach is right? Who's to say? I suppose what's right is whatever applies to the culture of the country you're playing in at the time. We would sneer at the softness of the Italians in waiting all that time to get themselves right again, but the argument from their angle is: 'When I come back, you want to get everything from me, you want to get the full product. An English player comes back five weeks early, but he doesn't play at his best for those five weeks. An Italian player might come back one week early, but he'll be just about right to start playing again at his peak. He'll be contributing more.'

I think foreign players are more scientific. With us, it's more about guts and playing for the shirt. The question of aggravating an injury is an important one. Because of our mentality, we are more likely to break down again or, more seriously, we are more likely to turn a little, niggling injury into a chronic, long-term one. It is hard for us to change, however, even though, standing back, it is quite easy to see the dangers in our over-enthusiasm.

George:   The problem with the short-termist approach you get over here might be that in the longer run, your career as a player is a little bit shorter as a result.

Pat:      That's definitely been the case for many, many players in this country where they've done that. Working with the union, I see them all the time. They're the people who come to our Benevolent Society, our Accident Insurance Society, looking for help with hip-replacements, major knee-operations and so on. These are chaps in their forties or fifties and older that have played football in the past, and a huge percentage of their injuries were caused by coming back and playing when they shouldn't have played. When you have an injury and it's painful, it's painful for a reason – it's your body telling you it hasn't healed yet and you shouldn't be playing on it. Yet we're expected to play through pain just about all the time. With the huge amount of games being played just now, everyone has got used to playing while not 100 per cent fit.

*George*:  Presumably you can mask the pain, hide the symptoms, using pain-killers, but the condition is still there . . .

*Pat*:  To some extent, but it's not so much pain-killing injections in particular. Most players of a certain age, at some stage of the season, are living on anti-inflammatories. That's the big one. Much more so than pain-killers. Players are quite obviously aware of the dangers of pain-killers, and will only use them for certain games in certain circumstances. They'll have the occasional jab in certain circumstances, for example to get through a particularly important game. But we all know now, as professionals, that you just can't live on that. You can't live on continual injections. The thing that players do is use anti-inflammatories, which do slightly mask an injury, because, by stopping the injured area becoming inflamed, it makes it much easier to play. Unfortunately, the next day, when the anti-inflammatories wear off, you're in pain again. So you keep taking them until the end of the season, when you have a real chance to rest and recover fully.

Again, that's the culture, it's expected of you, and there's actually very little complaint about it. The attitude from the fans' point of view is: 'Bloody hell – you're paid enough! For God's sake, get out there and tolerate a bit of pain!' I suppose there's a wee bit of that within the game as well as outside it. But I would be reluctant to blame clubs for that. You have to look at the culture of the game and, ultimately, it's down to the players themselves. They're like that. It's brave, sometimes it's stupid, and only with experience do you learn how to judge the situation. Even then, some of us continually get it wrong.

*George*:   And how important is the role of the physio in all this?
*Pat*:      All physios are qualified now. The FA and the PFA have
            helped make and enforce these changes, so you have to
            be a properly qualified physio . . .
*George*:   As opposed to the old days, when all you needed was
            your own bucket and sponge?
*Pat*:      Exactly. That's been quite a wrench for a lot of clubs,
            but it was a necessity. So now they all have properly
            qualified physios. But one of the tricks that physios pull
            is that when you're injured and you're with the physio-
            therapist, you don't sit on a table and have massages
            and work with different machines all the time, as
            people might imagine from seeing pictures of Gazza
            recovering, and so on. With a lot of the clubs, and cer-
            tainly the three major clubs that I've been with, Chelsea,
            Everton and Tranmere, you are worked incredibly hard
            doing weights, doing various kinds of cardiovascular
            stuff that obviously won't trouble your injury. Just
            because you're carrying an injury, that doesn't stop you
            working! Not a bit of it! There are plenty of ways of
            making you work without troubling whatever kind of
            injury you've got at the time. There's no injury on this
            earth that's going to stop you being worked hard. If
            you've got a leg injury, you'll do upper-body exercise,
            you'll do rowing and various other exercises. The
            attitude from a lot of the physios is: 'There may be some
            slackers out there and if we give them a cushy number
            in here, they'll hang about for a long time.'
               There's a bit of antagonism between a lot of players
            and a lot of physios, because many of the players get
            this feeling that the physios simply don't believe that
            they are quite seriously injured. Some physios may
            think: 'These players are just lazy malingerers who are
            after an easy life.' But if the physios work the players
            really hard, the players won't *want* to hang about in the
            treatment rooms – they'll want to get back to playing
            again as soon as is humanly possible. The manager
            often colludes with the physio in this respect – they
            claim they don't do it, but they do. They'll say to the

physio: 'Make sure the injured lads are worked incredibly hard when they're with you. I want it so they can't wait to get back! Playing and training with the first team will seem like a holiday compared to what I want you to put them through!'

Part of it, obviously, is making sure that your players are as fit as possible when they return to full training. The manager wants the player to be available for selection as soon as possible, with as little time as is feasible being wasted getting back to his 'match' fitness, hence all the cardiovascular exercise, building up your strength, etc, but in among that is still the issue of suspected slacking. It's infuriating! One of my biggest bugbears that has annoyed me throughout my whole career in football, and outside it too, is that all players tend to get tarred with the same brush and there's nothing we can do about it.

*George*:  When England manager Glenn Hoddle managed your old club Chelsea, there were rumours that he had more of a belief in faith-healing, and other scientifically 'un-conventional' approaches, than in conventional physio-therapy. I wonder to what extent he's not alone . . . how much do other players – and managers – go for these techniques?

*Pat*:  I've seen a few. Just like a lot of doctors and GPs now, I think a lot of physiotherapists are willing to try out some modern and rather unusual techniques. 'Holistic' medicine. That's the term, isn't it?

*George*:  Yes, 'holistic' relating to the fact that it's concerned with the whole person, the complete person, rather than just some discrete area of injury. A lot of the beliefs also spring from Chinese medicine . . .

*Pat*:  Well, the problem with some of the Chinese remedies is that if you take a cup of ginseng tea, there's a good chance that you'll fail a random drugs test, so you have to be very careful indeed what you consume. Anything involving potions and drugs is a minefield – you're certainly taking a chance if you go down that route, particularly if you don't know exactly what it is that you're taking, right down to the specific ingredients and even the chemical compounds.

George: So homeopathy is probably out?

Pat: Some parts of it are, but not other parts. I've come across advocates of aromatherapy. Another thing I've found, certainly with the physio we have at Tranmere, is that he quite frequently uses acupuncture. There are lots of different kinds of acupuncture, but he uses the original Chinese kind, setting light to the needles as he presses them into a specific part of your back for a problem you're having with, say, your toe. That sort of thing. It reflects quite a modern, open-minded approach.

George: And is this something to which a player would say 'Yes, I quite fancy trying this' or 'Not for me, thanks!' – or is it something that the player would be put through automatically if he happens to have that physio?

Pat: What you always find in this country – absolutely always! – is that players are so keen to get fit again and to get back to playing that they'll try *anything*. Anything at all, as long as it's legal. They'll go through any treatment at all, anything that's being offered. The slight exception to that at the moment is probably jabs.

George: With syringes, rather than acupuncture needles?

Pat: Yes. Cortisone is the big one which everyone is very wary of now. It's known that it leads to serious trouble, arthritis and so on, in later life. That's been shown so often now that we're all aware of it. As for other techniques, although some are laughed at and some aren't, generally, if a player is struggling and he can't get rid of something, he'll try as many different remedies as are offered, including a machine that appears to do absolutely nothing at all, other than show a dull, orange light when it is switched on . . . no feeling . . . no heat . . . no buzz. Actually, I wonder whether it's just an electronic placebo machine that our physio has had installed. In my experience, there's nothing over-stupid or excessively ridiculous being used that I'm aware of, though having said that, with Ivano Bonetti, the Italian player in our team, we watch his methods and they really seem alien to us! He has a completely different attitude to the rest of us, but the fact that the lads didn't laugh off his ideas – they were very, very intrigued and interested – suggests that today's players are quite an open-minded bunch.

He had this machine with him, 'The Translator', and I'm not sure how widely it's used but certainly AC Milan and Sampdoria and other teams use it in Italy. It attaches to whatever muscle in the body you want to work, so instead of doing an hour on the bike, you plug this thing in, strap it to your leg, and the pulses which it generates work your muscle. The muscle thus builds up and you can just sit and enjoy a cup of tea. He uses this religiously. He swears by it. Apparently, most of AC Milan's players used it throughout last year, and it certainly didn't seem to affect them in a negative way. You might have thought that the players would laugh at him, saying: 'Oh yeah? Anything to get away with not having to do so much work! Certainly beats running up and down the sand-dunes!' But they didn't. They were grafting away and he was sitting with his machine, reading the paper. I think it's important to be aware that the machine won't build your stamina in the way that pitting yourself against sand-dunes will, but it seems it can build up your muscles. Ivano stresses that it has to be used in conjunction with a wider fitness-plan.

*George*:  So it's like getting an electrical massage?

*Pat*:  Partly that, but I think it goes beyond that. It's something that none of our players had seen before, it was so modern, but two or three of them immediately took up the opportunity to borrow it and try it out on themselves. So there are some unusual ideas out there. You mentioned faith-healers. Two years ago, we were in a desperate position: in the play-off semi-finals, we lost the first game at home 3–1 to Reading, so in the away game we had to win heavily in order to get to the finals. It was so important that the manager at the time decided to bring in a sports psychologist with some very strange and unusual methods.

*George*:  Yes, you'll find a lot of variation in the methods adopted by sports psychologists. At the moment, anyone can call themselves a sports psychologist, so they might have a psychology background, a more general sports science background, or indeed no basis to what they're doing at all. A few of them are just smooth-talking quacks with a nice line in buzzwords and parlour games.

*Pat*:  One of the things that this guy did was that he got us all in a room, got us to move all the furniture away to the sides, and asked us to team up with the player with whom we worked most closely on the pitch. For me, it was Gary Stevens. He then said: 'Now hug each other, very, very tight . . .' which, in a macho sport like football, seemed very, very unusual. The next step was that the others had to part you, but you'd be working together as a duo to prevent them from doing that. I suppose it was quite obvious what he was working on, building closeness and trust and so on.

In another game, everyone got together in the group and one person became 'the outsider' who had to break into this group. It got very, very physical and it ended up with quite a lot of blood being spilled and everyone thoroughly bruised – but I have to say it worked! It definitely worked, because the next day, before the game, we went through a little routine he'd given us and the team spirit was just *exceptional*. The 'buzz' was superb. Everyone had been pumped up to perform for one another in quite an exceptional way. In order to pull something like that off, though, you have to have the right attitude throughout the team, with no-one sneering at what is being done.

Well, we managed a 0–0 draw away from home, which was good but not good enough. In the end, the best thing about this guy was simply that he got everyone talking.

*George*:  That's the long and the short of it, isn't it? Whatever the technique may be, however wacky, if it increases communication between players, it must be doing *something*.

Pat:        My difficulty with the whole thing, which is really my
            difficulty with football generally, is that rather than
            going out and *doing* the damn thing, putting it into
            practice, I just spent my time analysing the process,
            observing what was going on! I could understand all
            the underlying reasons why he was doing everything
            he did, but I think the idea was really to switch off from
            doing that and just get the underlying benefit from it.
                That's one of my failings, to analyse continually why
            people do things. But I could see that his games worked.
            They achieved what he had set out to achieve. So I was
            happy to go along with it and even back it.

George:     I suppose that in among all this, you have to look at the
            effect of placebos, things that have no medical or
            scientific reason for doing you any good beyond your
            own belief that they are doing so. These can work very
            well if you believe they are going to do so, of course.
            You can even alert people to the fact that the treatment
            or the pill they're taking is a placebo and it'll often *still*
            work just as well. You can say: 'Look, these tablets I'm
            giving you contain nothing but sugar, but I've a sneaky
            feeling that they might help you, and if you agree . . .'
            and people will take them and their condition will
            improve, even though they know there's nothing
            magical about what they're taking. I guess you could
            say it was a case of mind over matter – if you think, if
            you *believe* that something, however bizarre, however
            unproven, is going to help you, it generally can.

Pat:        Oh, people's beliefs can definitely influence their
            reactions to drugs, there's no doubt about that. I had a
            friend with whom I played five-a-side at college, and
            one night, a group of us chopped up some Bisodol
            tablets into a fine, white powder and told him it was
            cocaine. Well, he sniffed this powder and said he got a
            real buzz out of it!

George:     And think of the money he saved!

Pat:        I suppose that if you had *half a ton* of Bisodol up your
            nose, you probably would be flying. But in reality, it
            had to be a placebo effect.

*George*: When you look at people's reactions to drugs, they're generally very influenced by those around them. I mean, they might realise that they've taken some kind of stimulant, but whether they should get aggressive or just sit around and giggle or get very talkative, this is often very affected by how those around them behave. Anthropologists have tried this with tribes who are unfamiliar with what the effects of certain drugs are supposed to be. People look around and observe one another, in an effort to react similarly to other people. I wonder where these anthropologists get their funding . . . ?

*Pat*: When it comes to footballers, though, it'll always be the case that at the end of a gruelling 90 minutes, your muscles are telling you more than your mind ever will. For that reason, mind games can be great for doing things like increasing communication between players, but very limited in terms of what they can do to achieve *physical* improvement.

*George*: Let's get back to the present, and to your current position at Tranmere . . .

*Pat*: Well, I still find myself miles out of the team, which is a very unusual experience for me. Throughout my whole career, even if I've been returning from an injury, as soon as I've been fully fit, I've just been put straight back in the first team again. Footballers tend to be very impatient, and I'm no different. It's been 11 days now that I've been fully fit and I've missed three first-team games. I'm already beginning to think: 'Wait a minute! What's wrong here? Are they trying to get rid of me?'

*George*: You're beginning to feel a bit persecuted?

*Pat*: Yes, but I don't want to go to the manager, because he would just say: 'Hey, steady on! You've only played two reserve-team matches, you've missed a lot, and you've a lot of catching up to do.' So I'm fully fit and I've worked incredibly hard to achieve it – although, admittedly, match fitness is a different thing. I've missed three first-team games, not even having been brought into the squad, and I already feel hard done-by.

If I stand back from it, if it was someone else in my position, I'd be saying: 'Don't be daft! Get fully match fit!' It's just that when it's you, you begin to feel that it's something personal, that there's something wrong.

At this point in time, I feel I can't be quite sure. I just don't know. Maybe the manager wants to get rid of me, maybe I'm not being irrational. A couple of the lads have done well while I've been out . . .

*George*:   Lads who play in your position?

*Pat*:   Yes. So it's kind of difficult. Reserve-team games are tough. If you play badly in them, you're not going to get a chance in the first team, but if you play really well . . . well, it's only the reserves. It's easy to be negative about it and to feel you're banging your head against a brick wall.

*George*:   Just how different is the atmosphere in the reserves compared to that in the first team?

*Pat*:   The atmosphere is brilliant in our reserve team. Over the years, I've seen some established first-team players go into the reserves and they can't lift themselves for it. It is difficult sometimes to summon up the motivation to play at your best when you're in that position, and sometimes you feel you're being messed around and your attitude is to muck about and think: 'Well, I might be selected for the first team again. If it happens, it happens. If it doesn't, it doesn't.' That hasn't been the case at Tranmere, certainly since I've been here. The attitude of the players has been brilliant, very upbeat, and the games have been as enjoyable as first-team games. Because there is very, very little pressure in comparison to a first-team game, the experience – at least from that point of view – has been at least as enjoyable.

You do start to fear that there's no way back, though. I keep coming back to this, but I feel like it *already* and it's only been 11 days! Again, it's the culture of the game. You *have* to drive yourself forward. You'll do anything and everything to get back into that first team. The fact that you may be seen as playing in a comfort zone is completely taboo. 'Comfort zone' is such an offensive term. Any player tends to feel ashamed that anyone should think he was playing in one. 'You're playing in a comfort zone' is one of the most insulting comments you can throw at a British player.

George:  I'll remember that next time we visit Southampton!

Pat:  That's either very catty or else irrational spitefulness because you are a Newcastle fan. I mean, what has Matt ever done to you, other than crush your title hopes now and again single-handedly? Well, 'comfort zone' is insulting to me, anyway, if not to absolutely everyone to the same extent! I've learned something from the experience of playing reserve-team football, though. After my third game in the reserves, I felt totally exhausted and that's very unusual for me, because I like to keep myself very fit. I'm usually at least as fit, if not fitter, than anyone else on the park. It's only because I've been working so hard to demonstrate that I'm not caught in a comfort zone that I'm left feeling so tired. I've been working stupidly in order to prove myself. My running hasn't been intelligent. It's just been 45-minute bursts of running and running and running and running . . . But I hope I've learned my lesson after three matches of that. 'Re-learned' would be more precise, though, because it is something you learn instinctively very early in your career.

It's been the total opposite of the way I usually play, in fact. Normally, I'm thinking all the time, only making a run if the situation demands it or there is at least a chance of something positive coming from it. They always say that a player like Dalglish ran the first 10 yards in his head, and I've tried to be like that, too. If you are going to try and copy someone, you might as well try and copy the best. I can't believe, now that I'm back from injury, how little time it took me to forget to *think*. Unfortunately, to get back to match fitness – not simply physical fitness, but the fitness required to play well for 90 minutes of first-team football – you have to do quite a lot of that stupid running, regardless. But I think I've done enough of it now. That's my lesson learned.

George:   What are your feelings towards those players who currently occupy the positions you could play in within the first team? I know that, rationalising it, you wish them well, but from a purely emotional view, is that harder?

Pat:   To be totally honest, I really do think I'm fairly unusual in this respect. I commentated on the first-team game the other day, and I awarded the player who is currently playing in my preferred position Man of the Match. However, I had spotted something that he was doing wrong – he's a young lad – so at half-time, I came down and gave him some advice. I believe myself to be a total team player. This might surprise some people, who might see me as very much an individual player because of my individualist style of play when I have the ball, but I have always, *always* felt a team player.

The advice I gave him turned out to work very well for him in the second half of the game, and I was very happy to see that. So although I want to regain my position in the team, I certainly don't want any individual to do badly. I know that it's an unusual position to take. The readers may not believe it! From my conversations with other players, the attitude of those in a similar position has generally been: 'I want the team to do well, but I don't want the person who plays in my position to do well.' Occasionally, they don't even want the team to do so well. That's taking it too far, but not wanting the guy who's got your place to shine is very understandable. It's a very human attitude. I suppose my own attitude is: *I should be good enough. Whether he's playing well or not, I think I'm a better player than him and I should be able to show it.* This comes from having these attitudes bred into me both by my father and by Celtic Boys' Club, as I mentioned earlier. It has always stayed with me. If you're out of the team, you're expected to be on the bench shouting for them – that's not affected, the indoctrination runs so deep that it's part of me now. That's the way it is.

*In this session, as well as catching up with what Pat was doing, I wanted to ask him about his work with the Professional Footballers' Association, the players' union. Taking on the chairmanship of the union might have seemed like a cushy number, an honorary position with little to ruffle your feathers. Then came 'The Season of Sleaze' (1994–95), when bungs, bribes and violence were on everybody's lips. On top of this, Pat now found himself in a position where he looked in serious danger of leading the players of the First, Second and Third Divisions out on strike . . .*

Pat:    Well, I'd had this jab, but the team was struggling and I was asked by the manager to make myself available. I did it as a favour, because of all the difficulties that the team had, but I thought I had to rest it to allow it to recover fully. I was then made to play in a full reserve game the next night, which was a bit of a slap in the face, because I wasn't fully fit. I managed to get through the reserve game and as a direct result, I was finally back from injury and thinking: 'Wait a minute! Why am I not back in the first-team squad?' This is the normal and acceptable lack of patience which you get from professional footballers in this country. We all suffer from this slightly. After only two days' training, I was getting quite paranoid and questioning whether the manager rated me at all, which I knew – or *thought!* – was fairly ridiculous and insecure, considering it was only two days!

George:  How long did that feeling last?

Pat:    Well, the insecurity normally lasts until you get your first game – and in this case, that was still a few weeks away! Soon afterwards, there was a Wednesday night game for the reserves. I had run myself into the ground in the reserves, trying to impress the manager and force him to put me back into the first-team squad. Two of our team's players were substituted with about 20 minutes to go. It became obvious then that it was a tactical thing: they were being rested for Friday night's first-team game – and I wasn't. Those final 20 minutes were difficult for me, because it was clear that they were in contention for the next match and I was not. I became immediately very disappointed and my concentration went, which is very unusual for me – it had never happened to that extent before. After the game, I thought 'I'll correct that – I've *got* to correct that!' because I could see that the standard of my play had collapsed in those last 20 minutes. It was a direct result of having what I'd been working so hard for for the first 70 minutes swiped away from under my feet.

So I was thinking on the coach back from the game: 'Am I being paranoid? Should I call a meeting with the manager to find out where I stand?' Then, right in the middle of all this, we, the union, called a strike ballot!

It's a funny thing, but four or five years ago, I was at Everton when there was the last call for footballers to go out on strike. I was the union rep and also on the management committee. Extremely quickly, I dropped from the first team right down to the 'A' team – not the reserves, the 'A' team, which is even lower. I was there throughout the whole period when the possibility of strike action was threatened. Amazingly, now I'm at Tranmere, there was a call for strike action and again I was out of the first team, playing in the reserves and not even getting a *sniff* of first-team football.

*George*:  A spooky coincidence?

*Pat*:  I honestly, *honestly* would say it *is* coincidence. A lot of people would put two and two together and come up with the answer 'conspiracy'. It would be so easy to become bitter, to use that as an excuse for my absence from first-team football – it's a nice, self-deluding, confidence-boosting, ready-made excuse. But I refuse to accept that explanation.

*George*: Acting as a representative of other players can be a hazardous thing. I remember Garry Nelson talking about trying to put the case for his team to the management, while the other players just looked away or stared down at their shoes. It's the kind of behaviour that gets you put on transfer lists! As Terry Venables often says: 'The players are behind you 20 per cent!'

It's only now that I'm beginning to appreciate why Mark Dennis used to be QPR's PFA representative when I first met him. They obviously thought he'd get in so much trouble anyway that he'd be a natural choice – always give the job to a troublemaker! To what extent are you taking your life – or at least your career – into your own hands by accepting a chance to act as a players' representative?

*Pat*: There's always a bit of a worry that you'll rattle someone's cage – usually the manager's! But that is the concern of any union man in any industry. A football manager could easily justify dropping a player by saying: 'Union business is obviously going to be playing too much on your mind at the moment. You're going to have difficulty concentrating on playing.' I really do think it's coincidence this time that it coincides with me being out of the first team.

*George*: Tell me a little about the dispute. I believe the Football League are at the heart of it . . .

*Pat*: Not for the first time, it is the Football League that the PFA has fallen out with. We've had this agreement with them for many years: we were always due 10 per cent of the TV monies, because we had originally withdrawn any claim an individual player might have for TV appearance money. Instead of individual players getting little dribs and drabs here and there every time they appeared in a televised match, it was agreed that the PFA would get 10 per cent of the TV money from the Football League, and this would be filtered back into the clubs and to wider player-benefits such as education and training – it was not allowed to go into union coffers.

Now, we also have an Education Society, which is

financed jointly by the union itself, the Football League,
the Football Association and the Premier League. Each
body paid £84,000 last year, which isn't a huge amount
considering the money in football at the moment. This
year, however, the Football League refused to cough up
their full percentage, having already complained about
it last year. As a result, the Football Association, the
Premier League and the PFA paid extra to top up the
deficit missing from the Football League. The other
three bodies picked up the tab between them, as a
gesture of goodwill and understanding of the Football
League's concern about its finances.

Bearing that in mind, when the Football League announced that they were no longer going to honour their
original agreement to give us 10 per cent of the TV
money – which was now a much higher figure following their brand-new, increased deal with Sky TV – and
would instead pay us a 'generous discretionary sum',
we thought: 'Right! We simply can't trust them. We have
bent over backwards to help them in the past and this is
the thanks we get!' For goodness' sake, we are still
actually net *givers* to the Football League and its clubs,
shelling out half a million here and a million there. We
have also often taken only five per cent of the due
monies, and on occasion deferred payments altogether.

They want to maximise profits, of course. That's
understandable. But their outlook tends to be very, very
short-term. To some extent it has to be. It's the nature of
the business. You never know what's around the next
corner. The PFA, though, are in a different position. We
can afford to be a little more long-term in our approach.
We're not plagued by the same kinds of short-term
problems that affect the Football League and its clubs.
We therefore feel that we're entitled to our 10 per cent.
The 'discretionary fee' could very easily turn into: '. . .
Had a bit of bother this year, so we can't afford to give
you *anything*. Sorry.' If it hadn't been for their refusal to
pay that extra few grand last year, we might not have
been quite as paranoid about money where they're

concerned, had we not come across their previous attitude.

The other day, we had a meeting of the PFNCC (the Professional Footballers' Negotiating and Consultative Committee), which is the forum where all four bodies meet, and the Football League were very, very relaxed about our – the PFA's – call for industrial action. They made no effort whatsoever to come to any agreement to negotiate and quite obviously, from the way they were talking, wanted us to go ahead with the strike ballot! I was very taken aback by that. For an organisation that is so worried about its finances, all of a sudden, to take such a huge gamble with the money coming in from TV – the biggest revenue that they get! – staggered me. If we said that we would continue to play, but refused to do so in front of TV cameras, that would make their Sky deal much shakier – it might even fall through. For an organisation like the Football League, you'd expect some sign of weakness, some fear, some panic. There wasn't a *hint* of effort to show that they wanted to come to any agreement.

It doesn't compute. It doesn't make sense.

George:  Are they simply calling your bluff?

Pat:  Possibly. A number of things *could* be going on. You could ask the question: is someone payrolling this for them? We don't know. We have no idea. If we suspected it, we would have to take that consideration seriously. We haven't got enough money at the PFA to be light-hearted about it. We were certainly knocked sideways by this. We thought we'd been very reasonable. We said: 'Okay, okay. Maybe not 10 per cent. We'll be reasonable. We'll start negotiating a lower percentage . . .' They wouldn't budge a millimetre. It takes two sides to negotiate and everything was only coming from one side – ours.

The ballot papers have gone out now and they're obviously awaiting the result of the ballot. What do our members, the players, want? We, as a union, are very confident that we'll get a mandate for industrial action from the members. In the next week or so, we'll start pushing ahead with it. All of the feedback we've had from our members has been incredibly positive. The last time we balloted players, it was just those in what was then the First Division and is now the Premier League, and we got 90 per cent backing. Slightly more, actually. If we get anywhere near that again, it puts us in a very strong position. It does surprise me, though, that the Football League are so confident – almost *over*-confident.

George:  It's intriguing!

Pat:     It's certainly that. I find it fascinating. We'll just have to see what happens.

George:  If you were to all go out on strike, this would become a very short book . . .

Pat:     There are no meetings on the horizon. They're sticking to their guns and being absolutely rigid. There's the inevitable war of words going on at the moment, with a lot of information – a lot of *misinformation* – being thrown about in the papers and in the media. But who owns BSkyB?

George:  Rupert Murdoch.

Pat:     Precisely. And he owns *The Times*, the *Sun*, etc. He's not exactly a fan of the unions – we know what happened when he moved News International to Wapping! Who knows how deep this will get?

George:  Who knows how much of this our publishers will ask us to cut? Such strike action would be unprecedented in modern times, surely?

Pat:     Well, five years ago we came within inches of it. We would have gone ahead with it, but we got such a strong mandate from our members, as I mentioned, that the Premier League just capitulated. They were forming the new league from what was the old First Division, so maybe they weren't in the strongest position at the time, and they agreed to a five-year deal which, incidentally, runs out at the end of this season. Naturally, the Premier League, if they're to maximise *their* profits, would quite like us to have a less than favourable outcome on this one, so they've been sitting on the fence and not really getting involved!

*George*: Fearing that they'll be next.

*Pat*: If you were to be cynical, this 'fixture' against the Football League is just a warm-up for the big game against the Premier League next season. From our angle, a bad result in this one wouldn't bode well for the bigger game in the next round!

*George*: The other issue that has been in the press a bit this week was prompted by Channel 4's *Critical Eye* team, having televised Graham Taylor's managerial suicide in front of a hungry media, doing their programme about Paul Gascoigne. This was a more sympathetic portrayal – but I guess I'm not alone in finding Gazza more sympathetic than Graham Taylor – though it did raise the issue of alcohol as a team-building device. Up until now, the tabloids had had us believe that when Sheryl was giving birth, Paul was out on the bevvy with *friends*, but it now seems that these friends were none other than his Rangers team-mates and the bevvying was all part of the club's official – if unwritten – player-bonding policy. Now, frankly, I'm not hugely surprised. On those occasions when I've been for a night-out with, say, the lads from Dulwich Hamlet – admittedly a non-league side – a few swift libations were had, and very good for team spirit it was. Walter Smith has admitted to me that getting smashed together is a Rangers trick. The club's all-day 'lunches' are legendary in football circles. So what's your view – does a team that gets plastered in one another's company play better together?

*Pat*: Certainly, as I've said before, the pre-season tour is generally designed to build camaraderie and team spirit, and yes, it *does* involve a certain amount of drinking! It's everyone together, having a good time and, to use the buzz-words, indulging in a bit of 'male bonding'. You'd never use the term 'male bonding' with the team – the culture of football is far too blokeish for terms like that.

I have to admit, I missed the point completely when

I first started playing football. Everyone else would be playing drinking games and I'd be off to the art gallery or seeing the sights, or whatever.

George:     Yes. My friend John Kirkpatrick phoned to tell me that *Viz* were having a bit of fun recently with that side of your image, as they 'outed the brainy footballers who suffer in silence'!

Pat:        That was the only article that is true to life that I have ever read in *Viz*. We've mentioned the headline already, *The Agony of the Soccer Eggheads*, which is funny as well as accurate. It's one of the best headlines I have ever read, right up there with the headline in the *Coatbridge and Airdrie Advertiser* after a Scotland Under-18 game I played in. I scored one goal and the young Spurs striker of the time, Ally Dick, scored the other. And so it came to pass that the banner NEVIN AND DICK SHINE hit the news-stands of Lanarkshire. We suffering soccer eggheads seem to do most of our suffering on the pre-season tours, though. In a tour a few years ago with Tranmere, we went to Dublin and I was fined £20 for being a wimp and going to see *In the Name of the Father* at the cinema, instead of having a game of golf and a drink with the lads. God knows what the fine would have been if they had found out about my visit to the city's Gallery of Modern Art the previous day.

Worse happened the following year on a tour to the Isle of Man. My room-mate, a triallist, came back to the room at four in the morning, totally plastered. Much moaning and groaning followed as he threw himself on his bed – or at least attempted to. He totally missed and landed on the floor, smashing a table on the way down. By 4.30, he was snoring like a hippo with a cold and I wasn't getting a wink of sleep. At 5am, he stumbled up to go to the loo. Sadly, he got it wrong and when I opened my eyes, all I could see was him standing on top of my bed, relieving himself over my sheets. It does sound a bit pompous, but is that any way to treat the chairman of the union you are hoping to join? Not surprisingly, the rest of the team found it hilarious the next day, and so did I . . . well, the next week, anyway.

*George*: You must be really fit to be able to carry such serious drinking off. A seasoned drinker but incredibly fit professional that springs to mind is Paul McGrath.

*Pat*: One of the reasons, apart from my interest in the culture, that I would look around any city we were visiting on tour was that I didn't want to do the serious drinking, because it would compromise my fitness.

*George*: With the recent focus on alcoholic stars like Tony Adams and Paul Merson, some people are questioning the wisdom of a drink culture that works in direct opposition to players' fitness – even if some of them *can* carry it off for a long time.

*Pat*: I think there's a very thin dividing-line between what's *excessive* drinking and what isn't. Some clubs step over that line, and others don't. But there is definitely a potential benefit there. I mean, a lot of people, used to say that Liverpool were at least as big a 'drinking' team as any during their years of greatness in the seventies and eighties. The camaraderie and team spirit were just incredible. Certainly, Rangers are renowned for it now, and have been for a long time up in Scotland. The bonding that exists at that club – and it's almost painful to admit, as a Celtic supporter! – really is *exceptional*. The club has its own humour, its own banter within the group that doesn't involve anyone else.

*George*: A set of in-jokes, almost like rhyming slang in that it excludes those who don't understand it?

*Pat*: Yes – almost like the players' own *language*. It involves the whole team. There is, of course, their own rhyming slang, their own idiosyncratic use of odd vocabulary and language, and even types of intonation in speech that is only used by that group, within the group.

*George*: I think this was one of the things that attracted a prankster like Gazza. If a club's team spirit has reached legendary status, it can be a very good way of attracting players. Walter Smith told me that he thinks it has worked very much in Rangers' favour.

*Pat*: Definitely. Look at the Wimbledon 'Crazy Gang' thing.

All clubs have a slightly different spirit, and they all
use it in different ways. It's one of the things that make
a club unique, like having its own special signature.
Some clubs, of course, find team spirit in short supply,
and managers try to build it. I think if they could find
ways to do it using slightly *less* alcohol, they would,
but sometimes it does take a lot of alcohol, and it takes
a very long time! It's a question of knowing how far to
take it and – to bring in a cocktail metaphor – of getting
the mix right. Certainly Rangers, if you look at them as
a domestic force, have got the mix perfectly right, but if
you look at them as a European force . . .

George:   Too much rum or not enough pineapple in the pina
colada, metaphorically speaking?

Pat:   Yeah. You have to question the mix, but Rangers' failure
in Europe can't all be attributed to having too much
bevvy.

   Everyone is leaping on the Tony Adams bandwagon,
or talking about Paul Gascoigne, asking: 'Are they such
heavy drinkers *because* of football and its attendant
pressures? Has football pushed them into it? Do footballers tend to have addictive personalities?' To be
honest, I don't think there are any more footballers with
addictive personalities than there are people like that
in any other profession with similar pressures and
temptations.

George:   As a psychologist, I'd have to agree. There are addictive
personalities – whether it's drink, gambling, whatever –
in all jobs. It's only the sports stars, musicians and actors
that we tend to hear about. Paul Merson points out quite
movingly in his autobiography that he does feel different
to other players. He can't just have a couple of drinks
and then walk away. Once he's started, he can't stop.
Other players, even heavy social drinkers, will not have
that kind of personality, that kind of compulsion.

Pat:   Players like Merson and Adams have no choice but to
force themselves to drink nothing at all, and they would
be the first to admit it . . . Here I would like to applaud
their self-will and strength of character to have been

able to beat the demon drink and come back to playing at the very highest level. But to be fair, there is seldom huge pressure applied by a club, forcing its players to drink. There's a difference between it being the accepted culture and a club twisting your arm. Clubs can't *force* you to drink. However, there was one club that actually tried to make me drink and I simply said no. Well, I mean they tried to make me drink *too much* – I can't say I mind the odd drink! The manager threatened me with a fine if I didn't start bevvying. It was half in jest. Only *half*, though.

I think players drinking are an easy target for the tabloids, though. I think one of the reasons that Rangers were scared of Gazza spilling the beans a bit on the club's 'drink culture' was that they could anticipate the tabloid reaction. The tabloids are not interested in thinking the concept through. For them, it's just an easy headline. This, of course, is bad PR for Rangers FC, who are a large company, want to sell a lot of merchandise, want to be seen as a positive, forward-thinking and modern corporate body and probably don't appreciate this kind of publicity. I think that's why Walter Smith is happy to talk about it, while the more operational end of Rangers as a company are less keen.

George:  All of which might explain why Alex Ferguson sold players like Paul McGrath and Norman Whiteside. Bevvying may be good for team spirit, but the publicity surrounding it is bad for your share price. Anyway, it always smacks of humbug when journalists accuse *any* other group of people for drinking excessively.

Pat:  Their argument would be that they don't have to run about. It is frustrating for managers, though. There is something very alcohol-friendly about the British player's psyche. The players at AC Milan don't feel the need to go out drinking the way we do. With the season they're having now, that may be changing, though! There is just no history of it for Spanish or Italian players. But they'll no doubt have other traditions that we'd find odd.

Although I've never really gone for the heavy drink-

ing in any club that I've been at, I will go along sometimes and spend time with the lads on a drinking
session, and I will enjoy that time. It just happens that I
don't feel as comfortable as some other players drinking
*that* much. I can't completely condemn others for doing
so, though. I understand the reasons behind it, from the
point of view of our cultural identity and the positive
effect on the team spirit.

*George*:  I remember talking to Terry Venables – over a drink, I
have to admit – about the press criticism of the drinking
that went on in Hong Kong prior to the Euro 96 tournament, all that tequila and dentist's chair stuff at the
Jump Club, or whatever the place was called. He said
that, in all honesty, the current England side drinks less
than any other England team in history – including,
most certainly, the golden boys of '66. There are players
like David Seaman and Stuart Pearce who don't drink
at all. In fact, when players see how long a teetotal professional like Peter Beardsley has kept going – he must
be well into his fifties by now! – they may be inclined to
think that depriving themselves of the amber nectar
might well put two or three years onto their playing
career... and that represents no mean earnings-
potential in today's game.

*Pat*:  There is definitely more of that kind of thinking now –
a more professional attitude than has certainly existed
in the past. It's, as you say, a more *material* attitude a lot
of the time, but the two go together. Players see it not as
a game, but as a career, a business. I mean, can you see
David Platt going out on a bender? It stretches the
imagination a bit, doesn't it?

And it isn't always *necessary* to have the spirits flow-
ing to help the spirit flow. I was with the Scotland squad
from just before the European Championships in 1992
all the way through to 1996, and we didn't *have* to drink
– the team spirit was so incredible. Andy Roxburgh
started it and Craig Brown has worked on it to tremendous effect. How they managed to do it is very difficult
to say. It's not an easy thing to crystallise, but I think it

had a lot to do with the people who were in the squad at the time, and also Craig and Andy's team talks – how they timed them and the things they stressed. There was certainly a real empathy between the players and the supporters, who have a tremendous spirit. In fact, in 1992, much of it came from our supporters in Sweden, this wild, weird bunch of fanatical people who are not dangerous in any way, even though they like a drink much more than the players do. Their carefree but committed support, mixed with a healthy nationalism, a few drams and a wild enthusiasm, all rubbed off on the players.

*George*: Having been one of that group in '92, I have to say that even by the Tartan Army's usual standards, that was something special. The Swedish authorities loved it, too. The papers labelled us 'Jollygans', contrasting friendly drunken behaviour with the hooliganism that they had been so careful to try and avoid (naturally, the English fans could not be relied upon completely, but by '96, even they had begun to cotton on. I sometimes feel that Scotland supporters are *very deliberately* nice to everyone to make the English fans look worse). But that was an excellent experience. It was actually on my birthday that you beat the CIS 3–0, with you being brought down in the box to allow Gary McAllister to score from the penalty – a knack that seemed to desert him against the Auld Enemy in '96.

*Pat*: The fans will probably remember that 3–0 victory over the CIS with most affection, but for me, the game that sticks in my mind most was the 2–0 defeat by Germany at the same stadium. Scotland really bullied and battered Germany that day and although we lost, and from a distance it might seem like a sob story, it was one of the most incredible games I've ever seen. I was jumping into tackles with six-foot-three centre-halves – and winning them! I came on as substitute – with a broken ankle. I've never felt so strongly *part* of something as I did then.

*George*: Not at university, not at Chelsea, not at Everton?

*Pat*:      No. I really felt part of a team, part of a terrific group of people, but I also felt very *Scottish*, very much part of my country. It's a special feeling. That takes nothing away from the clubs I've been at. More so, it just stresses how special it was with Scotland. Sometimes it's very hard to build that up, sometimes it just happens, but it needs someone to push it in the right direction and I think Andy Roxburgh and Craig Brown did that so well at the time. It didn't need alcohol. It needed something else. You need something to lift you, lift your spirit. Maybe alcohol does that for some people, but sometimes supporters can do that to you – especially if they're as outstanding as they were that year. I remember the motorcycle police that drove in front of us on the way to the matches were wearing Scotland strips. Some of the Swedish people were crying as we left the tournament.

Realistically, it made me want to take a chance with my injury. It made me want to play through it and think, 'Sod the injury. These fans have travelled thousands of miles, they're living in tents, getting soaked. They have spent a lot of time and money and put up with a lot of discomfort, so you feel you have to give something back!' That was certainly one of the reasons I played while carrying that injury. Another was that I was at the end of my contract and I wanted a move. I'd been left out of two championships at the last minute before, and this was my one chance. I really didn't want to miss out on it again. For the six weeks leading up to the squad's trip to Sweden, I was hoping it would recover. I didn't know that the ankle was actually broken at the time. It was cracked along the base of the fibula and it was excruciatingly painful. I really couldn't kick a ball more than 10 or 20 yards.

But I'm glad I did it. When I was given the opportunities, I didn't let anyone down. I played my part in that competition and I did it quite well. With hindsight, I think I made the right decision. So I can't honestly say that the fans made me *forget* the pain, but for them, for my country and for myself, I was happy to go through it.

# SESSION 6
## There's Only Two Pat Nevins

*To find out in what way Pat differed from footballers in general and in what way he was very much like the others, I got him to complete a personality questionnaire about his typical or preferred behaviour. It covered 30 interconnected aspects of personality ('traits') and gave an interesting insight into what made Pat unique. First, however, I was interested to know to precisely what extent Pat would describe himself as a footballer at all, knowing he doesn't fit most people's stereotype. I could draw on my own experiences here, as I hardly strike most people as the typical psychologist, either . . .*

George:  I'm interested to talk about being a footballer and a player's sense of identity. Generally, when people ask someone who they are, one of the first things they'll mention is their job, what they do for a living. I sense that from what we've discussed before, you don't like to be thought of as 'Pat Nevin, the footballer' in the way that other players might. To what extent is that true?

Pat:  I like to make a distinction: being a footballer is what I *do*; it isn't what I *am*. The popular image of what a footballer is still doesn't correspond to me, even after all these years. I was very, very anti anybody seeing me in that light when I was younger. I had been a student, I was growing up and when I started playing football professionally – especially at Chelsea – the people I was associating with were more musicians, actors, dancers – even road-sweepers, although my road-sweeping mate Willie was a Wagnerian, Proustian aesthete. There weren't many other footballers. Nevertheless, over the last 15 years, I've had so many memorable experiences as a player that it no longer feels completely odd – as it did in my Chelsea days – for me to think of myself as a player.

If someone asks me what I do now, I say: 'I play football.' It still feels a little funny, but not as much as it did. I used to feel totally uncomfortable about it and I don't anymore. A lot of that has come from my work with the PFA. It's given me my position within football, so I feel duty-bound to present myself as a footballer in a positive light.

George:     The acceptable face of the game?

Pat:         If you like. I mean, you can see the paradox. It's laughable, really: if I don't see myself as a footballer, why on earth would I want to *represent* footballers? It's because I've spent a lot of time watching other players that I hope I now have a fuller understanding of their problems and difficulties and worries.

George:     I think it comes out in your writing. The piece about Gascoigne for *Arena* was a case in point. It was so different from the many pieces written about him by journalists and fans, and the new breed of journalist-fans, who I have a lot of time for (the Jim Whites, the Olivia Blairs and so on). Your angle was that you were a player who had played against him and mixed with him socially. It's so different to the usual angle, and you see things that we don't see. Being a footballer-journalist doesn't sound like a bad thing to be at all. If you had to pick one – I'm forcing you into a choice here, as psychologists often do! – which would you say is more 'you': the player or the writer?

Pat:         Player *spokesperson*, really. I like to think that in some of the articles I've written now, for the *Independent*, the *Sunday Times*, *Match of the Day* magazine and so on, I'm trying to provide new angles, new twists, which have been given to me through being a player.

George:     To some extent, what you've said about being a player parallels my attitude to being a psychologist. I'm always a little bit cautious about saying I'm a psychologist, because of the public perception of psychologists being so influenced by the '*Punch* cartoon' stereotype of what a psychologist is. Certain 'media tart' individuals, many of whom are not even Chartered Psychologists to start with, are quite happy to live up to that stereotype, but end up becoming caricatures of themselves.

Well, as a result of people like that, I tend not to introduce myself as a psychologist, first and foremost. I'd rather say I'm a Newcastle supporter, or a regular cinema-goer, or anything unconnected with my job, and then only later add what I do for a living. I get the impression that you're a bit like that when it comes to describing yourself as a footballer. Is that anything to do with the rather dodgy image of footballers that, again, the tabloids have helped to reinforce?

*Pat*:    The position that you describe taking up is one which I think I left behind about two or three years ago, after holding it for a very long time. The position I'm in now is enjoying the reactions of people when I do say that I'm a footballer! I'm so detached from the media-fashioned 'Pat Nevin, the footballer' side of my personality that I tend to think of it in the third person anyway. But when I answer that I'm a footballer, it is interesting to watch the reactions, and sometimes very funny! I play a little game in that I wait for them to introduce the stereotype into their conversation and then I squash it. Once I've done that, we have quite a level playing-field.

I do sometimes adopt your technique of talking about my other interests or some of the other jobs I do when I'm not playing football, and then come on to talking about the football later, but increasingly, I'm happy to kick off with 'the football thing': set up the generalisation, shatter it and then carry on with the conversation. I find it actually works very well – probably better than the other method of hiding the job!

*George*:    I think that's fair enough, but it doesn't work with everyone. With my last book, *I Think I'll Manage*, I was very careful to point out that while I was a psychologist, I was also a football fan and it was probably the latter that formed the major force in me writing the book. Fans tend to have their biases and their own slants on things, and I tried to make it clear that I would too, that the famous impartial objectivity that psychologists have to pretend to possess – but, of course, no human being can *really* have – would be taking second place to my views as a fan. Hence there were lots of digs at Arsenal, Alan Sugar, Alex Ferguson and my other *bêtes noires*. Now, one particular reviewer couldn't get his head round this at all, that it was possible to be a psychologist *and* a football fan. Surely you could only be one or the other? Surely the conflict between the two roles couldn't be resolved? It was like Jekyll and Hyde!

Anyway, he gave me a dreadful review as a result. Very low tolerance of ambiguity, as we say in the business. Plonker!

Pat:	On this theme, the reaction I get from my fellow players when I tell them I'm doing a book with a psychologist is very interesting.

George:	Yes, that sounds a fascinating perspective: the 'inside view'. From my own point of view, the reaction I get from psychologists tend to be positive, because they know what I'm like, they know that there are almost as many different kinds of psychologist out there as there are different kinds of people. They're fascinated that I'm doing a book with a player, but they're not surprised. My only problem is with people who are not psychologists, but who think they understand perfectly what psychologists are supposed to be like – they are, of course, the same people who think they know what footballers are like!

Pat:	I have to say, I haven't told many players that I'm doing it yet! I'll have to test it on some more players to gauge the reaction. I'm fairly wary of mentioning it, to be honest. When players hear you're writing a book, their first thought is going to be: 'Oh no! Exposés!' I'd have to explain in detail what it's all about, but I think that once the word got around, the reaction would be fairly negative. Players would be scared that I was going to strip bare their personal secrets.

George:	When, of course, you're only stripping bare your own!

One of the things people asked me a lot about my last book was: 'How did you get these football managers to talk to you so freely and openly?' And I don't think there was any particular technique to it. I mean, my psychological background might have played some small part – my 'bedside manner', as one reviewer put it – but more than anything else, it was probably my naiveté, in that I'm not an experienced journalist. I think that one of the wonderful things about a lot of the football books that are being written now – and this is also true of some of the interviews with players and managers in the fanzines, and in the newer glossy magazines as well – is that they're being written by genuine fans who come straight out and ask the questions that tired old newspaper hacks have learned over time not to ask, but which we all want answered.

*Pat*: You chose your managers very well, too.

*George*: Yes, that was certainly part of it. It wouldn't have worked with certain other managers. Having said that, if you ask people open, straightforward questions without any hidden agenda, you often get an honest answer!

*Pat*: Well, honesty and football management don't always go hand in hand!

*George*: You completed a questionnaire for me, which has proved quite illuminating in certain respects. It was one which I had given to a group of footballers from different clubs as part of some research I was doing with my colleague Stephen Smith. As a group, there was hardly anything to distinguish players as a whole from the general population of Britain. Some were more extrovert, others more introvert, some were more inclined to plan, others more spontaneous, and so on. The players, like people in Britain, reflected the whole spectrum of personality. I think it was Graham Taylor who once sagely observed that 'footballers are no different to human beings', and he was absolutely right – with one little exception. As a group, footballers were more competitive, worse losers if you like. This is fine in one respect, but in a team game, being individually competitive must somehow be channelled towards the great good of the team.

Interestingly, people in Britain, if anything, tend to play down how competitive they are. There is still this 'playing the game and taking part' thing, the Corinthian ethos. In America it's very different, but over here, this 'winning isn't everything, it's the only thing' attitude that they have across the Atlantic is somewhat frowned upon. We want Frank Bruno back in panto, not fighting Tyson – he might hurt himself! Only in this country would Eddie 'The Eagle' Edwards be seen as a sporting hero.

Now, this is fascinating from your own point of view, as you've emerged as someone who is quite a good loser, someone who doesn't need to win at all costs. This makes you different from the average player. What would you say about that point of view?

Pat:    I suppose it's a limitation of the way the questions are asked in the questionnaire, to some extent. I could understand why it came out that I'm a 'good loser', as it were. But it's nevertheless the case that I *absolutely hate losing*! I'm not necessarily a *bad* loser, but I *hate* losing. I compete with myself, not really anyone else. I don't need anyone else. I push myself very hard *against myself* in a lot of areas. I try to achieve – or even beat – what I think I'm capable of, what I should be capable of. Having been given certain talents, I like to push to the limit what I can do with them.

George:  What are you like after your team has lost? Are you one of these players who can't sleep afterwards? Can you shrug it off and look to the next game straight away?

Pat:    Losing is something I came to terms with quite early on in my career, when I was at Chelsea. I managed to get over it. To start with, I had set myself outrageous and unattainable standards of performance. I was incredibly disappointed when we didn't win, I was incredibly disappointed when we *did* win but I didn't play well. I remember doing an interview with someone, four or five years into my career, and he asked how satisfied I was with my form. I replied: 'Not particularly.' 'Oh, so you're playing badly?' he asked. Well, I wasn't, but if I'm honest about it, I've only really been satisfied with some four or five games in my entire career.

*George*: You set your sights *that* high?'

*Pat*: Yes. I have this ideal to which I try to live up. In my early days at Chelsea, I would never really enjoy the evening after a match, because I was pushing that perfectionist side of me forward too much. Then somebody said to me one night: 'You're really selfish, aren't you? We all want to have a nice time on a Saturday night, and you're in a bad mood!' I think that from that day on, I never acted grumpily after a match again. Since I've been married and now have a family, I know I could never do it again. I wouldn't dream of doing it, of putting my family through my disappointments. So I don't know if I'm hiding it now, if I'm submerging it somewhere deep down, or if I just live my life and compartmentalise things better, to the extent that football matters and family matters are given separate compartments. I certainly feel more relaxed now. It may seem as though I don't care about winning, but I really do. It's just that I can put it in that compartment and thus feel more at ease about it.

I suppose that someone in your profession or a psychiatrist might think: 'He's bottling up how he feels about losing. Tick . . . tick . . . tick . . . He's a bomb waiting to go off.' But it isn't that way at all. I suppose I've understood myself a bit better. I don't want other people to have to wallow in my own disappointment – that's a selfish attitude.

*George*: Well, you've certainly indicated, from the way you completed the questionnaire, that you do have slightly more of a tendency to keep your feelings and emotions in check, compared to other people. Now, this is interesting, because you're also an outgoing, extrovert kind of person, and for those who like to be with others and enjoy a laugh and a joke, keeping your feelings under control can be difficult. This is especially true if you have a pronounced independent streak and very strong views about things, as you do. It can always be a source of conflict – I'm like this myself, to a large extent – if you want on the one hand to be nice to everyone in the group and keep them happy, but on the other hand to put your very strong views across, particularly if you suspect that the others won't necessarily agree with them. Which is the stronger pull for you: saying what you feel, regardless, or holding back for the sake of harmony?

*Pat*:     It depends on the group, it really does. The biggest problem always comes when my two different peer groups meet. I end up stuck in the middle. I know how to act in the two groups – footballers and those who don't play football – but when the two groups meet, it really becomes a bit of a dilemma what to do. Generally, I think that when I'm with players, I hold back a bit more. When I'm with my other friends – and this is especially true of the friends I had in London during my time at Chelsea, who were an unusual, strange, wild set of people – I tended to be more likely to crack jokes and be in the middle of the conversation, 'the life and soul of the party', I suppose, even though there would be a lot of other strong personalities there. Maybe I felt more confident in that situation, because football was never really brought up in the conversation. I was actually *me*, as opposed to 'the player'. It was as though I'd cut away from the football side of my life, and I'd almost feel like a different person.

A perfect example of this happened just the other day, with all the Tranmere boys looking at me as though I was from another planet. We were playing a reserve-team game against Blackburn, who were already on the field, and Graeme Le Saux and Billy McKinlay applauded me on for a laugh because we are such good friends. When I am with them, I behave in an almost diametrically opposite way from when I'm with most other footballers. So the first thing we did was hug each other – particularly with 'Badger' McKinlay – in that

very matey, Scottish kind of way, and then we pro-
ceeded to have a real laugh.

The Tranmere players looked at me and I could see
that they just didn't understand. This wasn't the player
they knew or the *person* they knew. Suddenly I'd gone
all loud and was having an incredibly good time! It's
actually a side of my personality that is very difficult
for them to see. I walked across to them and they were
giving me completely bemused looks. It was a good
example of two different peer groups meeting – even
though Billy and Graeme Le Saux are both players, too.
I think it was the Scottish thing with Billy, as well.
People from Scotland tend to be more demonstrative in
expressing their affection for one another, especially
being part of that Scotland squad which had such a
wonderful group feeling.

George:   I can understand that completely. When I meet good
friends of mine from Scotland, like my mates Chris or
Stevie, we tend to greet one another in that way, too. I
suppose that to your team-mates, it might have looked
as though you liked your opponents better than you
liked them!

Pat:      That's true. I didn't think that way at the time, but I
think you're right – they probably did think that. I
thought they'd realise that it's just a different sort of
relationship I have with these particular players. But
this sort of reaction has gone on for as long as I can
remember, when two different peer groups of mine
have met and the reactions have just been too weird for
words.

          Having said that, I've never felt uncomfortable in
that situation. Generally speaking, when the two
groups have met, I've been the effervescent me. I suppose I adopt that role because as your questionnaire has
suggested, maybe that's the one that I do feel slightly
more at home with.

George:   One thing you have said that you're reserved about is
what you've achieved. Now, that's not so unusual.
Some players are very modest indeed. The public

stereotype, however, is probably that players are a bit on the arrogant side. I remember when I first met Mark Bright, he told me that I was lucky to be talking to someone as famous as he was. It's always people who are not quite as famous as they think they are who have to keep reminding you of the fact that they're celebrities. Gazza isn't like that at all. For all his wealth of talent – and wealth of wealth, come to that! – I've always found him very modest and reserved about his achievements. You've said in the questionnaire that you're *extremely* unlikely to go on about your successes, that you wouldn't blow your own trumpet. Just how true is that?

*Pat*:     I suppose one answer to that might be that I feel I haven't really achieved all that much, but compared to someone who has tried to play football and has never made it, I realise that's going to sound stupid.

*George*: Realistically, you've played for Chelsea, Everton, Scotland . . . You've scored some brilliant goals . . . You've been a hero to thousands of fans . . .

*Pat*:     I think it's something that goes straight back to childhood. If you're a decent footballer, it's going to attract a lot of jealousy. So rather than being loud and obvious about it, I hid it to the extent that when I was younger, even very close friends didn't know I played football, even though I was playing professionally. I went away to play for Scotland Under-18s in Finland and I was awarded Player of the Tournament in this European Under-18 Championship. Quite a lot of people only found out I played football as a result of reading about that in the back pages of the Scottish daily national newspapers.

*George*: Incredible! Not many players could have kept *that* quiet about their achievements, surely? That really does sound unusual.

*Pat*:     Well, I was starting a degree at around that time, and I suppose then I'd rather people knew I was doing that than doing anything else. Perhaps I didn't want them thinking that I spent all my time playing football. But since I've got older, what I think has taken over from that is simply an appreciation of the fact that while being good at playing football is all very well, you only have to listen to *Desert Island Discs* in the morning to know that there are a hell of a lot of people out there who have done far more important things than I have. Whenever I've set out to do something, it's been the same feeling. Trying my hand at journalism is a good example: by the time I was writing for the *Sunday Times* and the *Independent*, and they liked my stuff and were publishing it without changing it, that should have been a bigger buzz than it was. It felt nice for a moment, but then I thought: 'Ah, but there are plenty of better writers than me!' and that was it. There was no glow and no other glory attached to it.

One of the most difficult things that faces me in my future life is that at some point, I'm going to have to write a CV for a job. It frightens me to death, because I just don't know what I'm going to say!

*George:* That ties in with something else that came out when you completed the questionnaire. You said that you're not interested in selling and negotiating – when returning it, you said you'd make the world's worst sales rep! – but when it comes to writing a CV, there's an element of having to sell *yourself* – not perhaps to overstate, but certainly to stress what you've achieved very strongly – and it strikes me that this isn't something that would come easily to you . . .

*Pat:* I think that whatever you've achieved in life should speak for you, rather than you having to do it yourself. But I don't think I'm modest – I think I'm honest. I truly believe that. As for the CV, it's a nightmare, the idea of trying to *sell* myself.

*George:* Perhaps you just have a more global perspective on life. You mentioned that many other people have achieved far greater things, and in the end, even the best player in the world can only contribute to his team's performance and entertain his fans. But just acknowledging that is surely modest. I mean, you don't get Clint Eastwood saying: 'Well, in the end, I'm only an actor. All I do is entertain.'

*Pat*:        But you will get some actors who say that. Harrison
              Ford has said that. When they asked him about his
              philosophy of acting, whether he was a method actor
              or whatever, his classic reply was that he went to the
              'Let's Pretend' school of acting! He's very good at his
              job, but I don't know if that was really an overly modest
              comment. His view is: 'Don't muck about – I'm good at
              what I do, but I'm not doing anything other than pre-
              tending to be other people. Acting's got its place, it's
              not overly important in the wider scheme of things' –
              and of course, I feel that way about football.
                 I suppose he sees in the acting world that some
              people believe their own publicity machines and the
              media hype. If you are too wrapped up in that world,
              it's easy to lose a sensible perspective on life, and of
              course, football is just the same. An often overlooked
              reason why people lose a reasonable, level-headed per-
              spective when they achieve fame is that the general
              public fawn over them so much. They are treated like
              royalty, but when their popularity wanes, people are
              shocked when the ex-star can't cope or is unable to
              behave like Joe Bloggs again. I do feel a little pain for
              people in this situation, as it is not completely of their
              own making.

*George*:     I must say, I find being overhyped – as can happen in
              publishing, of course – to be a bit embarrassing some-
              times. When the publicity department starts sharpen-
              ing up its superlatives, I sometimes wonder whether
              occasional understatement might not do the trick just
              as effectively.

*Pat*:        I've got a fear of hype. It's something I'm scared of. I've
              read stuff about myself and understood that it's been
              hype at the time. I remember in my early playing days,
              when a lot of the tabloids were trying to do stories about
              me at Chelsea. My platform was always to try and
              change the subject by discussing another player instead.
              Then the journalists would go home and try and write
              an article about me and find that they couldn't.

*George*:     Through not having collected enough material?

*Pat*:      That's right. It was something I recognised very early on, that some of the tabloid journalists are very good at trying to get you to blow your own trumpet. Their editors have then said: 'What the hell is *this*? Go back and ask him some more questions and get proper answers this time!' That kind of to-ing and fro-ing lasted for a while.

*George*:   There's that phrase: 'Don't believe your own publicity', but to what extent do you think there is a danger of younger players doing just that? You only have to score a couple of goals now and suddenly you're the new Pele! There is simply so much coverage devoted to football now in the papers, on the radio and on TV, and there are so many journalists desperate for something to write about or make programmes about, that it's hard for a player not to fall for the hype – especially his own. Look at Tony Yeboah. He had a good start to last season for Leeds and suddenly he's on the cover of every magazine, in every paper, on the telly constantly. And it tends to be very short-term. Matt Le Tissier, Andy Cole . . . *Who's flavour of the month this time*? Can a player get carried away with all that?

*Pat*:      Because the hype was so heavy at Chelsea, and because I never believed it, the reality has never hurt particularly. I haven't 'come back down to earth with a bump', because I never believed I was that high-up in the first place. But I can see plenty of personalities in the game who will never be able to look at things in that light. I used to think they were stupid for not seeing through it, but they're not thick – they're just not that type of person. Some people, after all, thrive on being told how good they are, and they believe it if they read it again and again. There can be lots of reasons for it, as you'll know – maybe their parents didn't show them enough love when they were children, or whatever. Some haven't been praised that much in their lives and suddenly they see themselves in the papers being hyped out of all proportion. You can't blame them for being a little taken in by it.

Any opportunity I get to talk to young players, I do warn them not to take it too seriously. There are some who are masters at talking for a long time and not saying anything at all, not allowing themselves to be caught up in it. Alan Shearer is excellent at that. There's now also a media package for players, which we've organised with the help of responsible journalists. I did a Radio 4 documentary about the need for media training for footballers, so naturally the union said: 'Right! Go and bloody well help organise it, then!' So that's what we, the union, did and now all young players get the pack and are taught it through their YT tutoring. 'Don't believe the hype' is one of the messages of it. Don't let them build you up, only to pull you down.

My own motives in going into journalism are not self-exposure. Ever since I was 17, I just felt it would be providing a service if people got to understand players better. I *do* feel a little pride in some of the pieces I've written, where I've interviewed Stuart Pearce, Joe Royle and Graeme Le Saux. I felt I got information from them that they hadn't given to anyone before.

*George*:  I'd add your piece about Gazza to that. It wasn't an interview, but it showed great insight. Everyone has written their Gazza piece and some, even those by good writers like Pete Davies, have been woeful. Your *Arena* article struck a very true note, I thought. I've only met Gazza two or three times, but I could recognise him from your article.

And I suppose that takes us full-circle to where we began this session, talking about the concept of identity. It seems to me that you see yourself as not just someone who is a footballer *per se*, but someone who wants to communicate what it's like to be a footballer to other people, either from your own perspective or through talking to other players. This comes into your writing and your work for the union, the PFA.

# D'You Wanna Be in My Gang?

---

*The players' strike has been averted. Fans of teams outside the Premiership breathe a sigh of relief. Pat is feeling a sense of relief, too . . .*

George:  So, let's get up to date. It seems that your feeling of paranoia springing from being forced to play in the reserves has subsided?

Pat:  Yes. It had been a very odd feeling for me, not to be playing first-team football any more. I still felt I was playing well in the reserves, working hard in training, and I did begin to feel a little paranoid over the fact that I wasn't being included. I don't think that's too strong a word. That's how I felt at an emotional level, but, rationally, I still felt I was being a bit silly, that I was still only working my way back from injury and I shouldn't make too big a deal of it.

    I've been doing weights all season, staying as fit as possible, deliberately losing weight, and all of a sudden, as of last week, I've suddenly started feeling incredibly calm. I feel calmer now than I've probably felt for a year. I've been racking my brain to try and figure out why it happened. Although I'm naturally a calm person and don't usually let things get to me, for a while I had been getting slowly edgier. Then for a week or two I'd really been quite worried, thinking: 'This isn't right! It doesn't make sense!' Now, though, I feel really relaxed about everything. I think it's partly down to the fact that on Thursday, the breakthrough with the Football League finally happened. They buckled under the pressure and came to the negotiating table at the last minute.

George:  It's odd that they went for an eleventh-hour settlement, after being so utterly intransigent and uncompromising to start with.

Pat:     It appears that that was just a brilliant act. You were right. They had been calling our bluff, but we were completely sure about our position. Perhaps they thought we were going to change our minds and back down. They left it and did nothing, right up until the Thursday night, knowing that the strike-ballot result was coming back on Friday morning. We knew that the support for action had been fantastic, and maybe that was what they had been waiting for. The strong feeling of our membership was our trump card. Perhaps they thought that the feelings of the players in the lower divisions wouldn't run quite as strong, that we wouldn't get the support we'd hoped. When they discovered that we were going to get it after all, they talked. I believe our membership had once again voted over 90 per cent in favour of strike action. It was particularly impressive because it would have been harder for those players in the lower leagues to afford to go on strike. It is so heartening that they believe in and trust their union – but then again, they are right to do so!

So maybe the resolution of that dispute was one of the things that completely relaxed me. In addition to that, I'd got myself incredibly fit by working hard in the gym and continuing to do the weights all that time, and I had this realisation that for the first time in about six or seven months, I had managed to reach that plateau of fitness and I was *completely free of injury*. It had been a long time. I might not be in the first team, but I had total confidence in both my fitness and my ability. It just feels wonderful.

George:  Like a huge weight off your mind?

Pat:     Like that, even though I never used to think along those lines. I've never been a big worrier. I remember thinking this when filling in the personality questionnaire. Worrying excessively about things isn't really me.

George:  Yes, you certainly described yourself as someone who is not only relaxed and free of tension on a day-to-day basis, but also someone who doesn't get apprehensive or tense about specific events. In fact, a feeling of paranoia would seem very alien to your usual make-up indeed.

Pat:     I know. It is obvious now to say that tension over the union work was a problem and I'm only now returning to my normal self. It's really because every dark cloud that was looming on the horizon has gone. For every question and doubt, I was able to find an answer. Firstly, the PFA/Football League dispute sorted itself out. Secondly, I was able to dispel doubts over my fitness by getting fully fit. And finally, there was a good feeling from a *moral* point of view – this is probably the most interesting part.

I'm in a position where I'm earning quite a lot of money here at Tranmere. For a club of Tranmere's size, I get decent wages. If you're out of the team and not getting a game, not being played by the manager, the normal thing for a lot of players is to rush around trying to get a transfer. This is something I will not do, and haven't done in the past at any club while I've been under contract. So I'm making a lot of money and not getting a game, which could make me feel like a bit of a cheat, a bit of a fraud. But I feel quite good about it, morally. This is because I signed a three-year contract with Tranmere last year. At the end of last season, I turned down two teams, a Scottish Premier League team and an English Premier League team, because I wanted to show my loyalty to the club. I could have made a lot more money by moving. So now I feel that *the club* should show the same loyalty towards *me*, because I still think that I'm capable of playing well; or, if they want to get rid of me, *they* should go and organise it.

I therefore don't think I'm cheating anyone, as long as I play and train as well as I possibly can. I've put the ball in the club's court. It allows me to feel quite relaxed and happy with myself from a moral point of view. My conscience is clear and that matters to me. It's a very,

very big thing for me. I would feel terrible if I was picking up decent wages at a club and I wasn't trying, or had a bad attitude, or was past it and not capable of producing the goods on a Saturday afternoon. I always try to display a perfect attitude – or as close to it as I can possibly get. I hope that the fans realise this. I always try to be anything other than a 'passenger'.

*George*:  To what extent do you think other players struggle with the dilemma of the fact that their earnings don't necessarily get reflected in what they're delivering for the club? I remember the criticism of Eric Cantona, who continued to draw a very high wage for the whole of the time that he was suspended for kicking that fan. It must play on a player's mind if they feel they're getting paid for nothing, or for very little. Psychologists who study motivation call it equity theory – the belief that what you're putting in is matched fairly by what you're getting out, and that the same applies for others.

*Pat*:  I think a lot of players think about it the way I do – that as long as you're trying your best, the rest is in the hands of the manager. Certainly, a lot of the managers feel the opposite way, that players have no right to earn the money they do when they are not in the first team. Some of the managers from the old school, in particular, have a bit of a problem with it. They're jealous, really, of the high wages that players earn, which they never had the chance to earn themselves. I definitely think that it is an attitude that current players encounter.

*George*:  There's a famous story told by the late Tommy Trinder, when he was chairman of Fulham, about a player being upset that the wages successfully negotiated by another player, which were naturally paid all through the year, were higher than his own. 'But he's a better player than you are,' protested Trinder. 'Not during the bloody summer, he's not!' came the reply.

*Pat*:  I remember Tommy telling me that story himself on a chat show we were on – obviously he had told it to the rest of the world, too! It's a good illustration of how important it is to communicate it well. I'm hosting a phone-in radio show just now and some of the people phoning me up are naturally asking about my position at Tranmere. Also, a lot of fans have been writing to me and asking me what's going on. So I have to let them know that I'm very, very keen to get back in the first team, but it's also extremely important that I'm not snide about the team or the manager. You mustn't make bitchy remarks about the situation and about your team. It can have a negative effect on the support and on your team-mates, and always sounds petty, small-minded and selfish, anyway. It's always too easy to fall into that trap. Even remarks that are fairly veiled, people can generally see through. I try to be completely and utterly honest, so it's generally not a problem.

George:  I think there's a certain kind of fan – you'll find them writing articles in *When Saturday Comes*, a lot of the time! – that assumes a total cynicism on the part of *all* players. There's a feeling that players are just after the most expedient way of making lots and lots of money, that they're not troubled by moral dilemmas concerning the size of their bank balances one iota.

Pat:  There are almost certainly some players who are totally mercenary. I'm not going to deny they exist. But most of the players I've come across want to play and want to earn their wages. It affects a player's self-esteem as well, in a lot of cases. How many players do you know who go straight into the manager's office and ask for transfers when they're not getting a chance to play first-team football? I can tell you there are plenty. If they are transferred, it is quite possible they'll end up on lower wages, and they may have to uproot, move house and re-school the children, but at least they get the chance to play first-team football. That is just how important it can be for some players to have high self-esteem.

A big dilemma of the age concerns those players that are bought for huge amounts of money, with wages correspondingly high, and end up getting stuck in the reserves. In those situations, there isn't enough incentive for some individuals to give maximum effort. I believe it is a very small number, but it is a real problem for the game as a whole. It's a dilemma for clubs, for players and for the PFA, really.

To my mind, if you are one of the highly paid players concerned, you've signed a contract that is legally binding for a certain period of time, that you're going to be paid x amount to give the best that you can give. As long as you're doing that, it strikes me that it's morally and ethically OK to stay at the club. The player shouldn't chase other clubs, looking for a transfer under those circumstances and having to accept a reduction in wages. It is perfectly possible that it is the club that has made the error – that the player's style of play doesn't fit the rest of the team, or there has been a change of manager and the new one has different ideas, or the player doesn't fit a particular system and the club should have considered it more before buying that player. They should have done their research a little bit better. If the player is costing them that much, they should have spent a little more effort getting to know what they were buying.

The unforgivable thing is, of course, when you're not putting in the effort but you're still drawing the wage. You can see how managers, other players and fans would get very angry with that attitude, and from the PFA's point of view, it becomes difficult to back a player if they're clearly not firing on all cylinders.

In my current position at Tranmere, I'm turning up early – maybe an hour early – for training sessions, getting positive reactions from the lads. The manager can see how keen I am. No-one is going to say that I'm not giving my all.

Anyway, to bring us right up to date, there was a televised match against QPR and I thought there would be very little chance of me playing. Everyone, including the manager, could see that I was playing well, that I was 'on fire', to quote a football phrase. I thought perhaps that the manager's view had been affected by my performance in the second half of last year, when I didn't always play up to my usual standard. I had been playing with a groin injury which made it very difficult to turn quickly, and where I think I have a skill that sets me apart, it's my ability to do those very sharp turns. I'm not an exceptionally fast player, but I can turn remarkably quickly. Unfortunately, because of the groin injury, I couldn't do that in the last quarter of last season, and as such, my game was affected. Most players can give you their own version of this story at any given time. Because of the demands on players these days, most of us are playing with injuries throughout part of the season.

I should probably have communicated that to the manager at the time, but I was determined to play through that particular injury, partly to show loyalty and partly because I was desperate to get into the Scotland squad again – which didn't happen, in the end. My wife and I had had a baby who hadn't slept a full night in 18 months, which was also difficult for me – but much more difficult for my wife! So there were a few things slowing me down.

So I was going along to the QPR game, the only senior pro, I believe, who hadn't started a match this season and it was already nearing November. I arrived at the ground, not expecting the chance to play, but thinking: 'I'll see how it goes' – and the first thing that happened was a fan stopped me and said he was sorry to hear that I was leaving the club on a free transfer!

This stunned me somewhat, as you can imagine, particularly right before a game and an important, live televised one at that. It was a story which had been dropped, and I use that word advisedly, in the *People* by someone. The story used quotation marks and said I was 'fed up' and 'wanted away'. Now, I'd never spoken to the *People* – I'd never spoken in this way to *anyone*. I asked the manager about it and he just made a joke of it, neither saying yea or nay, really. He wouldn't reveal what had really happened, which gave me even more of a shock.

*George*:  I can imagine!

*Pat*:  And he then put me on the bench! I could make no
sense of this at all, but despite everything, I still had
that inner feeling of being relaxed and thought that if I
got my chance, I'd be really confident and do well. It
was only afterwards that I thought: 'Is he only playing
me now to put me in the shop window so he can sell
me?' That's the kind of thing that can go through a
player's mind as he's sitting on the bench. People don't
realise sometimes that all these sorts of thoughts are
going on inside a player's head while a match is being
played. Most players are professional enough and capable enough to focus on the job in hand, though.
Usually, as a breed, we can play well through some level
of uncertainty. However, if the papers say you're off on
Sunday morning and you're on the bench on Sunday
afternoon, your mind can't help but wander. Anyway,
we lost.

*George*:  Have there been other points in your career when you
felt you were being used in that kind of way?

*Pat*:  Not like this. My moves from Chelsea to Everton and
from Everton to Tranmere both came when my contract
was up, so it wasn't the same. For me, it has been 15
years of almost unbroken first-team football, so this
kind of experience is new to me. To accept in myself
that age is the problem, that this is the start of the end,
would be accepting defeat. To accept this would be to
plummet immediately. Over the next few days, all this
was going through my head, and, of course, I still
hadn't had a chance to discuss it properly with the
manager. When, eventually, I did, he just said: 'Just get
your head down and work really, really hard and take
your chance when it comes.' I've taken that at face
value, which I suppose is what you should do with
comments from your manager. This is what I needed
and wanted to hear.

Even since then, though, a number of agents have
told me that the club are trying to get rid of me – I don't
have my own agent, but this came out in conversation.

Again I asked the manager, and he told me there was no truth in the rumours.

*George*: It sounds very unsettling.

*Pat*: Well, you end up feeling very uncertain, but I'll just take the manager at his word at the moment.

*George*: It must be even harder if you are represented by an agent, because then you have two individuals of whom you can't be sure whether they're giving you the full story or not – the manager *and* the agent. I certainly know of one agent who will quite happily invent transfer speculation about his clients, just to keep their names in the papers and, presumably, their value up. I'm sure he's not alone, even if others are perhaps a little more subtle about it – I nearly gave away who it was with that comment!

*Pat*: I've seen it happen and I've known plenty of players who were featured in that kind of newspaper story, but I've always stayed away from that. I've no wish to take part in that hype. I always believe in being up front and that's why I've never had an agent as such. I feel that I shouldn't need one.

So, bringing us right up to date, after an unsuccessful run of about eight or nine games, the players went for a day out which turned into an evening out, with a view to building team spirit in very much the way we've discussed. We'll find out later this week if it worked. That was the Tuesday. On Wednesday the Football League and PFA met, and as I said, a negotiated settlement was reached – after five hours of talks. So for me, a number of loose ends were tied up and it spelt an end to a period of uncertainty and slight confusion about my position.

Maybe the reason that I'm always happy, I'm always relaxed and confident, is because I'm generally in control of all the things that happen in my life – and perhaps, for a very short time there, that control slipped from my grasp. But I seem to have pulled it all back now and am back in control again – of *most* of my life, anyway.

*George*: Certainly, a feeling of lack of control over what happens in your life can be profoundly unsettling and cause a lot of stress. If you feel that other influences – events, people, luck – are pulling you in directions over which you have no control, it's very unnerving.

*Pat*: Those influences are probably still acting now, but because I know they're happening, I know what's going on and I'm now much more relaxed about them, even if I can't fully control them.

*George*: You know which direction they're trying to pull you – you know the score?

*Pat*: Yes, I'm back in total relaxed mode – and it has a great effect on my football. Any time I get a chance now, I'll be ready. The only problem which remains is whether I can get that chance. The manager has decided to go for a 3–5–2 formation. I'm one of four players at the club who are looked upon as wingers, and of course 3–5–2 doesn't feature wingers! We still travel to the matches, but the system may not allow us to play! I don't see myself as a winger, anyway. I can fit into three or four other positions. I hope the manager doesn't just see me as an out-and-out winger. In any case, I'll be reminding the manager in the morning!

*George*: This varies a lot from player to player, doesn't it? You get certain players who can only play in one position, and you get others, like Paul Scholes at Manchester United or Steve Watson at Newcastle, trying to break into the team and winning a reputation as 'supersubs' who can come on and play in just about any position – even, probably, in goal if they were asked!

*Pat*: Brian McClair is a perfect example of that.

*George*: Yes, Manchester United have several of these players, which is very annoying! But some players think of themselves as *just* strikers or *just* wingers or whatever. I wonder what impact that makes on their attitude to the game?

*Pat*: You certainly get players who just play in one position, and when they're bought by a new club, the manager of that club will only think of them playing in that

particular position – not good news for players who
have taken that role at the club until then. It is also bad
news for the incoming player if the system is adapted
and the position is no longer there. Inflexibility in football is a recipe for obsolescence. I've always thought
adaptability vital, ever since I started playing football.
If I was asked to play at left-back, I'd do it. That isn't a
cliché – I would happily have a go at it! It's something
I cottoned onto early on in my career at Chelsea: you
really have to learn to be adaptable. If you play in a
particular position and suddenly the club acquires the
world's best player in that position, you're not going to
get a game. You're finished. Hence, you have to be
flexible. When I was between 18 and 20, this struck me
as the most simple and obvious thing in the world. I've
always made it very clear to the managers at each of
my clubs that I'm prepared to play in any position up
front – centre-forward, on the wing, behind the front
two, whatever. But I've also tried to work very hard on
my fitness and stressed that I would be happy to take a
midfield role – though because of my height, most managers are fairly wary of doing that.

My adaptability has worked a treat for me, particularly with the Scottish national squad. If you're seen
as that kind of player, then you can change according to
the demands of the game. If the game changes and the
system has to be modified, then you can be moved –
and not necessarily substituted! Certainly, if you want
to play international football, it's important to think that
way. International matches are so much more technical
and the tactics are invariably changed at least two or
three times during each match, by both teams. I think
there are very few internationals who don't have a good
measure of adaptability these days.

*George*: Another time when you have to be flexible is when
something really drastic happens. I remember last
season, up at St James' Park, Wimbledon's keeper had
to go off and Vinnie Jones stepped into the breach. He
was actually terrible as a goalkeeper, but he won the

respect of the fans – even the Newcastle fans – for being prepared to do it at all. It's a bit like Gareth Southgate missing that penalty. He was almost certainly not the best person to take it – but at least he had the bottle to volunteer when certain others (Paul Ince) were cowering on the halfway line. I think the fans really respect that kind of commitment, even if it seems foolhardy with hindsight.

Pat:      When something *that* unexpected happens, like the goalie getting injured, then any organisation just goes out the window and the instinct to stop the dam from bursting completely takes over. You often ask a winger to play in centre-midfield in that situation – or full-back! The control has just gone in that situation and very few managers have teams that are capable of adapting *that much*. To pull it off with any success, teams rely on exhausting effort and that special spirit that comes from feeling hard done-by. There's a set fall-back: you bring off the winger, throw on another defender, stick the centre-half in goal and try to hold back the tide.

I've already had one meeting with the manager this season where I've told him that if he doesn't want me to play in my usual position, I'm happy to play in many others and I'll fight to be the best in other positions. It gives me more options, more possibilities.

George:   Your position will be dictated to some extent by which foot you prefer to kick with, and I don't mean that in the sense that the term is used in Glasgow! About a decade ago now, I was studying handedness and *footedness* for my PhD, and certain researchers have shown that people who show left-handedness and left-footedness are actually more skilful at sport, rather than less. The left-lateralised have traditionally been branded clumsy, but this seems to apply more to people who show a mixture of preferences – they do some things with their right and others with their left, suggesting that they haven't developed to prefer either side strongly. The strongly left-lateralised seem, if anything, to be quite exceptional in sport. One theory which has

been suggested is that it springs from greater involvement of the *right* hemisphere of the brain in strongly
left-handed people. The right hemisphere is considered
a more 'instinctive' one, connected with art, music,
vision – and maybe having a good sporting brain. The
left hemisphere, which typically plays a stronger part
in the lives of right-handed, right-footed people, is more
about language, logic and cold, rational reasoning –
maybe not as suited for sporting excellence. If you
look at the disproportionate number of very successful
left-handed tennis players (McEnroe, Connors,
Navratilova, etc.) and southpaw boxers, the theory
could have something in it. To what extent have you
found left-footed players to have a more instinctive
talent? Is it all an old wives' tale?

*Pat*:      There are five left-footed players currently at Tranmere:
Cook; Rogers; Teale; McIntyre and Mahon. Each of
them strikes the ball uncommonly *sweetly*. It is all about
timing and balance, but I find it hard to think of a pro
footballer who is left-footed who isn't an exceptionally
fine striker of the ball. At Everton, Kevin Sheedy was
the same. With Scotland, John Collins is a fine example.
I could go on! There are dozens of right-footed players
who do not 'ping' the ball sweetly, but I can scarcely
think of a left-footer like that. I am convinced that there
is something in left-sidedness that is helpful in some
respects.

*George*:   Actually, one paper I read – I think it was from a Can-
adian journal – suggested that, in football in particular,
those who are cross-lateralised, i.e. prefer to kick with
the opposite foot to the hand they write with, were
particularly successful players. This would include
players like Chris Waddle (left-footed, right-handed). It
even extends to some keepers. Ray Clemence is a good
example.

*Pat*:      I haven't come across many of them, to be honest. My
younger brother is cross-lateralised and can lash a ball
much harder than I can. His cross-lateralisation is
amazing in his painting, as he is a talented artist who

paints with both hands. My father-in-law is the same: he plays golf left- *or* right-handed . . . sickening.

*George*: On the wider issue of versatility, you have a lot of strings to your bow. Beyond being a player, you write, you represent players on the union and so on. Is there ever criticism of having 'too many interests outside the game'? Terry Venables is often accused of this . . .

*Pat*: Well, if you look at my position, I have one more season of my contract to run after this one, and then I'll be 35, so it is sensible to look to the future with a few 'projects'. I still have the attitude I had when I started playing: I'm still dedicated to it and don't, if possible, let anything interfere with my levels of performance. But I need something else. I've got other ideas. I always remember there are other things in my life. It just so happens that for the last three or four years, I have been paid for doing those other things. The writing, in particular, is going well. So I've had that parachute all the time, just in case the engine packs in with the football.

I hope I've been observant enough, though, to notice that many of the people around me haven't had that 'parachute', and I think I've had more respect for them as a result. I still feel just as much an outsider, though, as I ever did. However, it's not an antagonistic outsider anymore – it's a more voyeuristic and often impressed outsider. In some ways I have been working with a safety-net. Many other players haven't. Their position needs more bravery.

*George*: Do you think football culture has changed much since you began as a player?

*Pat*: Certain aspects have, but in essence it hasn't changed that much. I haven't changed with it or nearer to it. It isn't as though I've evolved to fit it better. The difference is that when I was starting out at Chelsea, I was listening to Joy Division on the *John Peel Show* while the other players were listening to Billy Joel, and now they listen to Chris Evans on Radio 1 while I listen to Melvyn Bragg's *Start The Week* on Radio 4 as well as John Peel.

*George*: Not any more, they don't! [*This cheap reference to Chris*

*Evans' hurried departure from Radio 1 was added with the benefit of hindsight. It might be snide, but it amused the authors.*]

Pat: It's a different set of differences now and players really are a far more sophisticated bunch on the whole, any enjoyment of the *Chris Evans Show* apart, but my understanding of the tastes of others is better now. At least, I hope it is. It *should* be, if I'm representing them.

George: To what extent are you a father figure – or maybe an older-brother figure – to some of the young players at Tranmere Rovers?

Pat: I have absolutely no idea! I really don't know how they see me. This is something that's true not just of footballers but also of anyone else in the public eye – it's very hard for us to see precisely what our image is. It becomes so blurred and warped by the media that it becomes almost impossible to see it, particularly to obtain a balanced view of it. It goes back to Rabbie Burns' *To a Louse* and the gift of seeing ourselves as others see us. It's bad enough in everyday life – the poem says it all. But if you're in the public eye, it's even more difficult to appreciate how you're looked upon by people.

George: I'm going to resist mentioning Chris Evans again.

Pat: A perfect recent example of my own inability to do it came the other day, when I was one of the guests on the Liverpool leg of Vic and Bob's *Shooting Stars* live on stage. I went through that door and I had absolutely no idea what my reception was going to be, whether I would get booed or cheered or what! I had no idea what my reputation is with the general public (if you can call Reeves and Mortimer fans the general public) of Liverpool. I had just heard Gerry Marsden walk on ahead of me, and he got booed. I thought, 'Oh no! And he's a local lad!' Happily, it went fairly well.

George: Perhaps they consider him a sell-out like they do Cilla and Tarby – or like a lot of Glaswegians see Billy Connolly now.

Pat: I think his main problem with that audience is that he's a bit older! But it illustrates the point well. And I haven't a clue what the other Tranmere players make of me – or indeed, how footballers generally see me in my role as PFA chairman. I suppose it runs the whole gamut from those who have some respect for me for the fact that I do a lot of unpaid work for the union, to those who are suspicious and think I do it only to feather my own nest and secure a cushy job in the future.

George: Some might latch onto this paradox that you appear to want to do something good for the game, while always having placed yourself so much outside it.

Pat: That's accentuated in my articles. There are certainly occasions where I've been a little more of a 'union rep' in what I've written than someone with strong opinions about my fellow professionals. There's always the temptation to . . . how can I put this delicately? . . .

George: Make the game seem more squeaky-clean than it really is?

Pat: I suppose so, yes. It is rather strange representing players when I don't feel like one of them, yet in another way, I sometimes feel that's the best way to do it. Occasionally, the best person to represent the views of a group is someone who's just outside that group. When communicating the needs of that group to an audience, it sometimes helps if you're not totally submerged within the culture of that group.

George: I can see what you're saying. Most jobs have their own cultures and often those who can communicate on behalf of those who do a job are able to get outside that, forget the jargon and the idiosyncrasies that are unique to that job and which people on the outside won't understand. As you say, these people often make very effective representatives.

Pat: Well, I hope that may be true with me. But the main reason I do it is one of the oldest clichés in the book: I want to give something back. People may not believe me when I say it – 90 per cent probably won't! – but it's absolutely true. Football's been damn good to me. It has. I've travelled, I've earned a lot of money, I've met a lot of incredible people, I've enjoyed it – I *love* doing the job, the actual playing of matches and the training, too. I *do* want to give something back, I feel I owe a debt to the game. I'm sure a number of others feel the same.

George:   Pele once said that football had been his university.

Pat:   That comment owes a lot to one of my heroes, Albert Camus.

George:   That everything he'd learned in life, he'd learned from football? That's been corrupted now. People have it on T-shirts and the word 'football' has been replaced with 'Star Trek'! Frightening!

Pat:   But football *has* been brilliant for me. I've made a great deal out of it, I've had a great time as a result of football, and I've learned a great deal about myself and about other people. It is often said that football is a roller-coaster of extreme highs and lows – you see the extremes in people in this game, and how they cope with extreme situations. I do feel you see the essential man under these circumstances. So I really do owe the game something. I also think that, from within the game, I'm probably as well-placed as anyone to give not just a positive view of what it's like, but a *realistic* view of what it's like. There are not that many people around who have had some training on how to write about it, have been trained on how to talk about it and, most importantly, have been trained how to *do it* at the top level. Maybe the position I've found myself in, even if I'm not talking about myself – which, 90 per cent of the time, I haven't been, until this book – is an appropriate one for me. I don't feel ill at ease doing it, because most of the time I feel that footballers, whether they're like me or not, are a very misrepresented bunch, and I don't like that misrepresentation.

George:   On the theme of you being different, there's a story that when you first came to London to play for Chelsea, they were expecting some sharp-dressed, flash Glaswegian and they nearly couldn't find you at Euston station, because you were dressed so casually, even scruffily – like a student, presumably!

*Pat*:       Yes! That story goes on, in fact. They said that they had
             fixed up digs for me, though they had originally pro-
             mised me a flat. I just said I wasn't staying in digs, I'd
             rather go back home to Glasgow. They were shocked.
*George*:   Of course, in the end, you finished up in a flat just
             across the road from Scribes. What a splendid location!
*Pat*:       And you know what? I've never been to Scribes!
*George*:   You're missing the home of karaoke. You could give
             them a rendition of that Celtic classic, adapted from a
             favourite by the Proclaimers, 'When You Go Will You
             Send Back Souness to Sampdoria?' The other interesting
             thing about you coming to play for Chelsea is that you
             supported them, didn't you – despite being brought up
             in the East End of Glasgow?
*Pat*:       I didn't support them – that's just the way that these
             stories get twisted. But the first football strip I owned
             was a Chelsea strip. Utter fluke!
*George*:   It must have been embarrassing – it could so easily be
             mistaken for a Rangers kit! I notice it's not just you,
             either. Author Roddy Doyle was a Chelsea fan from
             childhood – and he's a Dubliner!
*Pat*:       It just *happened*, really! I was born in 1963 and I would
             have been bought my first football strip around 1969–
             70. Celtic had just won the European Cup. Everyone
             was a Celtic supporter, my brothers and all the boys
             around me of my age. My father offered to buy me a
             football strip, and I saw a picture in a magazine of this
             brilliant, simple blue strip – the Chelsea strip. It looked
             fantastic. So I asked my Dad for it and that was the first
             one he went out and bought for me. It was the look of
             the strip, the style of the team – and of course, no-one
             believed the story when I told it to journos at Chelsea
             years later.
*George*:   So aesthetic considerations were important to you, even
             then!
*Pat*:       It was too weird for words that I ended up playing for
             them!
*George*:   It's interesting how these things turn out sometimes. I
             know a Scottish Protestant family called the Clements –

the mother comes from Belfast, in fact – and their eldest son has grown up a Celtic supporter, apparently because his father accidentally bought him a green-and-white football shirt – it might even have been a T-shirt – when he was young! Naturally, they're all very disappointed, but what can you do?

*Pat*:      It's a funny thing, though. The feeling sort of impressed itself upon me. I definitely wanted Chelsea to beat Leeds in the FA Cup final in 1970. After that, I lost interest in them a bit.

*George*:   As did almost everyone else, except recent converts like David Mellor who apparently used to be a Fulham supporter before he linked up with John Major and turned blue. I think fans are very insecure about changing loyalty. It's seen as an unforgivable thing to do.

*Pat*:      You should know!

*George*:   Yes. Switching from Spurs to Newcastle just to annoy Alan Sugar was a wrench, but I don't regret it at all.

*Pat*:      You're right about people being very sensitive about it. I remember a bit from *Only An Excuse* with Jonathan Watson commenting on changing allegiances and players claiming always to have had a soft spot for their current team. As Graeme Souness, he said: 'Of course, I've always been a Liverpool supporter, but as a young boy, I used to skip school to go and watch Sampdoria play in the afternoon ... but of course, as a foetus, I was always a Rangers fan.'

*George*:   Yes, we must talk more about loyalty on some occasion. You get Mo Johnston getting all dewy-eyed at the prospect of returning to Celtic, supposedly playing all the old Glenn Daley songs on his car stereo as he drove up the M74 to Glasgow – and then, a month later, he signs for Rangers! These are mercenary times.

*Pat*:      Super Mo! One of the only players I've ever had a fight with. We were about 11 years old and playing together for a representative team. I think that, style and attitude-wise, we were opposite even then – I thought him far too flashy and arrogant. The team had the snappy title

of The Glasgow Catholic Schools Football Association
Representative Team. I wonder how good that looked
on his CV when he joined Rangers! Anyway, at an end-
of-season awards ceremony, we were actually scrap-
ping on our way up to collect our medals from a stage.
The manager was also my teacher at school, so I paid
heavily for that little outburst on the Monday morning.
The next time we played together was for the Scotland
national side. Happily, we had matured slightly by
then . . . I think! I could tell you stories about him all
night.

*George*: Mo all night? It doesn't bear thinking about. But returning to Chelsea, I suppose it's always been considered
the trendiest of the London clubs, what with the King's
Road nearby, swinging London and all that.

*Pat*: I remember feeling that when I arrived, and being told
all about it. I was very stylised at the time – stylised, as
opposed to *stylish*. I had a back-combed, spiky hairdo à
la Ian McCulloch from Echo and the Bunnymen, the
statutory Joy Division gloom-boom overcoat and all
that gear. The point that was possibly being missed by
some people was that this wasn't a new style as such,
or even an attempt to be stylish. It was *anti-style*.

*George*: One can lead to the other. Look at Jarvis Cocker today,
with his tank-tops and Joe 90 specs – my Mum mistakenly
thinks they're back in fashion again because of him!

*Pat*: It was very much in the post-punk tradition. Although
it was a very distinctive way of dressing, it was very
much opposed to the clubbing, having a good time,
high-living, hedonistic attitude that was, and to a
degree still is, the popular image of the professional
footballer. My position was in fact precisely the opposite: social attitude; bit of a leftie; concerned about 'real
life' issues and so on.

*George*: There's this view, perpetuated in magazines like *loaded*
– which I have to say I subscribe to, as it's great fun –
that football is all about mindless, shameless, *aimless*
hedonism. Is it really all about largin' it and enjoying
the good things in life?

Pat:     No. It quite simply isn't. It's a nice story, and it sells *loaded*, the back page of the *Sun* and so on, but it's a myth. A myth, however, that was popular enough to ensure I made every effort not to be seen in that light myself!

George:  I think a lot of this image is down to superannuated seventies players knocking out autobiographies about what lads they were – George Best, Stan Bowles, Frank Worthington and so on.

Pat:     There's a terrific story about this concerning Charlie Nicholas, a player with a very different image to me – the Stringfellow's/Victoria's man, and so on. He was once being taunted by a fan about how flash he was. The fan was saying that he could do anything Charlie could . . .

George:  Fail to score for Arsenal, that sort of thing?

Pat:     Exactly. And Charlie said: 'I bet you can't do *this*!', got out a £50 note and tore it up in front of him. Now, that's often told as a story about how flash Charlie was, but afterwards, when the guy had gone, Charlie gathered up all the pieces and sellotaped them together again! Nobody *really* had that kind of money to burn – or very few, anyway. Not very hedonistic, I'm sure you will agree.

There is a *degree* of hedonism among any group of young men who are well-paid, but you simply couldn't survive in football if you lived the life some fans imagine we live. You can see that it doesn't work, because those who try it can't keep it up, and it ends up damaging their careers – the Mersons, the Adamses, whatever. You just can't do it – the human body won't let you! Sooner or later, it catches up with you. It goes back to what we were discussing about the drink culture in football: yes, there is drinking; yes, there is the odd mad night-out; but players don't have a bucket-ful on a Friday night and then go out on a Saturday afternoon and play a great game of football. That is the stuff of legend – and it's a mythical legend precisely because it is simply not possible to do it consistently.

*George*: A lot of these people like to fuel that myth though, don't they? They like us to think that in the good old seventies, when mavericks walked the earth, this was part and parcel of the game.

*Pat*: It might have been *just about* possible then, but I don't think it's possible now. At Southampton, the new centre-half can do a hundred in 10.4 seconds. You can't do that on 10 bottles of Hooch a day.

*George*: I won't even try. Just how much has the average level of player-fitness shot up since the seventies?

*Pat*: Tremendously. It's the biggest and most important change in the last few decades. It really is quite incre-dible – even over the last five or ten years, it has changed dramatically. When I started playing for the Scotland Under-17s and Under-18s, Andy Roxburgh and Craig Brown were in charge – of course, they've both gone on to manage Scotland – and they gave us a 12-minute run to gauge our levels of fitness and stamina. I was pitted against all these young profes-sionals from all over Scotland, and I beat them all by two or three hundred yards – I was still a student at the time, but my fitness-level was very high. I used to be a middle-distance runner. That was my thing. Take a group of young professionals nowadays and I guaran-tee the young student Pat Nevin would not finish two or three hundred yards ahead of *them*. I did have a concern along those lines when I was only 23, as I've mentioned: a young, teenage full-back at Chelsea was so fast, he was really showing me up. Fortunately, as his subsequent England selection showed, it wasn't that I was getting bad – it was him being so good. Thank you, Graeme Le Saux, for making me worry about being past it even before my 24th birthday!

*George*: Student culture is not exactly *unknown* for its drinking.

*Pat*: I did a little bit, I have to say, but like many men in positions approaching pseudo-respectability, I am re-writing my past. The drinking and whatever nights as a student have been expertly air-brushed out of my history, with Stalinist efficiency. Back to those first four or five years as a full-time pro at Chelsea – if I wasn't getting by the left-back, full-back or whatever defender I was playing against through skill, I would run him and run him for 80 minutes, so that in those last 10 minutes, he couldn't stay with me. Although I'm older now, I look at young players today and I think it would have been much more difficult for me to do that in the modern game. Their level of fitness is just that much higher. In those days – and it's only the eighties we're talking about here – people who had the potential to be brilliant athletes didn't maximise it, whereas nowadays they do. It goes back to the fact that if you stay fitter longer today, your earning potential is so much greater than it ever used to be. Players are not dim. They know this, and have acted accordingly.

The drink culture in football, especially at the highest level, is nowhere near what it once was.

*George*: I suppose if you were to compare football culture further with student culture, students might stereotypically be seen as more tolerant of outsiders, of women in particular, of homosexuals. It's maybe more of a live-and-let-live culture, a more *socialist* culture, even? Is this true, though? Is football culture really that different?

*Pat*: Yes. Or it was when I first came into it, and I found the contrast very hard to take. My peer group before then was just so extraordinarily different to the peer group made up of all the young professionals I then played with. It was a mind-blowing difference. It covered everything: attitudes to life; attitudes to government;

attitudes to how you treat people; race; colour; the
sexes; sex itself . . . all these things. It was all so different. My own attitudes were very different to most of
my fellow professionals. The same went for what I
considered important in life, things that were worth
talking about and discussing. I was almost laughed out
of sight with my 'student' attitudes. You just couldn't
talk about literature, art or theatre to a group within a
football club. It was not on.

Over time, though, I've seen it slightly adapt. Footballers don't all read Proust now, of course, but some
actually do. Where I think I made a mistake before was
maybe thinking that students were a more representative cross-section of society than footballers were,
when in fact, I now believe it's the other way around.

*George*:   That's probably true. I remember giving a cross-section
of footballers at several clubs the same personality
questionnaire you completed earlier, and when it came
to their level of interest in the arts, there was actually
no difference in distribution or the range of interest they
expressed from the range expressed by a much wider
cross-section of the general population. Some hate
poetry – but some love it. Look at Cantona reading
Rimbaud and dabbling in abstract painting! It was a
perfect normal distribution, as the statisticians say.
There were those for whom art was a dirty word, those
who couldn't get enough, and the majority were somewhere in between – just like the population of Britain as
a whole.

*Pat*:      I'm very glad you said that, because I've thought that
for years, and I couldn't get any back-up.

*George*:   I mean, these were players at clubs like Sheffield United
and Crystal Palace, not clubs you'd normally associate
with any overt artistic leanings. Indeed, they're clubs
whose style of play might stretch to call itself 'cultured'!
So even at these clubs, you'll find art-lovers. But maybe
they keep quiet about it! It's something they'll admit in
an anonymous questionnaire, but not strike up a conversation about on the coach, possibly.

*Pat*: It's not just art. It's other aspects of life, too, that are just not hip to talk about – not just in football but in young, male culture, generally. Girls, conquests not relationships, nights out, having a laugh – those are the things to talk about. Subjects where you're showing your heart slightly more don't lend themselves to football team groups. To start with, they are large, laddish on the surface, and also, while you are working intensely close to them for a while, it's only for a short part of your life. Most of the players you play with, you'll be together with for two or three years. This isn't enough time to get into the kind of relationship where you can discuss things that are perhaps more personal to you. So perhaps football culture and most of the friendships within it will always have to stay at a certain level of depth – and not a very profound level – for that reason.

*George*: It's an interesting thing about male culture that if you look at stuff that's very popular like *Reservoir Dogs* or *Trainspotting*, it appears at a superficial level to be about very macho things like violence and crime and drug-taking and so on, but actually what Quentin Tarantino and particularly Irvine Welsh do very effectively is to weave in stuff about male vulnerability, about the fragility of the lad's ego, about things like the desperate need for friendship that many men share. I mean, there's a lot of shooting and blood in *Reservoir Dogs*, but at its heart, it's a story about the betrayal of friendship. I think *that's* what strikes such a chord with a male audience. You get it with *loaded* as well. Very often, it will go beyond the superficial hedonism and reveal something quite personal and occasionally profound about the attitude of the writer.

*Pat*: It's often said through humour. It's funny that you should mention *Trainspotting*, because it's the perfect example of it. There's a player at Tranmere who I've been talking to about *Trainspotting*. We both enjoyed the film – in fact, I found myself calling him Sick Boy the other day, he's very popular with the girls! Anyway, we were discussing the film, and the conversation got quite deep. We were talking about the amount of government money that has been spent on tackling drugs issues and how much effect that's likely to have compared to the effect of the film and, considering its cost, how much impact *that's* likely to have. I think *Trainspotting* will do more to steer people away from drugs than a hundred years of government action, because it actually hits home where it's supposed to hit home. However, we talked about the relationships between Begbie, Sick Boy, Rents, Spud and Tommy, and the comparisons within our club. It was discussed in a jokey way but it was a method of discussing trust, mistrust, fear and affection within the group as a whole.

*George*:   Yes. It's deeply ironic that some people have accused it of glamorising heroin addiction!

*Pat*:   Well, if you leave the cinema half an hour into the film, you might walk away with that impression – but the *whole film*? Anyway, that's very typical of what goes on in football culture. You can get into some quite deep discussions, but they're often initiated by talking about a film or a television programme. This somehow removes the stigma. Even so, you only know people for very short periods – two or three years, as I mentioned – so it's difficult to go too deep. People are wary about giving too much away, about baring their hearts too openly.

*George*:   I suppose that there's the possibility you may end up playing against one another on opposite sides in the not too distant future. Revealing any sensitivity or weakness could be used against you at a later date!

*Pat*:   There's that, but there's also the need to maintain independence. You can't grow too close as friends, become inseparable and, more importantly, dependent on one another, because in a couple of years' time, one of you may be living in Plymouth and the other in Aberdeen. It actually makes it easier for the club if relationships exist at a more superficial level. Humour – albeit often very intelligent humour – is what you get in place of depth.

*George*:   Terry Venables has got a bit in his novel with Gordon

Williams, *They Used to Play on Grass*, where a player is a really close friend of another, they'd die for one another and all of that. Then, six months later, the other player has left the club and been replaced with another, but this guy is now just as close a friend of the player who came in to replace his friend as he was of the original friend, who seems all but forgotten. Perhaps some players like to form really close friendships with *whoever happens to be their team-mate at the time*.

Pat:    There are people like that, but they're rare. It's not a common thing to transfer such intense feelings of friendship from one person to another arbitrarily. When it does happen so obviously at a football club, it is clear for everyone to see that the player needs the crutch of a confidant to deal with the group. It comes across as a sign of weakness and, just like any other weakness, it is quickly noticed and mercilessly sent up.

George:    Some players do seem to maintain enduring friendships, even though they have moved to different clubs in different parts of the country. It's said about Ian Wright and Mark Bright, for example. Their friendship was forged when they were at Crystal Palace together and is supposedly still very strong.

Pat:    I think intense situations, like relegation battles or good cup runs, can sometimes lead to strong friendships being created in quite a limited period of time. Friendships built early in a career also have a good chance of surviving, as players haven't yet realised that they will move and lose these mates all too regularly throughout their careers. But just like what you were saying about players' appreciation of art being no different from that of other people, I think it's the same with the formation of friendships. Players are a fairly normal breed in this respect. How many really close friends, not just 'pals', do any of us have? You might have a few where it gets a bit tactile – you hug one another when you meet and so on – but how many *really* close friends can most people number? There are other jobs where people relocate and move around a lot. The relationships will be just the same as in these jobs. There will be the usual slightly false over-friendliness that you find in what I would call 'colleague culture'.

George:   Football is very tactile, in fact. I remember that there were a lot of mutterings in the seventies about players kissing one another and leaping on top of one another to celebrate scoring. To the outsider, it seemed there was something sexual about it all. The amateur shrinks had a field day.

Pat:      They were, of course, wonderfully wrong – and not for the first time! From the outside, it does seem strange that all these lads can embrace and it is perfectly accept-able, but if you're a little unusual or eccentric – anything away from the norm – the immediate suspicion within the team tends to be that you are the gay one! It used to happen to me at Chelsea. It didn't affect me, though, because of my confidence both in myself and in my sexuality. I didn't even feel the need to parade girlfriends in front of the team. In fact, I would keep my girlfriend away from the team on purpose for other reasons, specifically because I like to keep parts of my life separate. Maybe that fuelled speculation for a while. Also, the fact that I'm not homophobic in any way again meant that it didn't bother me. But I think you have to be very self-confident for it not to bother you. I think other players may not be quite as self-confident and it bothers them much more.

George:   Other lightning-fast, culturally-aware colleagues from your Chelsea days?

Pat:      I feel sorry for players who struggle to deal with that sort of stick. As soon as it is spotted that they are both-ered by it, it gets worse. It is that sign of weakness again. So you might think that it's something unique to being a pro footballer that if you're interested in art or ballet or literature, you end up being called a bender by your work-mates. But I know that when I've played at West Ham, half the crowd were shouting that at me. So being called gay because you are different is nothing to do with footballers as such – the fans managed to show

the same ignorance, bias, simplistic and incorrect thinking. Or maybe they were just trying to wind me up!
Footballers just reflect society as a whole again. You can
see the rather predictable thinking: He has fairly unusual interests . . . He's weird . . . Why is he weird? . . .
Because he's different . . . Why do I worry about him
being different? . . . Because he scares me . . . Why does
he scare me? . . . Because he might be gay. You do
wonder why heterosexual men should have a hang-up
and fear of gay men, but it is definitely there.

*George*:  It's an interesting area, psychologically. I was talking to
Russell Edwards, the captain of Dulwich Hamlet.
They'd brought out this video of them in the showers,
ostensibly for the hen-night market, but it sold much
better among gay men. I asked how the players felt
about the fact that lots of gay men were buying videos
of them in the buff, and he said that most of the players
were very relaxed about it, that it was no big deal. In
fact, as a former player on Palace's books, he said that
pretty much every club has at least one player who is
either acknowledged to be gay or it is strongly rumoured
that he is, and the players generally don't mind a jot.

*Pat*:  Well, every club I've been at, there have been whispers
about some player. At Chelsea, they were probably
about me! But there is never any ostracising of those
players, as you might have thought. In fact, it would
probably shock a lot of people that such players are not
ostracised. Again, it is usually referred to through
humour. There are a lot of comments, but they are made
with laughter. They're not particularly harmful, vicious
comments, such as 'Get out of this club, you poof!' I've
never spotted that attitude.

*George*:  That's why I was surprised when Justin Fashanu left
Hearts citing prejudice over his sexuality as the main
reason. I know he was planning to dish the dirt on some
MPs with whom he might or might not have had a fling,
but was that all a smokescreen?

*Pat*:  Well, Justin's position is unusual. Let me rephrase that!
There were suggestions that he might have been a bit of

a Walter Mitty kind of character, prone to telling stories. Justin is quite an unusual character in all sorts of ways – I don't think we can relate it all just to his sexuality, or indeed blame that for his departure from Hearts. I just thought it was very noble of him to move from Airdrie to Hearts, allowing the Scottish papers to switch from calling him 'Queen of Diamonds' to calling him 'Queen of Hearts'. That was inspired!

*George*: Is it possible, then, that footballers are actually more tolerant than many people believe, that what appears to be very cruel to the outsider is just a humorous exchange between team-mates who know they can take it? Close, male friends might greet one another in a way that appears very insulting – However are you doing today, ya bastard? Not bad, ya wanker! – and certainly isn't the way they would greet strangers! Is there an element of that in some of the exchanges we see between players?

*Pat*: That strong, laddish humour is always there. The one taboo, the one thing you *never* do, is betray the group. That's the golden rule. If you do it, then things get absolutely vicious. All you can do then is get away and get out. Betraying the group is simply the worst evil you can do. But unless you do that, you can actually get away with quite a lot.

Going back to players' attitudes to being gay, I was going out with my girlfriend Annabel – who is now my wife! – and I was at a party in Wimbledon. It was a fancy-dress party. Being a bit stupid, as I was at the time, I dressed up as a schoolgirl. It *was* a fancy-dress party, after all!

*George*: Gary Lineker is now paid money by crisp manufacturers to do that.

*Pat*: That's true! We were with a particularly mad gang of mates, having a good time, when, halfway through this drunken evening, I remembered that the Chelsea players were at a party no more than three or four streets away in Wimbledon. 'Great!' I thought. 'I'll go along!' Of course, I'd forgotten one minor detail: one party was fancy-dress and the other wasn't. Anyway, I only cottoned-on as I stepped through the door. One of the players, I think it was Colin Pates, said: 'Cor! She's alright! I'd have her!' Followed rapidly by: 'Oh, no! It's Pat!'

All of the leg-pulling and humour that resulted from that exchange, though, was always affectionate, or at least unthreatening. I never encountered any aggression. I think all the other players considered me too strange for words at that time anyway, and therefore beyond bothering with.

*George*: That just reaches a level of absurdity that goes beyond the normal, though, doesn't it? I mean, if you really were a closet homosexual, it's unlikely you would dress like that for parties! It's like a lot of the very laddish heterosexuals who will attend the *Rocky Horror Show* in fishnets, suspenders and a basque. Nobody really suspects anything about their sexuality on that evidence. Actually, maybe some do! I was dressed like that on my birthday once. It also happened to be the 21st birthday of the show and a whole bunch of us went to see it at the Town and Country Club in Kentish Town. I remember it well, because it was the evening of that match between Ireland and Italy in the '94 World Cup. So we popped into a local pub before the show started to catch some of the match. Kentish Town has a big Irish community, so it was pretty packed and suddenly all these blokes in fishnets started turning up. One or two eyebrows were definitely raised, though almost everyone just found it funny. And of course, Ireland beat Italy, so everyone was in party mood later that night! I believe that you also attended one Tranmere Christmas party dressed as Michelle Pfeiffer's Catwoman from *Batman Returns*?

*Pat*: OK, so my obsession with Michelle Pfeiffer got a little out of hand for a bit, and on reflection, I probably looked a bit too good in the outfit. I should say here that Michelle does remind me of my wife! (Boy, do I know how to crawl.) If you do anything different, people will talk about it and they'll let you know about

|          |                                                                                 |
|----------|---------------------------------------------------------------------------------|

*George*:    it, but I've never encountered any hostility.

*George*:    Was having the nickname 'Weirdo' not the least bit offensive?

*Pat*:    Oh, no! Not at all! I took it as a compliment. I was happy being seen as different. Being called 'Weirdo' wasn't too vicious. You can tell, when people give you a nickname, whether it's in a friendly, funny or nasty way, and I certainly never felt any nastiness at Chelsea.

*George*:    You once described Chelsea as your happiest time as a player. Is that true?

*Pat*:    I think Chelsea and Tranmere are not that different, in terms of how much I've enjoyed my time there. Everton was sometimes too over-sophisticated. There were too many people who were very, very professional and wanted to maximise their position at the club. It got to the extent of talking behind team-mates' backs. That led to a cliquishness that was poisonous for the team spirit. It wasn't a 'fun' club for a while. Everyone knows that a happy-go-lucky atmosphere has, does and probably always will exist at Chelsea. It exists at Tranmere as well, though. You mentioned the Catwoman costume at the Christmas party. This year I'm going as Father Jack out of *Father Ted*. Our parties are absolutely legendary! I've had Andy Thorn say that even the Wimbledon Crazy Gang parties were nothing like Tranmere's!

*George*:    It's interesting that Chelsea can be such a fun club with Ken Bates at the helm. A lot of fans regard him as a sort of despot figure with a white beard. Is he that bad, or is it an image thing?

*Pat*:    It's difficult to know for sure, because of the relationship I had with him. I think he was very wary of me. I kept him at arm's length all the time I was there. My attitude has always been never to deal with the upper echelons of any club, if I can help it. In my years at Chelsea, my approach was always to come in, do my job and go out again. For years, I never once set foot in the players' bar or went up to the directors' lounges.

    The first dealings I had with him were over a new contract, and, happily, my confidence and my position saw me through what was a wonderful bit of games-manship on his part. I told him I was going back up to Scotland, I'd had enough. I was earning less than all the reserves and I'd just been voted Player of the Year, having helped the club get promotion to what was then the First Division and is now the Premiership. After a couple of meetings, he told me to go away and come back with a wage that I wanted. Well, I asked a couple of the senior pros and returned with a piece of paper. He took one look at it, sniffed, as he does quite a bit, ripped it up, walked out of the room, got into his Rolls-Royce and drove away. I was 19 at the time and I sup-pose it was designed to make me feel very small, insignificant and guilty that I'd angered the chairman.

Actually, I didn't feel like that at all! I had a wee look in his drawers, saw some of the other players' contracts and gauged that I wasn't asking for too much at all. I stuck to my guns and the chairman eventually gave me every bit of it – apart from one flight that I'd requested!

I remember him writing that I was an incredibly difficult young man to deal with. Well, that was because I was in a strong position. If I didn't sign a new contract, I'd have been quite happy returning to my degree studies, so I had absolutely nothing to lose. *Of course* I was incredibly difficult to deal with!

George: I'd imagine *he* isn't exactly easy to deal with!

Pat: No. But he wasn't used to 19-year-olds standing up to him. I learned a great lesson from the experience: you need to fight for every penny you get in football. It may be construed as being greedy, but I'd always been nice and thought people would simply pay me what I was worth. Sadly, that doesn't happen.

George: It doesn't necessarily happen in the world of pro-fessional psychology either, I have to say!

Pat: I try to be nice in business, though. I'm a landlord now, and the tenants who rent my flat will tell you that I'm very helpful indeed! I shouldn't take too much away from Ken, though. He did give me some fantastic advice, and I find myself always coming down on his side. He saved a club that I love, after all. Our politics, personalities and outlooks may be at opposite ends of any spectrum you care to mention, though.

George:   You amaze me!

Pat:   Just before I left Chelsea, I remember us having one of those wonderful discussions where we spoke for two hours and never said one word. We were both playing a game that I can only describe as verbal and tactical tennis. He knew I was leaving the club. I knew I was leaving the club. He didn't want to speak out of turn, because he thought I would go to the papers and slag him off for getting rid of me. Meanwhile, he wanted me to say something that would allow *him* to go the papers and claim my demands were unreasonable, that I'd asked for 10 grand a week, or whatever. So we played this verbal tennis across the table at a restaurant on the Old Brompton Road for a couple of hours and then shook hands, walked away and kind of smirked as we did so, knowing, without saying, what we'd both been up to for that whole period, appreciating the other's point of view.

Actually, I was in the stronger position. Ken had effectively lost in a way, because it left me in a position where I could go to the papers and say: 'Ken Bates didn't offer me a penny. I'm off! I would have stayed, I could have stayed, but Ken gave me no incentive to do so.' The one error he made with his business dealings with me – and I don't think he made many – was that he didn't know that I'm honourable. I would never stitch Chelsea Football Club up in the papers – I love it too much.

George:   The starting-point in business is that you don't assume *anyone* is honourable! I guess that philosophy has worked for Ken more often than against him – but not when dealing with you.

Pat:   In the end, I can see why a lot of people dislike him intensely but on balance, I'm actually quite fond of him.

George:   And on that note of benevolence and goodwill, let's call it a day.

# Knowing Me, Knowing You (Aha!)

*We had been discussing in some depth a number of issues pertaining to the culture of the game. It was time to handle one of the big ones: loyalty. This was particularly pertinent to Pat's current circumstances. At this stage, it looked as though he would be leaving Tranmere Rovers – and not through choice. As always, however, he was keeping his spirits up – indeed, later in the session, he was to turn the tables and start probing me on why I was a fan!*

*George*: I suppose that, to be loyal, you need to be a bit of a people person to start with, to have a strong need for the company of others. After all, if you're quite happy on your own, the notion of sticking up for other people might not even occur to you. We've talked a little about the friendships in football already, but are there some people who are very difficult to feel friendly towards and therefore quite hard to integrate into a team, form a striking-partnership with, or anything else?

*Pat*: It's very much a matter of luck. I think striking-partners in particular do *try* to be best friends, but if they're total opposites, it's just not going to happen. There's definitely luck involved, but there tends to be an element of effort as well. With football, people's reputations go before them. You might have two players who know one another 'from afar'. Each is aware of what the other is like as a player and is also likely to be aware of the other's 'image', whatever that may be. You'll get, say, a couple of wingers who have been on opposing sides for a number of years and were kind of nodding acquaintances, rather than anything stronger, suddenly finding themselves playing in the same team. They'll tend to look for something they have in common. It could be anything – simply the fact that they're a couple of good-looking lads, for example. They may think: 'Hey! We're playing together now, but we should also be good mates! We could be quite cool together going out on the town!'

I've certainly seen that happen. The whole laddish, matey, 'we're going to be pals' thing has been set up even before the two players have got to know one another. It's premeditated. But I've also seen that badly backfire, where a player is expecting the footballer joining the club to be someone who he'll get on with like a house on fire, and the guy turns out to be a bit unusual or different in some way. It could be that the new arrival is not particularly interested in being a flashy personality, contrary to prior expectation. So it can work, but it's sometimes a disaster.

George:   It sounds a bit like *Blind Date*!

Pat:      Well, you're the expert on that, having been a contestant on the show – and worse still, been daft enough to own up to it! But there are similarities, definitely.

George:   Psychologists talk about 'attribution theory', letting your expectations about outcomes influence how you behave. Sometimes you can perhaps get the player to be, in your eyes at least, exactly what you want them to be, even if *he* doesn't see himself in that way.

Pat:      It's possible, but again, it won't always work.

George:   Thinking about Chelsea, I remember reading Kerry Dixon's autobiography a few years ago and he was talking about his relationship with David Speedie. This was certainly the most revealing aspect of the book. Initially, they didn't seem to get on at all – there was a lot of rivalry between them. This culminated in fisticuffs in the dressing-room – or possibly even on the pitch – but thereafter, they apparently became very good friends. Naturally, it must be an extreme dislike to start with if it gets physical like that, but I wonder how often a player, once he has seen the other's point of view, starts acting differently towards him?

Pat:      That's definitely happened with me. I think it's particularly an issue with David Speedie, actually. It's something about David personally. I had the same problem myself. We absolutely abhorred each other. It was real dislike for a long time, but now I'd look back on that time at Chelsea and say he was the player with whom I developed a better on-pitch understanding than any other in my whole career.

The reason we hated each other was because we were polar opposites, as personalities go. Kerry and I probably had more in common. David had a very antagonistic attitude to life. It was a real up-front nastiness, but only on the field. Kerry and I were probably a couple of 'nice boys'. When two players really dislike one another very intensely, there's no way that that can be kept a secret. Footballers are like old women when it comes to gossip, so it gets round the club in no time at all and rapidly becomes a standing joke, which all the players are in on. On occasion, some kind of clash occurs: a blazing row; coming to blows, like Speedie and Kerry; even getting sent off for fighting – remember Graeme Le Saux's fury at David Batty when the two were playing for Blackburn and it was all going wrong? Either that happens, or alternatively, the joking reaches such epidemic proportions, and the whole thing becomes so utterly ridiculous, that the players find it impossible to take their mutual antagonism seriously any more.

In both cases, the players end up having a laugh at themselves and go on to understand one another and appreciate the differences between themselves slightly better. That was certainly the case with David and me, and I'm sure it was true of David and Kerry, too. It's just a question of getting points of view across and sometimes people are slow to do that, which is where a lot of antagonism can spring from in the first place. David and I understood each other after fate drew us together unexpectedly in that Scotland squad I mentioned earlier in the book. With the new understanding, I was able to see his on-field attitudes in a different light, and I think it could be said that there was rarely any problem from then on in.

*George*: One of the things I've noticed about you is that you will always give credit where it's due for the way someone plays football, however much you may dislike them personally. This can certainly have its parallels in an office environment – someone who is seen to be an expert or have particular talent in a certain area could well be someone others are prepared to work alongside, however repugnant they may find him or her as a human being. The legendary animosity between Emlyn Hughes and Tommy Smith would be an example of that from the world of football, and there must be thousands of others in offices and factories around the country.

It's interesting, though, that friendship can play a very direct part in a team's success. The late Maurice Yaffe, a psychologist brought in by Crystal Palace in one of the earliest-known pieces of psychological research concerning football in this country, found that players who like one another play together better. A player is more likely to pass the ball to a friend, for example. It seems the most obvious finding in the world, but when you have situations where it is possible to play reasonably well without liking your striking-partner at all, it is probably food for thought.

*Pat*: One of the big differences between a football environment and maybe an office environment is that in football, because it is such a close-knit thing and probably also because it is so male-dominated, if two people dislike one another with a vengeance it's simply *impossible* to keep it a secret. You don't get any subtle political nuances or undercurrents – everyone knows! The hatreds and resentments therefore tend to be out in the open, but you still have to work alongside people even if you can't stand them. Frequently, people don't even *attempt* to hide it. It doesn't need to come to blows: two people just don't like each other. I've seen it at every single club I've ever been at. You can see the clashes from the moment you first come across these people.

Everyone knows who hates whose guts. Sometimes, of course, it's that old cliché – the reason for their animosity is that they're just far too alike.

You get that a lot. You can have two very strong personalities and both of them want to be the funny guy or the social hub of the club, the leader of the pack or, more commonly, the golden boy with the fans. Unlike in an office, there's no sneaky politics, no clever manoeuvring. If there's any subtlety there to start off with, it certainly doesn't last long. The culture of the game is to shout at each other. You can't brush things under the carpet. With the intensity of emotion that you get on the field, nothing could ever remain hidden for long. This is, of course, a good thing, because festering bad blood poisons the spirit of a club, and it's infectious. The next stage is cliques, and within football it is fairly widely recognised that cliques lead to defeats.

What you say about friends passing to each other more often is absolutely true. If you have an understanding with another player, you look up, you see them and you have an empathy with them. You can second-guess their thinking, the way they run – it's almost telepathic. I suppose I've contradicted myself by saying that Speedie and I had such a strong on-pitch understanding, despite the fact that we were polar opposites off the field – but that was the exception that proves the rule! It was such an understanding of one another's play, despite the fact that we were so different in temperament, that it was a real freak occurrence.

I think that some managers have taken what Maurice Yaffe and Malcolm Allison, who brought him in at Palace, found and developed it further. This thing about friends passing to each other is a very fundamental truth. If you look at Andy Roxburgh and Craig Brown's management and coaching of the Scotland squad, it is very apparent that those ideas were being developed there. They tried to group players together on the field in triangles, based on whether they played together and were friends at club level. Thus, you had Tommy Boyd as left-back, John Collins outside him on the left-hand side and inside of him you'd have Paul McStay – all Celtic players at the time. Those three acted as a little triangle. There was no-one from the Scotland side between them, it was just themselves. If you looked across the park, you would probably see another little triangle, quite often an Aberdeen threesome. Very frequently, there would be a Rangers triumvirate, too.

*George*: ... Which I suppose begs the question: do you feel it is a good idea to play someone who may not be as technically gifted, but who is better-liked by his team-mates?

*Pat*: What *I* feel might be slightly affected by the fact that there were unlikely to be two other Tranmere Rovers players in the squad! But given that we're talking about friendships, it wouldn't necessarily have to be three team-mates. It could be two team-mates and a close friend, for instance. Most frequently, it was two team-mates and a chap who used to play with them three or four years ago, or something along those lines. I don't know whether it was a subconscious thing or not, but in the case of the Scotland squad, it goes back to the days before even Andy Roxburgh in that, rather than playing Alan Hansen at the back, Scotland would often play the Aberdeen duo of Willie Miller and Alex McLeish, and immediately behind them would be Jim Leighton, the Aberdeen keeper. It was another 'triangle of understanding'.

It works at the very obvious level that these people play together week in, week out, so they know one another's game very well. But at a more psychological level, when you're in an international squad, you don't know all your team-mates that well, you may not have fans of your particular club behind you, there is a lot more that's uncertain and it gives you that additional bit of reassurance or comfort to have people whose play you know intimately around you. Naturally, you can break out of that when you need to interact with the rest of the team. It helps. It also builds loyalty wonderfully for when you get back to club football.

George: So that's why Alan Hansen didn't go to the World Cup in Mexico – he disappeared as a result of the Aberdeen Triangle!

Pat: Yes, it was tough on Alan but it can be justified very convincingly in terms of its effects on team morale, whether that is at club level or international level.

George: It's something the fans often find difficult to understand. Their club may have one outstanding player and they're desperate to see him achieve international honours. They resent this 'doesn't fit in' argument. Look at Matt Le Tissier – where are you going to find another two internationals to make up a triangle playing for Southampton?

Pat: There's no doubt that having an understanding with other players, being a better 'team' player, can come above technical excellence in terms of what managers value. It happens at international level and, to a lesser extent, at club level too. It's an understanding that goes well beyond being conversant with another footballer's style of play on the field. Some of the greatest partnerships have been like that. Certainly for me, those players I've achieved a real understanding with on the field have also been very good friends.

George: David Speedie excepted?

Pat: In the end, 10 years after the fact, I would say that David is now a friend. A bit of mellowing, some time, some maturing, but most importantly that better understanding of each other finally did the trick. We always respected each other's ability, and that is important.

George: Do players like that, who had very strong partnerships, remain in close touch, even if they move to different clubs – people who were once inseparable like Vinnie Jones and John Fashanu, or Mark Bright and Ian Wright? If Steve McManaman and Robbie Fowler were to end up playing at different clubs, would their friendship still flourish? Indeed, how far did John Fashanu and Hans Segers' friendship stretch?

Pat: Very often, that friendship really only reoccurs if you

happen to meet up again, but you wouldn't actually
drive 200 miles to spend some time with them. I can't
speak for the players you mentioned, but the big problem in football is that the friendships are so transient.
As I've already said: with any friend you make, you're
always aware that circumstances could change overnight and one of you could leave the club. But everyone
makes a few really close friendships. I certainly have,
perhaps three or four. It's strange, really: if you consider
the hundreds and hundreds of players I've played with
and got on well with, it's quite a small number that I'd
make the effort to go and visit. But that's the nature of
the game: you're thrown together in the first place and
you tend to end up being torn apart.

More often than not, you meet the friends who stay
very close to you early on in your playing career. You've
grown up together as players. However, because
neither of you has known a life with a wife and children
before, it's easy to grow completely apart within three
or four years.

*George*:   Psychologists have observed this outside football, too.
As people get older, and particularly start families, their
circles of friends get smaller. Certainly, the friendships
that tend to be most enduring are often ones made in
the late teens and early twenties. In the early twenties,
people report having more friends than at any other
time in their life, though often these friendships are
quite superficial.

*Pat*:   That's the thing about football – that circle of friends
you make at that time is typically absolutely huge. It
tends to involve all the players that you play with and
quite a few hangers-on and *their* hangers-on. I think this
inability to go into too much depth in friendships because you know, pragmatically, that they are necessarily
quite fragile through circumstance, can be quite
emotionally scarring for some young players. You know
that time is limited. You know you're going to lose them
as mates, being realistic about it. I can think of one close
friend from my Chelsea days who I was with practically

every day, a player called John Millar who now plays for Raith Rovers, and I haven't spoken to him for over a year. At Chelsea, it would be unusual to go for more than two or three days without having a chat, having a laugh together. Now we scarcely talk from one year's end to another. That's just the way it is. There's nothing you can do about it. If you look closely at the game, that might be one possible reason why footballers tend to marry quite young – they're after a one-to-one relationship that isn't going to break down. At least, wherever you go, your wife is likely to follow.

In football, if you want a long-term relationship, your only options are to get married – or sign a 10-year contract!

*George*:   I wonder also what the effect is on those who are getting too old to play the game. Do you think that a lot of people pursue coaching careers in part because they want to hang onto the social side that goes with the game? It's often said that one of the most psychologically damaging things about enforced unemployment, or even voluntary retirement or redundancy, is that very quickly, you begin to miss some of the informal social relationships that existed in the workplace, those with people you wouldn't necessarily say were your *friends* but were nice to chat to in a corridor or visit in their office. Very often, people say that they had simply no idea just how much they'd miss the people they worked alongside, even people they never really liked all that much. Leaving football, whether it's early, through injury, or at what is a very young age to retire, and moving away from a very buoyant social atmosphere, must be very difficult for many ex-players.

*Pat*:   For my part, I know that I am not going to feel that sense of loss, but that's because of my very specific approach to the game and attitude surrounding it, which I've been talking about. But it's true. I know a lot of former players now out of the game and they always say: 'I miss the lads. I miss the day-to-day stuff.' I notice that some of the lads who are pushing retirement-age start coming into the club with no other purpose than just being there, because they sense it's about to end. They don't even come to kick a ball around – just *walking into the place* is enough and feeling the importance of it in their lives. It's not something they pay much attention to for their first 10 or 12 years in the game, but for the last two or three it suddenly smacks them in the face! The effect is very marked. You do indeed see them chasing after their union reps, desperate to take a coaching qualification that might keep them in the game a little bit longer. They want to be part of it for longer, by whatever means, and it isn't just in order to secure a job, to make money to survive.

Tranmere is interesting from this point of view. A lot of the players grew up together as local boys. I see a lot of those who have left being drawn back to the place. It's a compulsion. I can name five or six who love to return. They want to come to the Christmas party, to the end-of-season do. They want to go to Magaluf at the end of the season with the lads who still play here. They come out with the players after a match. It may be that the social atmosphere at Tranmere is exceptionally good. This might not be true for every club. But it's definitely the case that players on the point of retirement do realise they are going to miss the game passionately, and they really get drawn into it and realise its importance as the days tick away.

There's a bit of an Orson Welles scenario going on. A lot of footballers start off as 'sensible young chaps', they get married early and are really quite mature in their outlook. Then as they get older and older, they start *acting* younger and younger. They feel their youth slipping away, so they get more and more laddish. It's as though they're living their lives backwards. You know that *Spitting Image* sketch about Orson Welles living his life backwards: all his best stuff, the stuff that should be the pinnacle of his achievements, occurs very early on in his life – he directs his masterpiece, *Citizen Kane*, in his twenties and by the time he's mature in years, he's reduced to doing voice-overs for Carlsberg and advertising sherry.

*George*: Yes. Definite echoes of George Best, there. Except he's partaking of the booze more than advertising it. When I studied the personality of players with my colleague Stephen Smith, one of the findings to emerge was that the senior pros at a club, that is to say the older, more experienced players like you, tend to be more team-spirited and supportive. Is this something that grows with time, or is it simply the case that you have to have a team mentality to survive any length of time in the game?

*Pat*: As you get older, you realise more and more the importance of the relationships you've made within the game. Most players wouldn't use that terminology, they'd say: 'I fancy a night-out with the lads tonight.' But that's really a recognition of the importance of football in your own life, and especially the social side of it. You start enjoying it more, you take care to be part of it to a greater extent. I certainly feel a good deal of that around me now from other older players.

*George*: We've talked a lot about the bonds forged within a club. Now, I understand, you've been told by your manager at Tranmere that they will 'allow' you to go. That must seem like a hell of a betrayal of your loyalty.

*Pat*: As you know, I turned down a Scottish Premier League club and an English Premiership club at the end of last season to stay here at Tranmere and show my loyalty. You often hear from fans or from certain journalists that there's no loyalty in the game any more, that the players are simply chasing money, but I do try to be loyal.

*George*: Can I ask to what extent you think such an attitude is typical? Last season, for example, if you take a player like Dean Holdsworth, almost every programme he appeared on he was stressing his desperation to leave Wimbledon. He felt he was going unrecognised, but money might have had something to do with it. He was almost like Alan Partridge on the radio, desperate to get his break on the telly. [*Later in the season, Vinnie Jones actually threatened to sue his own club – again Wimbledon – in an effort to move to another.*]

Pat:      Some people, probably including Dean, are very keen to get ahead and are very open about it. They are openly and overtly ambitious. Fans have an understanding of that point of view, I think. This desperation to move ahead, to maximise what you can do with the talent that you have, to advance your career, isn't unique to football, so I think there is likely to be some understanding of that position from the supporters.

George:   Mark McGhee was one *manager* who never made any secret of his strong need for career advancement, never hid his view that managing Leicester City was just another rung of the ladder for him, but the supporters of Leicester City never forgave him when he left them for Wolves. Mind you, they haven't done badly under his replacement, Martin O'Neill.

Pat:      Maybe it's a club thing. Certain clubs won't tolerate their trusted servants skipping off to pastures new just for the money. Celtic certainly won't, and neither will Newcastle.

George:   No. A lot of my friends won't forgive Gazza for going to Tottenham – let alone Chris Waddle! [*Later in the season, Waddle was to break the ultimate taboo, losing him the two or three fans he might still have had on Tyneside. He joined Sunderland.*]

Pat:      The attitude of fans of these clubs is: 'Why the hell would they want to go anywhere else? They're supposed to be happy at this club! This is the *top*!' These clubs have indoctrinated the fans very effectively, and that includes me! *I* can't think of any good enough reason why someone would want to leave Celtic.

George:   Paul Ince leaving West Ham for Man U is another excellent example of that.

Pat:      Precisely.

George:   When you look at a player like Paul McStay, one of the last great one-club players, do you think he has been at Celtic forever because of loyalty alone, that if you cut him, he bleeds green-and-white and all that?

Pat:    I think even he would quite like to have moved on at certain points in his career, but the right offer never came – he's been maybe 99 per cent loyal. At Celtic at the moment, you have the intriguing example of Pierre Van Hooijdonk, a player who professes no loyalty to the club whatsoever and makes no secret of the fact that he wants out. That would have amazed, shocked and stunned Celtic supporters in the past. The thought of having a player who is totally indifferent about playing for Celtic rather than anyone else is hard for these fans to take. They are not accustomed to what they would see as such overt, mercenary attitudes. [*Van Hooijdonk moved to Nottingham Forest, who were relegated at the end of the season.*] I personally value loyalty very, very highly. The fact that I was brought up with the attitudes of the old Celtic Football Club, through having been in the Boys' Club, all contributes.

George:    What about Peter Grant?

Pat:    Well, for loyalty, Peter is a great example. If he were ever to leave Celtic, it wouldn't be because he wanted to go but because the club no longer wanted him. He would bleed green blood. That's the position I find myself in now, with Tranmere, if they no longer want me. So while it's always the players that people slag off for being disloyal, I feel it can be seen the other way round. I'm prepared to give my all to Tranmere and I will be upset if they are not loyal to me.

George:    Is it very disheartening?

Pat:    It is, though I'm not trying to moan on about it. You accept it within the job. As soon as you're perceived as being not good enough for whoever the manager is at the time, then the club will want to lose you immediately. It always makes me laugh when any club complains about lack of loyalty from its players. I've never, ever taken that comment seriously, ever since the early days of my career, because loyalty has to go both ways, and you know there will be no loyalty towards you once you're perceived as being of less use than you once were. You'll be shown the door.

I have to feel – and do feel – within myself that I've shown a level of loyalty that is respectable. It's not a question of how fans feel at this moment – first I have to convince myself. It's an attitude that led me to blow about a year of my career at Everton, a very important year of my career. Howard Kendall and I did not see eye-to-eye, but I was determined to stay that extra year, honour my contract and show him that I was a good footballer. I was very green, really, and felt I'd been very naïve by the end of that year. It didn't matter how well I played, I had absolutely no chance. The manager had probably made up his mind before he'd even seen me play.

George:　Is there a sense of history repeating itself at the moment?

Pat:　Certainly all the same things are happening again that happened to me during my final year at Everton. I still hate the idea of walking away from a fight, though. I think I may be naïve to have these highfalutin ideals. Some other players might say: 'Let's be sensible about this, I'll cut my losses and go,' but I couldn't do that to fans who have come to watch every week and I couldn't do it to myself. I want to show I'm a fighter.

Up until last week, this attitude wasn't showing any return at all at Tranmere Rovers, as it didn't for a long time at Everton. What happened at Everton is almost the same as what has happened here at Tranmere: after a period of about four months, I was substitute, I came off the bench and I scored. At Everton, Kendall told me that scoring goals wouldn't make any difference, so then I knew what the score was. This time, I've come on, having been given my first real chance, made the first couple of goals, helped make the third and been awarded Man of the Match. Whether what happened at Everton will happen here with John Aldridge, I'm not sure, but my previous experiences have made me very wary.

George:　Did you play last night at Reading?

*Pat*:     Yes, I did. I ran my heart out. It was my second game in four days, not having played a first-team game all season before that. You certainly don't get match-fit to the same level, playing in the reserves. You can slog away at the weights and everything else, but match-fitness is something you simply don't get unless you've had a couple of games in the first team.

I'll wait and see what happens in the next three or four weeks. Anything is possible, but at least I'm being given a chance this time.

*George*:  Having broken back into the first team, it's conceivable that you'll now stay in it for a while . . .

*Pat*:     What I think is far more likely is that as soon as I have one bad game, I'll be dropped and I'll find it incredibly difficult to force my way back in again. Maybe I'm being paranoid. As I've mentioned before, paranoia runs high in professional football.

*George*:  Under the circumstances, I can well believe it.

*Pat*:     It's impossible to have a balanced overview from within the situation. People outside it and ex-players can give you a far more balanced view. I expect to drop back to the bench next Saturday, because I didn't score a goal last night. Looking at the wider picture, what would really upset me, really break my heart, would be if I was to leave a club and then get really barracked by the fans for being disloyal. For all the reasons discussed throughout this book, the faith of the fans is incredibly important to me. To some other players it is not as important. I'm not saying I'm right and they're wrong, but it's just the way I am. I feel I am a very loyal person, willing to show clubs more loyalty than they sometimes show me.

It has angered me over the years that people perceive footballers as a fundamentally disloyal bunch, and people outside the game do fail to realise that that loyalty only goes one way. Having said that, a lot of clubs do show their players loyalty, particularly if they are recovering from injury. In those circumstances, clubs tend to stick by players.

*George*:   A lot must hinge on whoever is the manager at the time,
            too . . .
*Pat*:      Without a doubt – and if a new manager comes along,
            everything turns upside-down. That was my experi-
            ence at Everton. But in the end, clubs are businesses, so
            they're not in a position where they can show loyalty to
            any individual player out of mere sentiment. That's
            what confuses me. Why are they so offended when the
            boot is on the other foot and the club is no longer good
            enough for the player?
                 What has emerged over the last decade as quite a
            sophisticated new argument from the fans – it may be
            an old argument, but it seems new to me – is basically:
            'We're more loyal to the club than you players. You're
            all just a transient bunch. In 15 years' time, we'll still be
            here and you won't.' I was a bit shocked to hear that at
            first. At Chelsea, certainly at Celtic, the attitude used to
            be: 'Wow! He plays for my club! What a hero!' and that
            was the top and bottom line.
*George*:   To be frank, I'm not even sure if that long-term loyalty
            is even true of supporters any more . . .
*Pat*:      Well, not of you, anyway!
*George*:   When I 'came out of the closet' about having switched
            my support from Spurs, whom I had followed for many
            years, to Newcastle United, I thought I'd better do it
            loudly. I did a thing for one of the Toon fanzines, *Talk of
            the Toon*, where I threw myself at the mercy of public
            opinion. Particularly at a time when Newcastle fans
            were finding it hard to meet the newly-escalating ticket
            prices, when the new, trendy middle-class supporters
            was moving in on the game, I thought they'd rip me to
            shreds for being a turncoat, a glory-hunter, etc. One of
            the editors, 'Decker' Graham, told me that he expected
            the same. 'This is just typical of the kind of rootless,
            mercenary bastards that Newcastle now attracts. Where
            were you when we were shite?' was the line I expected.
            After all, I'm no more a Geordie than . . . well, Pavel
            Srnicek.
                 But there was nothing. Nothing at all. Eventually one

person wrote in, but that was more an anti-Spurs letter than anything about the wisdom of changing your colours. Look at Nick Hornby, for whom loyalty is something of a euphemism for obsession: did he support Arsenal while he was a student? Of course not! He supported Cambridge United. Is it mere coincidence that Arsenal were in the doldrums at the time? In my defence, I'd like to refute any rumours that I'm a glory-hunter, at least: Newcastle United have won nothing (save the coming top of the First Division and getting promoted to the Premiership) since I've supported them!

It's hard for supporters now. What exactly do they remain loyal *to*? Taking Millwall as an example, they have changed players, board, managers (obviously), even their *stadium*. Nothing is as it was any more. There's very little for the traditionalist to cling on to. Poor Danny Baker!

Pat:     Perhaps even among the fans, attitudes are changing, but certainly I've been hearing a lot more people saying: 'You're only wearing the shirt,' rather than: 'It's great to have you – or whoever – here playing for us.' There's an acknowledgement of the fact that in five years' time, a player is likely to be elsewhere – in 10 years' time, it's pretty much a certainty. So although there is still a fair amount of undeserved hero-worship for some players, it is being balanced by a more pragmatic, realistic approach from some fans.

George:  The flip side of that, from the point of view of the fans, is that it's now very dangerous to slag off your opponents' players too much, because in a couple of months, they could well be playing for you!

Pat:     It's no longer about individuals. Individuals move around much more than they ever did. As a fan, if you are going to stay loyal to a club, it's the *name* that you can be reasonably sure will survive – even that is never certain. As you say of Millwall, almost everything else can change and probably will. What they are loyal to is those eight letters and a tradition and a history. In a way, supporters are more and more adopting this rational attitude and maybe that's not an entirely bad thing. As fans understand what goes on in football more, how the game works, they are less sentimental about it. In certain areas, the heart is taking second place to the head. Rationality in football! Whatever next?

I can understand the loyalty, though. Each club has a certain mystique, a certain aura about it. I could tell you things about Celtic that no other club could boast, things that make it truly unique as an institution. I could probably do the same with Everton. I've understood the loyalty of the fans during my time with these clubs. Chelsea is definitely a case in point. There are a number of things that give it uniqueness, an atmosphere, a culture all of its own. That's what the fans tap into. It comes back to what we were talking about before, a sense of identity. Saying 'I'm a Chelsea supporter' makes you a slightly different kind of Londoner from a West Ham supporter or an Arsenal supporter.

*George*: I wonder what would have happened if Celtic had moved its stadium to Cambuslang, as had been the plan at one point. Would that sense of identity have been compromised?

*Pat*: I doubt it. The history is so strong, so deep. There's so much of it, and it's so touching. I'm talking as a fan, here. That wouldn't be lost on any supporter, even if the club was relocated. If it's the Hoops, it's the Hoops and it doesn't matter where they're kicking the ball. If fans travel from all around the world to see them, what's a few miles' difference? I'm sure they would have managed Cambuslang.

I am happy, though, that they decided to redevelop Paradise instead. It is sometimes pretty strange for me, talking about certain clubs. I haven't lost that habit of devoutly following the club I supported as a boy, but I have to say I don't really come across this strength of feeling from many other players. Maybe when you get too close to something, it loses its mystique and it is difficult to see any club as anything other than big business.

There have been a number of times in my career when a move to my beloved Celtic looked imminent, but it always fell through at the last moment for all sorts of extraordinary reasons. It was disappointing at the time but, looking back on it, maybe it was for the best. When I stop playing, I will be able to follow my team around the country with my scarf on and there won't be any background bad feeling about them for me. Excuse the Flaubert quote, but it fits too well: 'Idols must not be touched; the gilt comes off in your hands.'

*George:*  Going back to Chelsea, I was watching a documentary about Terry Venables' playing days at the club the other day, and his run-ins with Tommy Docherty, who was then the manager. It's interesting that the team spirit at the time was very high, but Terry, as the captain, was a bit of a ring-leader for the players who didn't seem to have a great deal of respect for Docherty. I wonder whether you feel it is possible for team spirit to flourish without very effective management?

*Pat:*  I'd go further. I think it is possible for team spirit to be very good sometimes *because* of bad management. A bad manager can sometimes bind the team more cohesively and make them play for one another more than a good one! It's something I thought about when reading your book, *I Think I'll Manage*. It didn't come up in it, but then it was written from the point of view of the managers and no manager would admit to the fact that team spirit may be high because his players have ganged up in their mutual loathing of him. In the case of the managers you picked, that may never have been true anyway, but it does come up with some regularity in football.

Managers will have weaknesses and players are sharp. They know. They can see those weaknesses. The good managers I've known have two choices: know what you're doing all the time, or be able to bluff that you know what you're doing all the time! When a manager fails to take one of those two routes and loses control, the players are on him like a shot. Players don't miss anything. They're much more astute than people sometimes think. Once they've spotted that chink in the armour, it's not that huge a jump to having *total* lack of confidence in the manager.

If that happens, a number of outcomes are possible. The team can just fall apart and become a number of disparate individuals. When that occurs, you've got trouble and it becomes really hard to pull them back together unless you've got an incredibly strong figure within the club, or a small group of people in the club that can pull it together.

*George*: That sounds like Spurs under Ardiles. In fact, it sounds increasingly like Spurs full-stop.

*Pat*: That may well have happened with Ardiles, though I'm sure the players didn't dislike Ossie – he is almost impossible to dislike. The side splintered. It can happen without the chairman knowing, without the fans knowing and definitely without the press knowing for a very long time. On one or two occasions in my career, players have sussed that this was happening, that the team was fragmenting, and three or four of them have got together and pulled the others along, introducing a bit of cohesion again. The attitude of the group is: 'We need to do this for ourselves.'

Sometimes there can be an antagonism towards the manager. That can help bind the team. They are no longer doing things because of the manager, they're doing them *in spite of* the manager.

*George*: It can happen in other organisations, too. You can get a company whose employees have totally lost faith in their board of directors, or the manager of a particular department, but their mutual contempt for this group or individual can bind them together very effectively. It's almost worth recruiting somebody particularly useless and unpleasant on occasion, just to focus people's hostility on him or her and turn it away from one another! If people take pride in their own work, companies at all levels in this country might be functioning effectively in spite of their management, rather than because of it. This country prides itself on its managers. Everyone wants to be one. But many of them might not actually be any good!

Pat: It's particularly true in football, because of the cult of the manager. At some point, probably in the mid-seventies, everyone decided that the manager was the most vital person in any football club – much more so than any player.

George: It's similar to film directors. They're seen as the *auteurs*, far more important than the actors. I guess that managers are seen as the auteurs of the game today.

Pat: Before the seventies, the players were the stars and the manager was just someone who gently led them in the right direction.

George: Of course, John Harvey-Jones, the guru of management in industry, actually said that he turned around ICI not by any brilliant management on his own part, but by creating the conditions that allowed other people to manage. It's very fashionable now in organisations to manage in an 'empowering' way, allowing your employees to grow and develop. In practice, of course, it can simply mean that the manager does nothing at all and just lets those in his or her charge sink or swim. 'Empowerment' and 'delegation' can frequently be euphemisms for not doing anything. It gives you more time on the golf course.

Pat: Loss of faith in the manager is a funny situation for a football club to get into, because you would have thought that management and tactics were fundament-ally important on a day-to-day basis. Yet it's possible for players to hold their manager in total contempt, but still play very well.

George: That's certainly true of one manager I know of – I won't name him, but he has what's probably an undeserved reputation for being very good. Behind his back, his players loathed him. They felt he was completely out of touch, the jokes that they told in the dressing-room weren't understood by him because he paid so little attention to what was happening with his players. It was as though he had nothing but contempt for his players – and one or two of them openly reciprocated that contempt. Yet the press loved him. I sometimes think that some of the managers who have successfully courted the press have done it at the expense of getting any respect from their players. Indeed, perhaps *because* they get so little respect from their players, they've tried to find an audience that will listen to them – and the papers often provide a willing ear. The contrast between what any fan reading the papers might think and certain people's reputations within the game is quite startling sometimes.

*Pat*: Yes. The papers are very good at coming up with labels for people: 'wayward' George Best; 'bohemian' Pat Nevin. The ones they pick for managers tend to be things like 'wily, old . . .' or 'shrewd, tight-lipped . . .' and players tend to adopt these, too, but use them with a huge sense of irony, because they know that certain managers are a long way off the various sobriquets they've been handed by journalists. They may be very far from wily!

*George*: Though not that far from old?

*Pat*: It depends! But if you've been to university and you're a footballer, people will just assume you're super-intelligent. They wouldn't do that in any other walk of life. A graduate is no more likely to be a successful football manager than he is to shine in any other kind of managerial role. Although I haven't completed my degree, people assume that I'm incredibly intelligent for having gone to college at all. I just laugh at that! The trouble is, the more you deny it, the more the label sticks and the worse it gets. You just have to shut up and let it go.

*George*: With the average educational qualifications of players increasing all the time, it's likely that that kind of lazy stereotyping will change.

*Pat*: I think so. It's very much a media-driven thing again. They like to put people into neat pigeon-holes. I've tried to avoid stereotyping the individuals I've interviewed for the media – I like to start with a blank sheet, as it were – because I know how easily other journalists stereotype me. A lot of what is written about me could just be clipped together from previous articles, without a shred of insight: egghead; eccentric; aesthete . . . It's a reputation that's followed me. At Chelsea, I think I was blissfully unaware of how such reputations are fashioned, but by the time I signed for Everton, I'd had five years of that kind of coverage from the London press (and if you want the media covering your every move constantly – or even if you don't! – London is definitely the place to be) and I certainly felt it a bit there. By the time I came to Tranmere, I was aware that there would be a wariness and a certain stand-offishness from some of the players because I had this reputation for being a bit weird, and the temptation then was to be over-laddish, over-matey, swear more regularly than you normally would. But it just wasn't me, so there was no point in trying.

I always maintain that footballers are generally a sharp bunch of people and they will suss you out very quickly if you're putting on an act. That's the recurring theme to everything we've been talking about in this session: whether it's players, managers or anyone coming into the club to have a wee sniff around – psychologists! – players can usually see through them very sharply. You've got to be a smooth operator to pull the wool over their eyes.

And if they don't see through you immediately, they will eventually. It's like trying to impress a new girl-friend by acting very cool. Eventually, if you get married to her, she'll suss out that you're not! A football club is very like that. There's no point in being someone you're not for the first couple of weeks after joining – unless you want to keep the charade up for three years! There's a kind of unwritten set of rules about how you act when you join a club for the first time – though, obviously, they're going to be written now: it doesn't matter what sort of personality you are, whether you're a joker, a wit, sharp with dry one-liners or anything, you start off cautious, checking out the atmosphere and who the other characters are in the club. It's almost like joining the army. There's that initial reserve. You don't go in with all guns blazing into a group of 30 others who already know one another well. Well, perhaps Gazza could. But not many could. You've got to have real strength of character to do it. So instead, you start out cautious and wait for your niche to develop. You go in, keep your head down, bide your time and wait for the right time for your personality to develop.

I remember not heeding this accepted code of practice, and I made a dreadful error. I was quite old when I made it, too. I arrived at Everton determined to be myself and I sat at the back of the coach with Neville Southall. I didn't realise how much I was being wound-up for an hour or so. It was excellent, exceptionally well done. He was firing off the one-liners, and I was very into some of the alternative comedians at the time and I could just about do an hour and a half's worth of Jerry Sadowitz-type material. I thought I could match him joke-for-joke and he went along with it, but in reality he was pulling me in like a fish, catching me off-guard as if to show me up and say: 'You've been giving too much away. You're being too loud. You're being too smart.' About a week later, I realised and thought: 'I'd better shut up a wee bit!'

*George*:   But isn't Neville Southall seen as a bit of an unusual footballer himself – always on the periphery of the team and so on?

*Pat*:   I guess that's why I thought I could get away with all this comedy patter on him. I thought he'd be a fellow eccentric, a kindred spirit. And he *is* unusual, but he's very different from me. He's a very bad example if you're looking for stereotypic footballers, because he's like no-one else in the game! He's a stunning example of a one-off, exceptionally good at what he does best, which is winding people up! Oh, and he's not a bad goalie, either.

Anyway, I think it's time *I* did a bit of winding up. I

thought I'd probe you a bit for a change. Why are you a football fan? I need to know these things. Do you have an excuse?

*George*: Does a fan need an excuse? Yes, I suppose they do. Well, it's nothing quite as dramatic as a friend of mine who claims he had a dream in which the ghost of Herbert Chapman appeared at the foot of his bed and told him to support Arsenal. I guess that's a better excuse than Nick Hornby's. It needs to be something pretty dramatic if you're going to support Arsenal.

I've never been that head-over-heels about a particular club, but I love watching the game. None of my family were particular fans. My Dad would watch the big matches and that was about it – he follows it much more closely now, in fact. I was certainly never a good player. I was always played at left-back and I was never really a Julian Dicks or a Stuart Pearce. My heart was never really in it. It's hard to place just where the fascination came from. I think it could have sprung from being really keen on Disney's *Bedknobs and Broomsticks* when I was very young – about seven or thereabouts. Remember the scene where the two teams of cartoon animals play football?

*Pat*: I've played in a few games like that.

*George*: So that was the start of it. Later, I remember watching the '76 European Championship final very vividly. As a Czech, I never thought we stood a chance against the Germans, and then we won on penalties. Twenty years later, I was watching the Euro 96 finals at Scribes – I should have gone to Wembley, really – thinking: 'If only we were to beat them on penalties again . . .' But it wasn't to be.

The psychology of the game has always really interested me. I first visited Scotland around the time of the '78 World Cup in Argentina, and I've supported them ever since. That campaign might have been enough to put a lot of people off football for life, but it fascinated me. I wondered what was going through Willie Johnston's mind as he was sent back from Argentina for failing that drugs test and what effect it was having on the morale of the squad. So I was interested in that side of the game, even in my early teens. I was living in Exeter at this time, but supporting Exeter City was always a joke. Exeter is much more a rugby town. They did have one good cup run, when they made it to the quarter-finals of the FA Cup in '81 – beating Leicester and Newcastle – and Spurs knocked them out, which I secretly found rather funny. No-one should be forced to watch Exeter City. It's like being a music fan and having to watch village-hall productions of *The Pirates of Penzance* all your life.

Anyway, when I moved to London as a student, I started going to White Hart Lane on a regular basis. I liked the sense of a big club in a big city. If I'd stayed in Prague, where I was born, I'm sure I would have ended up supporting Slavia or Sparta. I fell in with a bunch of lads – all of whom were from Exeter as well, funnily enough – who used to go regularly. I loved the social side of it. For someone like Hornby, being a fan is very much a solitary obsession. It was always much more of a group thing for me: the pub before and after; the post-mortem; the anticipation of the next match.

Well, when Alan Sugar booted out Terry Venables, I, like a lot of the fans, was very upset. I was getting quite disillusioned with how the game was going at that point, and this was the final straw. The club had teetered on the brink of disaster in '91, but had managed to win the FA Cup and been saved. Now, the club where I'd marvelled at the likes of Hoddle and Gazza – definitely the most talented player I've seen in all my time as a supporter – was being reduced to a property being tossed about by various conflicting commercial interests. I felt I couldn't go back. If football in the nineties was all about consumer choice, then I felt the only way I could exercise mine was by not coming back, not putting any more money Alan Sugar's way.

I have to confess that I had already been to see Newcastle play a few times at this stage with friends. It was a more acceptable thing to do when they were in a different division to Spurs. However, a combination of the Toon's hugely enjoyable football, which was to win promotion at the end of the season, and superb atmosphere among the fans, coupled with events at Spurs, pushed me to do the unthinkable . . .

So, accompanied by a quasi-Masonic ritual involving downing bottles of Newcastle Brown and singing hits by Lindisfarne with mock reverence, I changed sides. And that's me. A Czech who spent his childhood in Exeter and now supports the Tartan and Toon armies. It happens all the time.

*Pat*: That takes care of the 'where', but I still don't fully understand the 'why'!

*George*: More than anything now, it's the social aspect. It's sharing the experience of something unique with a bunch of mates. That particular match is going to happen only once, but you know you've been there. Sweden '92 is an excellent example. I went there with one really good mate and made another really good mate, who I met there for the first time. And it was an excellent spirit among the supporters. It was like one big family. I can always look back and say I was part of that.

*Pat*: I remember being interviewed by a journalist at the time about how great the atmosphere was and how wonderful the fans were, and about how beating the CIS so dramatically was great consolation, and saying: 'I'm pissed off with moral victories! I'd like to see some other kind of victory!'

But when you first started going to matches, was it always with other people?

*George*: No. I would occasionally go on my own. You're right. There must be something more to it than the social aspect.

*Pat*: If you're a Scotland fan on the basis of what happened in '78, then maybe you're a masochist!

*George*: But even in Argentina, there was a certain amount of glory in the debacle. The victory over Holland was one glimmer of light in all the darkness. Perhaps I'm just a natural optimist. Research suggests that optimists remember the good times and forget about the bad times without even trying. I've already forgotten the Charity Shield this season, for example, but I won't forget beating Man United 5–0 in a hurry. Last season was a huge disappointment to Geordie fans, and as we now know, it broke Kevin Keegan. We came so close, but that doesn't stop me thinking that good times could still be round the corner. Maybe not this season, but soon.

Nowadays, even if I've been to a terrible match with friends, there is still the sense of having shared the experience and, I suppose, the male bonding that goes with that. And there's still the fascination with the individuals in the team and how they interact in pursuit of a common goal. Football is one of the most vivid illustrations of that.

Pat:      But is that the central appeal? That's certainly not why football got to me . . .

George:  I'm not sure. I'm not a great team-player myself – a lot of my best work I do alone. But I do admire team spirit and successful team-work, just as I admire other things I'm not particularly good at – singing, for example. I like to socialise in teams, but work largely on my own.

Pat:      That makes us polar opposites. I like to work in teams.

George:  But you need to work in a team by nature of what you do. And you don't socialise entirely on your own, either. But that probably makes me more attuned to being a fan than being a player. If I had any skill as a footballer – which I certainly don't – I might still struggle to be a good team-player. It would depend who my teammates were. I like to think I'd be better than Stan Collymore. But I do admire those who can bring out the best in a team. That may be one reason why I chose football management as the subject of my first book.

Pat:      It strikes me that you've always been something of an outsider. You came to this country at the age of . . .

George:  Four.

Pat:      So it would have taken a while to learn the language. In your current profession as a psychologist, you'd definitely be an outsider from a football point of view. Players would always see a specialist of that sort as being outside the team, not really part of it. Yet the fascination with football remains. It seems to have captured your imagination.

*George*:  Perhaps it goes with being an outsider a little, but there's an element of not quite believing the simplistic picture of the game portrayed by the media and wanting to know what really goes on, what the culture of football is really like. Increasingly, the image of football is being crafted by agents and spin-doctors every bit as much as acting or the music business. Fanzines like *When Saturday Comes* pontificate in great detail about what goes in the game, yet when it comes down to it, a lot of the information they have about it has come from sources like the *Sun*! The fans are forced to see everything through a gauze. Only those, like you, on the inside know what really goes on. Journalists, it seems to me, are rarely told anything just for the sake of it. There always seems to be a hidden agenda involved.

*Pat*:  You're absolutely right about that!

*George*:  But as an outsider, it fascinates me. I guess that's why we're here.

*Pat*:  Interestingly, while you're interested in what really goes on in the game, it always fascinates me why people become fans. That's why I asked the question, really. A lot of the time, it's inbred, and that's easy to explain: it's indoctrination. That's not very interesting – but that's me. People like me are stuck with that. I was born into a tradition of supporting Celtic and that's that.

It's when you go beyond that to see why people are pulled towards football. That always interests me. There are millions of reasons. I've known people who are gay who have become football supporters just to be part of the lads' set, a set they've never felt part of before. I've known people who are very insular, who watch the game just to be part of a group. These are often people who are famous – often really, *really* famous – but their fame has prevented them from being part of the gang.

*George*:   Like David Mellor?

*Pat*:   No comment. But I find it difficult to pin you down at all. I'm looking for some new kind of grouping.

*George*:   Perhaps it's that old psychologist thing of studying what you're no good at. Those with bad memories study memory, those prone to stress study stress, and those with no personality study personality. Needless to say, many occupational psychologists would be unemployable if they tried any other kind of job – and as for sexologists . . . ! So perhaps football has particular appeal to me because I've always been so bad at it.

*Pat*:   Yes, that makes sense. We're always fascinated by things we haven't mastered, things we don't fully understand. It's like that with love: in old Spencer Tracy/Katharine Hepburn/Cary Grant films, you always get the theme that the person they hate is actually the one they're secretly infatuated with and in love with.

*George*:   This doesn't extend to Terry Christian in most people's cases, though.

*Pat*:   No. But football fans are fascinating. You see so many people who love the game who, in their *real* lives, shouldn't.

*George*:   There might be a certain amount of chance, too. If Scotland had been astonishingly successful in '78, I might never have got to thinking about the psychological aspects of being a player, and then we wouldn't have a book. It's a funny old game, eh?

# Hard Times

*When I next caught up with Pat, he was turning the corner on what had been an exceptionally difficult period in his life. The pressure of his injuries, speaking commitments, PFA work, uncertainty over his future at Tranmere and a period of illness had taken a greater toll than Pat had ever imagined possible. This was one of the most sombre conversations we were to have . . .*

Pat: Well, things weren't looking too bright for me at Tranmere again. I remember walking off from the game that I talked about, the one where I'd been voted Man of the Match, with everybody cheering around me, but actually feeling quite down. I was uncertain what the future held, but I knew that the next three games were all away, and if I didn't score I'd probably be out of the first team again.

Anyway, Reading was the next match, on a Tuesday, which we've spoken about already, but I've had some additional thoughts about it since then. It was definitely the roughest time I've been given by an opponent *ever* in domestic football. The refereeing was totally inadequate – I tend to think of it as inadequate nowadays, rather than feeling I've been cheated – but I was being kicked and punched off the ball throughout the game. What was most annoying of all, though, was that despite my having played only one first-team game all season until then, the Reading management had singled me out as the one to do a serious man-marking job on! In a funny way, I felt that I was more highly regarded by their manager than my own! Seeing me as a threat was a mark of respect. I wish I could get that recognition at my club at the moment. There's nothing more infuriating than being highly rated by the wrong people!

To some extent, I was a victim of how football works: it's customary for the club you're due to play to send someone to the match just before the one against them and report back who the danger players are. Well, given that I'd had such a good game, making three goals, it was no great surprise that Reading had been given instructions to mark me out of the game. If I'd had a stinker the previous game, I'd have been fine!

Anyway, the Reading game was a bad one for me and I didn't shine the next Saturday either, though I worked incredibly hard defensively. This led to me being dropped and ending up on the bench against Barnsley, which I wasn't unduly depressed about, in a way. It was another away game that no-one was relishing and, probably for the first time in my life, I could handle being dropped. It's really unusual for me to feel that way. In the 800 or so professional games that I've played, I can't have felt that way more than once or twice. In fact, we lost that game 3–0, so maybe it was just as well I didn't play. If I'd played in all three away games and we'd lost all three, the finger of blame could easily have been directed at me.

However, I was keen to be back in the team for the game the following Saturday, which was at home. Well, the best-laid schemes of mice and men and all that . . . I tweaked my hamstring.

*George*:  How long do you think that will keep you out?

*Pat*:  I've no idea. I have never damaged a hamstring in my career. I've heard that quick people get hamstring injuries – so mine certainly contradicts that! I'm not the quickest of players over short distances. We'll just have to see how it goes.

*George*:  So in a sense, it's almost back to square one, just like at the start of the season?

*Pat*:  To some extent, yes. But at least the home fans saw me play really well in the one match I played at home. They've also seen me work incredibly hard and come off totally exhausted, so I hope they realise that I'm not simply past it or cruising, and it really is just circumstances that have kept me out.

George: So there should be no doubting your loyalty. How much mail do you get from fans?

Pat: I get quite a lot and, increasingly, the odd bit of e-mail. What I really want fans to know whenever I'm at a club is that I'm not some fancy-dan who doesn't try. I would hate it if any fan believed that. Catholic guilt with the Protestant work ethic again! Terrible, isn't it?

George: But not unique. My friend Stephen Smith is just the same. It must be something about Celtic supporters. Jock Stein was a Protestant, wasn't he? That's maybe where it comes from! Is that attitude a rare one in football?

Pat: No. There are a hell of a lot of Scottish players like that. A lot of players who I was brought up with and have played with are like that. It's an attitude among Scottish players – in fact, among Scots in general, particularly those working in England.

Certainly, for me, being able to accept the fact that I wasn't picked and was only on the bench was a rare thing. It was very unlike me. It'll probably be another 300 games – fingers crossed! – before I feel like that again.

George: It wasn't just you – it was probably highly affected by your circumstances at the time.

Pat: I'm glad you said that. I wouldn't want any readers thinking I'm losing my commitment, appetite or drive! For me, one of the key things about playing football is how much I enjoy it and how fortunate I feel to be doing it for a living. I accept that there are other players who take it for granted more, who are a bit blasé about it. Often it's very good players, child prodigies who have never really known anything else. Yet there's still the culture here, certainly in Scotland but also in Britain more generally, that you should always work as hard as you can. Sometimes, it should be said, this work ethic can be to the detriment of quality play.

*George*:   It certainly extends to the workplace more generally. In Britain, we work longer hours for less pay than anywhere else in Europe – and even, I think, the States and Japan.

*Pat*:       When you have a player who isn't pulling his weight, a lot of people think that it's always the manager who will pull him into line, but as often as not, it's one of the other players. It takes someone with a strong personality to do it. If you have such players in your team, though, it can become quite effective at regulating itself, without much managerial input. If the group realises that someone in their number is mucking about and not putting in the necessary effort, they feel as cheated as the fans do.

The fans, however, don't always realise who these regulators in the team are, these players who act as the glue, holding the rest of the team together.

*George*:   Can it sometimes be the ones who get a bad press, like Julian Dicks or Vinnie Jones (when he's not battling with his club for more money)?

*Pat*:       In my very early days at Chelsea, we had a player called Tony McAndrew who was probably the least popular player in the side, as far as the supporters were concerned. But among the players, everyone had total respect for him. He was very, very professional and possessed all the 'right' attitudes a player should have. An example of this is that when you're in the reserves and you hear that the first team have lost, you're not really supposed to cheer! It shouldn't turn into a battle between two sides from the same club, just because you haven't been selected for the first team.

Well, Tony was such a strong character that if anyone celebrated the first team's misfortune, he'd be down their throats so quickly that they wouldn't know what had hit them. It helped the *whole club*, the entire ethos seemed to emanate from him. The manager, John Neal, understood this. He was very interested in people and understood the importance of having specific types of characters at the club – very similar to Joe Kinnear in that respect – and knew that although Tony was unpopular with the fans, it was vital to have him as part of the team. He may not have been the best player we ever had, but John Neal made him captain and I certainly respected him as much as any player I have played with.

When I left Chelsea, people spoke to me about that time and what a good side it had been just after I joined. It could have been a great side, we were fourth or fifth best in the country at that time, after all. But this team that had been so close-knit, full of players who had grown up quickly together, just seemed to break up. A lot of people attributed that to the time when the manager left. Others singled out the departure of certain high-profile players – Speedie, Niedzwiecki or myself – or the arrival of others, but it all really changed when Tony left. Not one supporter raised an eyebrow at the time. No-one mourned his passing. Yet it was definitely his influence that had kept the team together. I wasn't a strong enough character in the club at the time to keep it going. He was the binding force with the right direction and without him, the group spirit and structure fell apart in comparison to what it had been. The players who were strong personalities who stepped in to fill his shoes took the club in all sorts of questionable directions, and things were never quite the same again.

The supporters often miss things like that. To all intents and purposes, it looked the same team after he'd gone and very few fans thought of him as significant in any way. But he was the glue. He held it together – along with a manager who understood and appreciated that.

*George*: It's amazing how quickly things can flip. I remember QPR in the late eighties, the first club I'd ever done any research at. Jim Smith was very respected as the manager there. There was a kind of social heart of the club and it centred around some quite unlikely players: Mark Dennis, the Julian Dicks of the eighties; Martin Allen; Wayne Fereday; Les Ferdinand – no-one had

heard of him then! They were doing very well then,
even topping the First Division – what's now the
Premier League – for a while. When Jim Smith left,
Trevor Francis came in and the club disintegrated. Most
of those players went to different clubs. I think Trevor
was determined to be heavy-handed because Cloughie
had taken the mickey out of him in the papers and
warned he'd be too soft a touch. Well, he went right the
other way – most famously, not releasing Martin Allen
from a game so that he could be present at the birth of
his son. He lost the spirit of the club practically overnight.

*Pat*:     You have to be sensitive to 'people issues' as a football
manager. It's like any other kind of management. Now,
a lot of the top names are not necessarily the best at that
side of things, but the clever ones get a good second-in-
command. This link-man is the hand, the eye, the ear
closer than the manager's to what's really going on
within the group on personal levels. It could be an older
pro still playing, a coach or an officially-identified assistant manager. If you've got someone like that who really
understands the team dynamic and who can liaise
effectively between the manager and the players,
you've got a good chance of building a winning team.
A sense of that dynamic is the easiest thing in the world
for the manager to miss. They'll all tell you that they
have to step back a bit when they take the job. They
might have other great talents, but if they don't have a
feel for what's really going on in the team because
they've become remote from it, and they don't have a
good number-two to tell them, then it can be very
dangerous.

The deputy, the number two, is a very interesting
position. I'm not sure I'd want to do it, but of all the
coaching or management roles, that's probably the one
that would keep me entertained longest. Even very
respected managers like Joe Royle at Everton [*Joe was to
lose his job later in the season, surprising many*], who have
a good rapport with the players, need a good second-

in-command. In Joe's case, it's Willie Donachie who the players completely trust and can talk to at their own level. If a manager finds someone like that, they'll take them all over the country with them, wherever they go, whatever club they move to. They're a deputy for life.

*George*:   That was certainly true of Terry Venables and Ted Buxton, and now of Glenn Hoddle and John Gorman.

*Pat*:   The classic was Clough and Taylor. When you have a bond that good, you know it's going to take a very long time to build something like that again. That's why these partnerships can last so long. Typically, there's someone very well-known and a less-conspicuous assistant working with them. In a sense, these deputies are the unsung heroes of football management. The difficulty is that you have to be careful with the egos. It's best if the number two has no wish to bask in the limelight of the number one, if they harbour no ambitions in that direction themselves and are content to remain in the shadows. Of course, if there is any clash of egos, it's unlikely that such a pair would have started working together in the first place. If you pushed Alex Ferguson at Man U, he would be willing to underline the extraordinary importance of Brian Kidd in the club's success.

*George*:   What about at Tranmere? Is there such a character between the players and John Aldridge?

*Pat*:   It's a relationship that's being built up at the moment. There is a chap called Ray Matthias who was here with the previous regime, and John has also brought in Kevin Sheedy as a reserve-team coach. Now, through no deliberate act, maybe through no-one's choice but the players' own, he has become very respected and taken on part of that role.

*George*:   It's interesting how that can happen, isn't it? At Dulwich Hamlet it was always Johnny Johnson, who was actually the goalkeeping coach. But he was definitely the link between the players and the manager, much more so than the official assistant-manager.

*Pat*:   John Aldridge likes to be one of the lads. He was always very integral to the teams he played in, but he's learning the ropes as a manager – and he'll be the first to admit that – and coping with each dilemma as it occurs. Now, it's difficult to do that while you're trying to run the team, while you're in the spotlight and while you're still trying to play. It's easy to miss something. I notice that what Kevin Sheedy does takes a little of the pressure off the manager. When Ray does it too, it has a very positive effect on the manager. He seems more relaxed as a result.

I could see myself in that kind of supporting role somewhere. I'm not saying I will pursue it, but I know that I'll never be a manager, yet being an assistant is more attractive. The effort that I make to understand what players are about would pay off in a role of that sort.

George: And how do you see the team dynamic at Tranmere developing over the next six months, as that role becomes more clearly defined?

Pat: The trick is always to know where the dividing lines are, not to step on people's toes. John has always followed the Liverpool model, that's very close to his heart. It's almost become a bit of a joke, this endless conveyor-belt of grey-haired men trundling out from the Boot Room and all turning out to be terrific managers. I think those people were listened to very carefully by the likes of Shankly, Paisley and Kenny, and if Aldridge is following that model, I think the role of someone like Kevin Sheedy will become more and more apparent. But there are other possibilities. There's a guy called Steve Mungall whose role might also grow in importance over time. Whoever ends up doing it, it is obviously imperative to the manager – any manager – that the team functions successfully as a group.

George: You do sometimes get the number twos moving into the limelight. Ted Buxton has become manager of the Chinese international side. Walter Smith has taken over from Graeme Souness at Rangers with a lot of success.

Does he now have to find another intermediary between him and the players?

Pat:    Walter Smith is the classic example of the role that I'm talking about. He was so good in that position under Souness that I think anyone can still talk to him, regardless of their level in the club, even though he is now the manager. In the game in general, before Souness left, there were already suggestions that Smith was the real brains of the operation. It is impossible to know how true that was, though.

I first came across Walter when I was 14 and he was still at Dundee United. He tried to sign me then. I was up there, involved in a training session with about 40 other kids, and he walked up to me and took me to one side. There seemed no obvious reason why he should have singled me out, but he spoke to me for about 20 minutes before showing me what he thought I should try.

It was a simple thing and I found it odd at the time: he said I was kicking the ball incorrectly. And I was! I had learned always to bend the ball, never to kick straight – I was trying to be clever. He said I could still do the things I was doing, but there were other things I was unable to do because I wasn't addressing the ball correctly. It was almost like the way David Leadbetter took Nick Faldo's golf swing and completely remodelled it, stripping it down to the basics and reconstructing it.

I was immediately really impressed by Walter because in that situation, if anyone is spending time with you, it means they might be interested in signing you and are impressed by what they've seen, yet he was simultaneously giving me advice that would change the fundamentals of my game. At the time, Walter was assistant to Jim McLean, who, if you remember, was one of the most abrasive and least player-friendly managers ever. In order to be successful, which he undoubtedly was, he needed a second-in-command who really understood the game and also the personalities of the players, and he got that in Walter. Walter was absolutely phenomenal. McLean certainly had many strengths, particularly his grasp of tactics, but he would definitely have been less effective without Walter Smith.

Walter was tactically brilliant, too. He was actually moved into the Scottish national team set-up and he did some very effective coaching there. He didn't particularly want the job of Andy Roxburgh's assistant, which Craig Brown took instead, but he was very influential with the Under-21s and even with the first team for a good five or six years. Everybody had huge respect for him and word of mouth got round very quickly. Souness was a player at that time, and that's where the bond between them would have first been forged.

Having said that, Walter Smith has been successful as a manager but that isn't necessarily true of all these mediators. In fact, many of them wouldn't have the skill or maybe the presence to be managers. It tends to take a very different kind of character, normally. Some, like Walter, can step into it, but that's rare. Normally, the deputy remains a deputy because he's so comfortable doing that and so well-suited to the role. Walter has been astute enough to recognise the importance of a good man in the liaison role, so he poached one of the best, Archie Knox, from Ferguson at Manchester United.

The Second in Command may not have, for example, the instantaneous talent for spotting a good player that some managers do. It can be some kid playing at Marine or somewhere, and a good manager might see in that kid the makings of a First Division – even Premier League – footballer. These managers don't work at it, it's just an instinct, a gift. That should never be underestimated, even if the manager is not the most natural communicator with his players. That talent to pick players is certainly one I don't possess – I couldn't be a manager for that reason alone. I would have to work with someone who does.

So you need both individuals and they complement one another. Where one has weaknesses, the other has strengths. All the same, the personality cult that has grown up around managers is probably slightly unfair. The number-twos deserve credit, too – sometimes just as much, if not more. Maybe it's time to redress the balance.

*George*: Someone actually suggested to me that I write a book about the number twos in the game, as a sequel to the one about managers.

*Pat*: I think that would be very difficult to do, because the classic number-twos learn very quickly *not* to take centre-stage, *not* to take a huge proportion of the credit and so on. Consequently, they'd probably avoid taking part in a book which publicised their role and put the spotlight on them. They haven't got that need for recognition, that ego. If they lifted the lid on their contribution, they'd lose the confidence of their manager and jeopardise their position as confidant, so it would be hard to get them to open up candidly in the way that the managers you interviewed did. It would be a fascinating book if you could do it, but how possible it would be to get near the reality of their experiences is something I'd wonder about.

*George*: Have your thoughts about management changed since the beginning of the season? At that point, it seemed very far from your mind.

*Pat*: No, there has been no change at all. The role I'm talking about is a very specific one, and anything else wouldn't appeal at all. As you spend more time in football, you come to realise just how specific many people's jobs really are. I'm not equating myself in any way with Kenny Dalglish, but I think what Kenny does at any club he goes to is he tells them very specifically the kind of things he considers himself to be good at. He then lets the club use those skills to their advantage by building his job around their organisation. Unlike some managers, he lets others deal with areas he doesn't feel he is qualified for.

Now, if I went to a club, I'd tell them that the number-two job is one I would like to do, but I wouldn't want to be doing a lot of the driving all round the country every other night looking at players, which forms an important part of many assistants' jobs. I could be useful, in the long term, in that liaison role between the boss and the players, spending time with the group and working out where the group may be lacking in certain respects. But I think it wouldn't happen, realistically, unless the job was very tailored to my interests, because there are certain aspects even of the assistant's role that don't appeal at all. But my instinct for understanding the group dynamic is very strong. When a player leaves and it's about to crumble, as it did at Chelsea, I could spot that almost instantly and would perhaps be able to help the manager rebuild team spirit quickly and effectively. At Chelsea, the problem was that I couldn't do anything about it, but I was much younger then and I think I've learned from what happened. I've been in similar situations since, but unfortunately I've left the club at the same time as the key player, or I've not been in a position to do anything about it because of my relationship with the manager at the time.

George:   Well, taking everything full circle, where do you now see your long-term future with Tranmere?

Pat:      That's a good question in the context of what's been happening to me right now. Something happened to me this week that has never happened before, and because I've promised to be honest in this book, I should talk about it: I got depressed. It had never happened to me before. I'd been in bad moods before, but throughout all the things that have happened to me in my career, good and bad, I'd never felt as bad as I did recently. I've always accepted that there will be bad times on the field and separated it from my *real* life.

Perhaps it was the combination of things. There were a couple of injuries at the wrong time, the two games that the team lost, all the union activity surrounding the threat of the strike, and then I was ill as well, which

I think was very important in affecting how I felt. The whole stress of it all finally got to me in a way it never had before, and for about three days I was really, really down in a very bad way. There were other niggling things going on, too. There were problems concerning my flat in London and sorting out Gordon Taylor's contract with the PFA which might have contributed, but I really felt rotten.

It's never been me. Well, it *was*: I was one of those angst-ridden young thinkers at school and college, but everyone goes through that. This was different. This trough was a new low for me. I sat in a darkened room trying to work out what was happening to me and I thought that, being realistic, my career as a footballer was now coming to an end. I've probably got 18 months at the most, and the way my opportunities are looking at Tranmere now, it could be less. My contract is secure for 18 months anyway, unless the club sell me – but either way, I'm fairly financially secure over that time, so it wasn't money worries. But I think my physical illness at the time made it worse. It contributed to my bleak mood. It was frightening that I'd never felt this way before, though. I told you early on in the book that I don't suffer from the stresses and strains of the game, and here I was, suffering. I think it's because I'm a bit of a control-freak and I had momentarily lost control of what was happening in my life.

I didn't turn to drugs, or get into the biggest paralytic drunken stupor I've ever been in, which is what the media often likes to imply is the natural reaction for players when they get in that state. But I can certainly appreciate a little more now how it actually feels when the stress is really getting to some players.

I am often asked to do presentations to groups of people or to attend charity events – as most players do, though strangely, it is rarely reported in the papers – and after three days of feeling like this, I was due to attend two presentations in one day. One of these was for young achievers who had succeeded in things despite personal difficulties. It had been organised months ahead, but it was heaven-sent in that I needed to attend something like that at this particular moment in my life.

I went along to see all these kids with disabilities and hardships to whom I was presenting these awards, and it made me think: 'What am I bloody worrying about?' I realised that the way I was feeling was stupid. I would have come to that conclusion eventually anyway, but it was quite odd that that event had come at that time. It really brought me out of my depression. I thought: 'Hey! Wait a minute! I'm not someone who gets depressed over things like this. I've got a different attitude, I've got other strings to my bow. Football isn't, as Shankly so incorrectly said, more important than life.' I thought, 'Just get back out there and enjoy life!'

George:    It's intereseting that you say that. I'm like you in that I never get depressed, but there have been a couple of periods in my life when I *have* been, and in both cases it coincided with a lot of problems and difficulties all happening at once, the sheer volume of setbacks and bad news. There was the feeling you mentioned, of no longer believing you're in control of your life. Like you, I like to feel that I'm in control of what's happening to me, and I had lost that control. Research suggests that almost everyone has felt like that at some point.

Pat:       I can imagine the reaction from some of my fellow players. They'd just say: 'Well, don't do so much, you're taking too much on' – which I definitely was. But how can you say no, particularly if the requests come from children's charities? You'd feel even worse if you *did* say no!

It's difficult sometimes to draw a distinction between being a bit down and depression. If you're really depressed, I think it begins to affect you physically as well, and if you play professional football, it can affect your training, your preparation and of course, in turn, your play. If you're not sleeping well, and it's really

affecting you a lot, you then can't really function properly as a professional footballer.

George:  Does it affect many players?

Pat:  I think it does, and many find their own ways around
it. It's quite obvious that many do. Having a drink is
one way. Boosting your self-esteem by hanging around
with a lot of people who'll tell you how brilliant you
are is another I've seen. It's a way of building your
confidence back up again.

But it can hit you really hard, something I didn't ever
think would happen to me until it did. I suppose it's
something you shouldn't be embarrassed about. But
when you consider the stress that someone like Kenny
Dalglish was under at Liverpool when he resigned, it's
very hard to judge unless you've been there. Of course,
he had to cope with a great deal, especially following
the Hillsborough disaster.

There's an attitude among some fans that players
should cope with the pressure because that's what
they're paid for, and I was in broad agreement with that
for a long time, but something happened at Chelsea that
made me change my mind.

After a couple of years playing at Chelsea, I was
fairly unconcerned about the so-called pressures of the
game. Having said that, the papers have been kind to
me. I haven't been a 'target' for them in the way that
Julian Dicks has, or had them make intrusions into my
private life like they did with Dean Holdsworth. The
truly hurtful things that people have written about me
could be counted on the fingers of one hand – and that's
over 15 years in the game. In fact, I'd have a couple of
fingers left over. I've been lucky in that respect.

Anyway, this friend of mine called Doug Rougvie,
who I counted as a mate off the pitch, came to Chelsea.
He's the loveliest bloke you'll ever meet – but he doesn't
necessarily *look* like the loveliest bloke you'll ever meet.
He's a great big Scottish Highlander and when he
played for Aberdeen, he was a bit of a legend, a bit of a
cult figure. Everyone knew he wasn't the most skilful

of players, but he was wholehearted and he tackled everything. He was a monster on the field and he looked as though he had been hewn out of granite. That stature and style made him a legend among Aberdonians.

He came to Chelsea to replace left-back Joey Jones, who was also a cult figure. Left-backs often are: Dicks, Pearcey, etc. However, the media quickly turned him into a figure of fun, making great play of the fact that they considered him ugly. That was offensive enough, but then he made a couple of mistakes and they labelled him stupid as well. They would write that he was a totally awful footballer and he became ridiculed in certain sections of the press.

He had put me up in his house for a wee while, so I spent some time with him and his family and I began to see just what an impact this negative press could have on a player. For me, after a match, I'd go and see a play on the South Bank and forget about it, but others would read the papers. Imagine being in that position, knowing that everyone you know is likely to see those same papers. You'd get so much stick in them, you'd throw them aside and turn on the telly instead, but there would be some smug commentator with that standard cliché: 'What on earth was he thinking about?' in that tone of mock-disbelief. There weren't too many ex-players doing it in those days. Well, one or two exceptionally smug ex-players, maybe. So you turn the telly off and try and forget about it. You try and talk to your kids, but they've been getting stick at school from other kids calling their Dad useless. So the stress transfers to members of your family. It's difficult to talk to your wife, because she was at the game and heard all the personal abuse aimed at you by 30,000 people in the stadium who have all turned on you.

It's easy for me to say it's a great job, there's no stress and everything's wonderful, but when it becomes a problem that is at once so big that the whole country can read about it and simultaneously so small that it affects the relationships with your wife and children, it must feel as though your whole life is caving in around you. Doug didn't suffer all these problems, but I've known players who have suffered each of them. It made a huge impression on me, not only because it was so extreme but because he was the most likeable lad you could hope to meet, and someone I've always really respected as a person and as a player. In some respects, he was a good player, too. He was a very effective marker, for instance. It had never really made the same impact on me before. I finally understood how painful it can be if things do not go well for you in this game.

*George*: There must be half-a-dozen players in that position now – at least!

*Pat*: Jason Lee is an obvious example and so is Julian Dicks. His kids started getting stick at school over the incident when he was accused of stamping on John Spencer's head – despite the fact that John didn't want to take the matter further. I think that's one of the things that players find very, very difficult to handle. You'd think players' kids have it easy, that they're popular because their father is a famous player and he does a glamorous job, and that all the other kids are jealous. Well, frequently they *are* – and kids can be *very* jealous and very evil. If the newspapers have given them some ammunition, they can be terribly cruel and that's the hardest thing for a father to take, whether he's a professional footballer or does any other job. There is also the feeling on top of that that you're the one who caused it, that you're the reason for your son or daughter's sadness.

I don't want to paint a dark picture of what it's like to be a player – *of course* it can be a brilliant job and loads of fun, but when things are not going well, people should be honest and admit that there are aspects of the job that are not so pleasant, rather than perpetuate the myth and carry on pretending it's fortune and glory all the way. No matter how much money you're earning, that may not be any comfort when the kids are crying. Some people claim they could put up with any kind of pressure, as long as they had the money. I think that's nonsense. It makes many things easier, but some of the richest people in the world kill themselves!

Anyway, I'm feeling a lot better now, and I'd feel even better if I could get my bloody computer to work.

# SESSION 10
# Boys Don't Cry

*They say the night is always darkest before the dawn, and for Pat, things were certainly beginning to look up. His hamstring injury only kept him out for one game, which Tranmere lost 2–0. At the next home game, against Huddersfield, he came on as a substitute. The sides drew 1–1. He then played in Tranmere's 2–1 away win over West Brom, and at the next home game scored both goals in the 2–1 victory over Swindon – missing a penalty into the bargain.*

Pat:     It was good to be back in the side and also good that Tranmere were winning again after what had been a terrible run. To score two goals in front of the home crowd after such a long time felt wonderful. It's a cliché, but you really do dream about things like that. It also gave it more of an edge that it was against Swindon – there had always been a friction between ourselves and Swindon, going back for several years. There was a mysterious lights-failure during one of our encounters and we've never really trusted them since. In addition to that, of course, they knocked us out of the play-offs. So there has been bad feeling between the two sides for a while.

George:   Of course, when Swindon were promoted, all manner of fishy goings-on involving Lou Macari soon got them demoted again, so you could well have been right not to trust them.

Pat:     It was an odd game, though – or at least the way I felt about it afterwards was odd. I didn't feel happy. I'd never before scored two goals in front of a home crowd against unpopular opposition and walked away feeling unhappy, but instead of driving home feeling delighted, I actually felt deflated after the game. It was partly

because just before I came off, I'd missed the penalty –
which didn't bother me, but the manager was furious
at my lack of professionalism, taking it when I wasn't
in fact the designated penalty-taker.

*George*: How did it compare with that classic penalty-miss
while you were at Chelsea, which we talked about in
our first session?

*Pat*: It wasn't quite as bad. But the comparison is a valid
one. I cared equally little about missing it, because, once
again, we'd won anyway so it didn't really matter that
much. The Chelsea miss I actually laughed about –
though I disguised it – whereas this time, I just shrugged my shoulders. I expect John Aldridge would rather
have been on to score the penalty himself. So he had
dampened my happiness a little – with some justification, it should be said – but there was also the feeling
that I was in a period of transition. I acutely felt at that
moment that there might not be many more highs like
this left for me at Tranmere, that I might be leaving
soon. And that thought, for some reason, took the shine
off it.

It was back to the knowledge that: 'I can't keep this
level of performance up forever. At some point, I'll have
a bad game, and this will be the excuse to drop me and
eventually to get rid of me. If I'm out of the team, there
is nothing I can do to show the fans what I'm capable
of.' On the other hand, though, it removed the pressure
that I had been feeling and lifted it from my shoulders
completely. I felt that it didn't matter what I did anymore, that the consequences would be the same.

*George*: So there was no more fear of underperformance, fear of
failure?

*Pat*: No, that had gone. There was no more compulsion to
try too hard, to overwork myself unnecessarily, even
counter-productively.

Anyway, the next challenge was the FA Cup match
against Carlisle, which we lost 1–0, knocking us out. I
felt very relaxed during the game, for the reasons I've
explained, and thought I played quite well. We were

away from home but were by far the better team for most of the game. We just couldn't score.

Then John Aldridge was sent off for swearing at the referee. It's interesting, because when I came on against Huddersfield in a recent game, I had been booked and that's quite unusual for me. It went down the line and the ball was out. It was definitely our throw-in, but the referee gave it against us and I reacted, which is something I don't usually do. It was quite a limited reaction, not a 'Fuck off, ref!' or kicking the ball away. All that happened was the ball was in my hands and I bounced it rather high. So I was booked for 'bouncing the ball in a dissentful manner'.

*George*:   What a shocker!

*Pat*:   Quite. Anyway, the manager got the booking-form through and he decided to fine me £200 for that. John Aldridge informed me that that was his decision, the day before the FA Cup tie with Carlisle. I was pretty disappointed with him. I had never been fined before in my entire career. I thought it was quite a harsh decision. It's particularly true that when you're a seasoned pro – Gordon Strachan and Bryan Robson are both good examples of this – you do apply pressure on the referee and try and influence what he does. It's part of the game. You do it by talking to him, or through whatever other means are available. You learn over time that that's part of the game, that the older pros do have that clout, if that's not too strong a word, that influence. Certainly, when I was younger and Robbo used to do it while I was playing against him, I'd be fuming. I remember once being booted in the air by Bryan Robson and complaining about it. The referee just turned to me and shouted: 'Shut up, sonny!' Then he turned to Bryan Robson and said: 'Look, come on, Bryan, old boy!' I was livid about it at the time, but I've come to accept that that's how the game works.

So I argued to the manager that all I had been doing was bouncing the ball and that I had been expressing my frustration at an unfair decision. I had expected the manager to support me, to see that I was trying to do my bit for the team by influencing the ref, but he chose to fine me for it. I therefore felt I had to tell him that I'd make no further attempts to influence referees from now on beyond talking to them. If I get pulled down, I won't shout at them or make gestures at them. I'll just stand up and walk away. I'm not going to risk getting booked and then fined 200 quid again. He replied that if that's the way I wanted to play it, then so be it. The fine was meant in some ways to be a bit of a laugh, and the money would be used positively for the team.

Anyway, the following night, he was sent off himself for swearing.

George:   A hilarious irony, indeed. I hope he fined himself.

Pat:      He did. He fined himself more than twice what he fined me. He'd left himself in a bit of a corner. He smirked at me knowingly afterwards. It helped defuse things between us slightly. He'd also fined a player in the reserves for dissent – he'd given him the maximum fine possible – so he wasn't picking on me or anything. That's just his approach. Most managers don't fine you heavily for these things.

George:   How do the size and the frequency of fines vary within the game?

Pat:      It depends very much on the club. There are a number of ways of doing it. One way is that the club will fine you according to a code which, for my sins, I helped to draft through the PFNCC and the money goes back into the club. It has various suggested fines which I can't remember off the top of my head, but it's something like 15 per cent of your week's wages for dissent, 50 per cent if you're late for the team coach for the second time on a match day, and so on. So that structure is in place, and if managers choose to follow that structure, then they can. I can't really complain when I've been fined to the letter of the law, according to a code I helped to draft! Another player in the team was fined the same amount as me for an equally small offence.

          However, the way that John Aldridge has done it is

better, because rather than the money going back into the club – which obviously annoys families of players, because it means that in effect the club doesn't pay them the usual amount in a particular week – the way the manager did it was to put all the fine money into the players' pool. So you shrug your shoulders and accept it, feeling that at least the lads all get a drink out of it. It's a much better method from the point of view of team spirit than the club keeping the money itself.

George: Presumably, you're one of the players who will be having a drink out of your fine – so you'll be able to get some of it back.

Pat: Oh, definitely. I'll be on the next night-out with the lads, eating and drinking my share. It reminds me of something that happened a while back with the Scotland squad. Scotland make these videos and sell them. Some of them are videos for disabled kids, others have coaching skills as their theme. I featured in some of these, demonstrating keepie-uppie and various technical tricks which I do well. Andy Roxburgh and Craig Brown always encouraged me to take part in these videos and I became their 'star' for a while!

I was in Canada with the Scotland squad just before the build-up to Euro 92, having dinner in a restaurant in Toronto, and Andy Roxburgh told me that there was someone there who wanted to meet me: the chief executive of Umbro in America. 'Er . . . okay,' I said, wondering what he wanted to talk to me for – I'm Puma! Still, it was Umbro who were paying for the dinner, so it seemed polite.

'I'm very glad I could talk to you, Pat,' he said, 'because we used you in our advert which we ran throughout the States this year.'

'Eh?' I said.

'You remember, keeping the ball up, balancing it on your head, flicking it back over your head and then volleying it?' Well, I'd done this quite a few times for the cameras, but never for Umbro. It transpired that they had obtained the footage from one of the Scotland coaching videos! Well, at this point, the dollar signs clicked into my eyes like a Fred Quimby cartoon character.

*George*:   This was despite the fact that you were wearing Puma boots?

*Pat*:   Yes. I was told they had used Pele and America's top woman player in the same advert. So I was just about to say: 'Hang on a minute. Where's my money? You've used me in a nationwide advertising campaign without asking me and I don't even wear your boots,' when Andy Roxburgh shot me a glare that said: 'Don't say it, Pat!' Instead I just said: 'Oh. Right. Very good. Maybe I'll get to see the advert myself one day . . .' and went back to join the players.

I was sitting next to Brian McClair and told him what had happened, that Umbro had used me in their advert without my permission and hadn't paid me a bean. Then Brian pointed out that it was Umbro who were picking up the tab for our dinner that night. This was indeed true, so I ordered a couple of bottles of Opus One, which is the best wine that has ever been made in America and cost 150 dollars a bottle in this restaurant. So we had these two beautiful bottles of Opus One. Thank you, Umbro, if you're reading this!

Which takes me back to the fact that my fine money is going into the players' pool. Well, if you pay for it, you're certainly going to drink some of it! This time it is going towards a Chinese meal followed by a night-out in Liverpool.

All this aside, though, it was very disappointing to go out of the FA Cup in such a fashion. We were by miles the better side and there was a lot of bad feeling afterwards towards the ref and our opponents, much of it springing from the manager's unfortunate sending-off. There has been something of a bad feeling at the club since then. We'd had a bit of a good run, and this FA Cup result has shattered that. The confidence just seems to have fallen apart over a few days. It's not what *should* have happened. We'd won the last couple of games and were looking a good, positive side. But *Carlisle*! Third Division . . . !

Maybe it's up to the older players in the club to make sure that the younger boys don't lose confidence completely. Those of us who have been there before will have to try and convince the younger players that we're still a good side, to prevent confidence from draining away. We have to remind them that it was only one bad result and it wasn't even too bad a display.

I've found myself speaking to the press quite a lot lately about financial problems at Tranmere Rovers, about which there are a lot of rumours currently rippling round the club, and this is affecting confidence, too – some players are actually worrying whether or not their wages will be paid. If we'd won the FA Cup tie, we'd have been playing Sheffield Wednesday at home, which would have been very good for the club's finances. So there is the embarrassment of the defeat itself, but there are also the longer-term financial implications that are leaving everyone a little bit unsettled at the moment. This makes Saturday's game away at Oxford very important indeed. [*In fact, Tranmere were to lose 2–1.*]

George: And I understand that you've had another jab?

Pat: Yes. I got that just before I scored the two goals against Swindon. It's the old foot-injury back again, just like at the beginning of the season, the sharp pain that feels as though you have a nail through your foot. It's one of those injuries that you can feel coming: it starts off as a slight, niggly irritation, but you know it's building up and you know it's going to reach the stage when it's unbearable and you're going to need a jab. It's hard pitches and rock-hard ground that have brought it back on. Anyway, I was in agony, so I had to get a jab. I had played through the pain against West Brom, had the jab on Monday and played against Swindon on Friday.

There's always the danger of going overboard on the jabs, but my career is coming to an end anyway and at this stage you have learned when and where to take those calculated risks. I was back in the team, I'd grabbed my chance and I felt I needed to capitalise on it, to carry on playing and not take any more time out.

It's pretty painful as the needle goes in. Just like last time, I was told to jump down and the pain would be gone. Well, I did and it wasn't quite gone. He'd just missed part of it – so I had to go through it a second time. The pain was fairly acute and the relief wasn't immediate this time, though ten days later, it now feels nearly brand-new. There's still a tiny bit of pain, but it's almost gone.

*George*: And how long are the effects of this jab expected to last?

*Pat*: With luck, this should see me through to the end of the season. If that happens I'll be really pleased, because then I'll be able to rest it over the summer. Then, during what will almost certainly be my last ever summer of pre-season training, I'll not overdo it and put too much strain on my foot in the run-up to the season, having learned the hard way from what happened this season. I won't run on hard ground, just on soft sand, and do a lot more cycling instead of running. It's strange that I'm already thinking about pre-season training for next season and it's only January, but that's the way I need to plan it with these jabs. Everyone always talks about only thinking about the next game and taking each one as it comes. In actual fact, that's not always the case – especially if you're a bit of an old git like me. In fact, during the next pre-season I felt so good I forgot it all and in the first week of the sand dunes I was second fastest in the whole club after Gary 'the Machine' Stevens. So much for 'good' intentions.

*George*: That's something that showed up in the research on the personality of players that Stephen Smith and I carried out: the older the player, the greater that player's inclination to be a planner, to think ahead. Maybe the younger professionals really *do* take each game as it comes and don't *want* to look too far into the future, given some of the uncertainty and unpredictability in the game that we have already discussed.

*Pat*:      I was listening to Steve Redgrave recently and he was
            discussing people who are very successful in sport,
            how they tend to be very competitive risk-takers. I see a
            lot of that in football, and it's definitely easier to take
            risks if you're young, if you're footloose and fancy-free.
            As you get older and the responsibilities of having a
            family begin to take over, it's harder to be quite as
            impulsive.

            That may sound like an over-simplification, but cer-
            tain memories really bring it home to me. I remember
            going to see Kenny Dalglish when he was just breaking
            into the Celtic side and he was such an outstanding
            player. He was supremely arrogant, not in the sense of
            boasting but in the audacity of what he would try and
            the self-confidence with which he went about it. If he
            failed at something, if something went drastically
            wrong, he wouldn't care – he'd just try something
            equally audacious. Of course, he had all the other
            qualities that go with being a great player as well, but it
            was his sense of adventure, the fact that he'd always
            try the unexpected, that really struck me.

            I tell people that now and they look at me quizzically,
            as if they don't really believe me. What they saw in
            Kenny's later years as a player was pure, calculated
            brilliance, but importantly it was *calculated*. They didn't
            see the devil-may-care attitude that characterised his
            early days at Celtic. So even with a player of the talent
            of Kenny, the risk-taking tapered off as he got older and
            his approach became much more planned and precise.

            After experience, one of the most important factors
            here is coaching. Coaches generally don't encourage
            players to do outlandish and outrageous things – it
            makes them much harder to coach. So players learn.
            They become less impulsive, but sometimes that's sad
            because it may make them less exciting to watch.

*George*:   I wonder if maybe we're seeing some of that with Eric
            Cantona this season?

*Pat*:      That's certainly possible. I wonder how true it is of
            other professions that risk-taking declines with age?

*George*:　It's certainly true that, generally speaking, younger people are more inclined to be impulsive. In the office, this might manifest itself in more junior staff having a lot of fresh ideas or being particularly vocal in meetings. As time goes on, they might find that their ideas are not adopted or their contributions not encouraged, and their devil-may-care enthusiasm is 'knocked out of them' a bit. It sounds a bit cynical, but I'm sure an element of that goes on. Fear of failure may become a stronger driving-force. The fear that taking too big a risk could cost you your promotion, maybe even your job, becomes an overriding one.

*Pat*:　It's this that is my only gripe with Danny Baker. He understands the heart and soul of the football fan so well, and I've been an admirer of his for many years, but he is always so hard on players who are older. He knows deep down the kind of pressures they're under, he appreciates that it's harder for them to go hell-for-leather at their age, yet he gives them a lot of stick. There are some players, of course, who will keep taking the risks. Eric Cantona is one I would have nominated, but as you mention, even he's been quieter this season. Maybe even he is being affected by the British trend for playing a 'safer' game.

*George*:　Gazza maybe? Perhaps that's why he and Danny are such good friends. [*Danny Baker is no stranger to risk-taking from his own point of view. Despite being no spring chicken, his impulsivity in delivering his show on Radio 5 Live, characteristic perhaps of younger performers like Chris Evans, particularly the risk he took in speaking out against the quality of refereeing in the Premiership, was to lose Baker his job with the BBC later in the season. As a risk-taker himself, it's probably not surprising that he admires this in players.*]

*Pat*:　There's an analogy with musicians. Young bands are raw and energetic. They take risks with their music because they don't know what they're doing. There's a greatness about them because they're so natural. Unfortunately, so often these bands settle into a formula, and

it's not a million miles from what happens to footballers.

*George*: They become the Premiership equivalent of . . .

*Pat*: U2!

*George*: Or even Paul McCartney!

*Pat*: Precisely. It's a learning process, too. The risks don't
come off that often, so you go with what is more likely
to work, and you end up playing safe. You can't play
like Brazil all the time and get away with it.

*George*: As many managers have found out. Ossie Ardiles,
obviously. Kevin Keegan too, in the end.

*Pat*: But I love all that youthful exuberance and sense of
adventure. That's why I like new bands – especially
seeing them live. Ninety-nine per cent of the time, my
favourite musicians are under 24 at any given time. The
footballing equivalent of exciting new bands are most
likely to be found nowadays among the African nations.
That's where you'll currently see youthful exuberance
at its most brilliant. When England beat the Cameroon
side in Italia 90, it was the most disappointed I have
ever been with a result in my life. I was close to tears
watching that. And it wasn't an anti-Englishness – it
definitely wasn't! If England had lost, there would have
been a little bit of smirking from the Scots boys,
obviously, but it was an appreciation of the pure, joyful,
naïve brilliance with which the Cameroons played.

So it does sadden me a bit when I see older players
not acting quite as impulsively as they did when they
were at their young, brilliant best, but I accept it. After
all, it's happened to me to an extent! However, with my
contract safe till the end of my career, and the feeling
that John Aldridge may not keep me long in the team
anyway, I can now afford to start doing more out-
landish, risky things again! I found myself, when playing against Carlisle, doing a set of turns that I hadn't
done since my Chelsea days.

One thing I definitely hate is the idea that complacency must come with age. That isn't true of me, and
I think you won't find it true of many Scottish players.

My work-rate is more intense now than it has ever been. The change in style hasn't been complacency, just more readiness than before to play the percentages.

George: Given that one of the things that may prompt more caution in older players is the sense that their careers are coming to an end, what do you make of ex-players and their attitudes?

Pat: I'll be one myself soon, so I'd better take care in answering, but a lot of what I see is very depressing. I see these players who I remember from their heyday and I often wish they didn't talk. In fact, I frequently wish they were invisible, because they now look very different to the way they did – they have acquired that distinctive 'ex-player' shape. There are exceptions, but a great many look back at their playing years and you realise that *that is all they've ever had. That is all their life was.* The rest of their life has been quite pallid by comparison – the playing was the only thing that was *real* to them. There are plenty, of course, whose subsequent living is based on reminiscing about the period in which they played.

George: It's always the same names, isn't it? George Best, Stan Bowles, Frank Worthington, Alan Hudson . . .

Pat: A lot of these people are continually reliving their life in the game, keeping it going by hankering back to it . . . again and again and again and again . . .

George: I suppose there aren't many jobs where people retire in their thirties, where, if you're still playing in your late thirties, like Peter Beardsley or Gordon Strachan, you're considered an old man – indeed, if you're a goalkeeper in your forties, you're considered old beyond anyone's wildest comprehension.

Pat: There's that aspect to it. There is also the contrast between the excitement of the game and the fact that few things can measure up to that. It's a bit like people who continually go on about the war, people who might have had a 'good war'. They can't stop talking about it. It was their finest hour. The same is true of many an ex-player recounting his career. It was making a difference, being part of something bigger. I do understand the reasons for it.

*George*: It comes back to your sense of identity. Once a soldier, always a soldier. The war may be over, but what you were during the war became so closely identified with you, so much part of you, that you *are* a soldier and you remain one forever. By the same token, once a player . . .

*Pat*: That's definitely true. They watch games now – naturally, reminiscing about the old days, about when the game was 'better'. Maybe there is a need to feel that, because it brings a greater sense of self-worth. There seems to be a need to feel they are still as important as they once were. Sometimes it's as though they are not just watching the game, they are watching life go by, more than taking part in it.

Maybe nothing can ever recapture the thrill of football and maybe nothing can replace the distinct sense of certainty that goes with it: the fact that there are clear-cut winners and losers. There is a structure to football with everything in black and white, no shades of grey. At the end of every week, you've either managed to get a result or you haven't. Real life and real jobs are more complicated and less precise. I'm always reminded of the old jailbird in *The Shawshank Redemption*. He hangs himself because there are no certainties for him on the outside. There is no place for him and he has little understanding of the world. Of course, we don't despise him – we pity him, though not in a patronising way.

*George*: I hate to single out Alex Ferguson for praise, but I remember him saying, in a reflective moment, that it wasn't religion that was the opium of the masses in football – it was nostalgia.

*Pat*: And nostalgia isn't what it was! Exactly. I don't want to sound as though I'm knocking all these ex-players, because I can understand how they feel. It has been a very real fear of mine since I was 17 that I'm going to end up like that, that 20 years down the line that'll be me. That's why I've tried to find other strings to my bow. Even at the age of 17, when I was first entering the professional game, I had seen the sadness of these people. I very much hope that the attitude I take, which is a determination to be different from what I have seen, will mean that I don't end up just watching games and making negative, bitter and jealous comments about them.

*George*:  It's interesting to observe people just on the edge of that change from player to ex-player. It's almost as if they have started trying out their after-dinner speeches early, so they can be completely polished by the time they are needed.

*Pat*:  I think players can get dragged into that a bit. A good example of how to sidestep that is often provided by Gary Lineker. Others are always going on about his playing career, especially on *They Think It's All Over* and *Football Focus*, and you get the impression sometimes that he would rather not keep reliving it, but would prefer to talk about something else. He will often quietly change the subject in a subtle way and start talking about other players.

The players that make me feel most sad are the ones I have very fond memories of, ones I watched play and really admired. I suppose, like most fans, I only want to see them through the idolising eyes of a starstruck child.

Certainly, for current players, it's never a good idea to look back. Don't dwell on past triumphs. The minute you start doing so, it's almost like an admission to yourself that you've begun to lose it. Even though I'm coming to the end of my career, I have plenty of plans for what I want to do next. You've got to have that, you need fresh challenges. The minute you run out of those, you start to grow old, and that's really what I'm trying to say here: some ex-players grow old too soon by living in the past, when they should be enjoying the present and looking to the future.

*George*:  Do you think that when you're 40, people will still come up to you and say: 'You're Pat Nevin, *the footballer*!'

*Pat*: I hope not. I really hope not. I wouldn't want that to be me. At 40, I'm no longer going to be a footballer. I'm going to be something else.

*George*: The evening after our last meeting, I went to the British Psychological Society's conference in Blackpool and I went to see *Evita* with my mate Chris Clement. There's a classic line in it when she's on her tour of Europe, drumming up support for Peron's regime. She's in post-war Italy and they're shouting and throwing things at her, because they have just got rid of Mussolini and see Peron as another fascist. She's exasperated by all this and laments: 'They called me a whore! They actually called me a whore!' But a dignitary accompanying her points out that people still call him an Admiral and he hasn't been to sea for years! Maybe that's what it's like when you're a player. You're stuck with the label forever.

*Pat*: Perhaps ex-players *don't* talk about their playing days all the time. Perhaps they have fuller lives and we only ever *see* them talking about the past. All the same, when I've met them away from TV studios, when they are just having a drink in a wee pub or restaurant, they're *still* talking about the same subject! It isn't always their own fault, though. People often seem to want to talk to them about nothing else other than their heyday in the game.

Having said that, through the PFA I do come across a lot of ex-players and many of them have gone into other businesses now. Some of them are physios, some are cleaning windows and others are directing companies. There is a lot of variety out there in terms of what the future holds for ex-players. Those who live sadly in the past are only one section of the larger group that comprises ex-players. I also think that players are getting more sophisticated as people and therefore that players of the future will probably spend less time banging on about the good old days than they do now. Players are not only better-qualified now than ever before but, wages being higher, now have better financial grounding to help them start their post-football futures.

I accept that football isn't a normal nine-to-five job, that it tends to take over your whole life. I understand that. But it should only take it over during your football career – not for ever, not for the rest of your life. It's not fair on your children for one thing. If all they ever get is, 'Oh aye, you're the footballer's kid,' then it can affect them. That's one of the reasons that I'm glad I never played at the highest level in Scotland. Children of players at Rangers and Celtic get singled-out a great deal and have to carry it with them for the rest of their lives.

*George:* Is that why you don't display any football memorabilia in your house, as your children are growing up?

*Pat:* Partly that, but also because my friends would think it incredibly crass. I've given my medals to my Dad, and they're lying somewhere safe that I won't mention. Most of the strips that I've acquired over my career have been given away to charities. The rest are in a black bin-liner somewhere. Other bits and pieces tend to be stuck in the loft.

*George:* That's quite a contrast with a player like Tony Cottee, who keeps a scrap book of all the press-cuttings that mention him.

*Pat:* I remember going along to Tony Cottee's house once. At Everton, we were room-mates. We are very, very different in many ways. He's very much a 'classic' Londoner and in certain ways I'm a typical Scot, or at least a typical Northerner. Our political views are very different. Despite all that, we actually liked one another very much. We respected our differences and had some great conversations.

So I went to his house. It was an enormous and beautiful house. We called it Southfork, after the ranch in *Dallas*. He took me down to the huge snooker-room he had in the basement, and he had all his strips hanging up behind glass – he had all his shorts and socks displayed, too! At the time, I laughed. I said, 'Jeez-o, Tony! This is a bit much, isn't it?' But over time, I have thought to myself that if football is such an important part of your life, then why not? I've read Tony's autobiography and he makes no attempt to disguise how much he loves the game, how incredibly important it is to him. It's a huge part of him. I just don't want it to be quite such a huge part of me!

*George*:    Is it precisely a player like Tony who has most to lose when he eventually retires from the game, someone whose life it dominates so strongly?

*Pat*:        I can see why you would think that, but in Tony's case, I don't think it will affect him too badly. He's got a sharp mind and he's not the kind of player who will start drinking heavily and getting all misty-eyed about the past. But the PFA has opened my eyes to the dilemmas facing some old pros a bit more. Many didn't make a great deal out of the game and came out of it without other skills but with plenty of chronic disabling injuries. Some of them have to look back to the good old days as an escape from some particularly bad old days now. Turning into the cliché of the ex-player has, as I say, been a fear since I was 17, but seeing some of these players – brilliant people, many of them – coming to the PFA for help because they have fallen on hard times has had a deep effect on me.

*George*:    That happened with Danny Blanchflower, didn't it?

*Pat*:        Oh, there are hundreds of them. I could go on all night about the famous and not-so-famous names who have found themselves struggling upon leaving the game. It wasn't all that well-paid in the past, after all.

Most only come to us when they are in really dire financial straits. They feel as if they have had to swallow a lot of pride and go 'cap in hand' to the union, *their* union. Of course, they could not be more wrong – these are the men who made the game great. The memories of them and their abilities are the foundations on which the game has stood for over a century. Without them or their input, the modern players wouldn't earn what they do and the game wouldn't be as popular as it is. The PFA, and indeed football, owes them a debt of gratitude and not vice versa.

*George*: It is important to remember that there are some great former players now struggling in their seventies, as opposed to struggling to get out of *the* seventies, like Alan Hudson and his ilk.

I'd like to expand on another subject that we've mentioned briefly before, but I would like to open up a bit more: keeping the tensions of being a player bottled up and not letting others know how much pressure you're under.

*Pat*: It's integral to the culture of the game that players don't admit to feeling the pressure, that they keep it to themselves. But it does take its toll: I've seen players vomiting with anxiety, either out on the pitch or off it, because they are afraid of being dropped, scared of being transferred, getting a lot of stick in the media, or are just plain nervous. Players will never own up to the fact that these may be the symptoms of stress. They'll say: 'Oh, I've been a bit ill. I've had a virus,' or something like that. It's a bit like being in a family that's too close-knit and gossipy: you're even frightened to tell your best mate in case the manager finds out, thinks you're not coping and drops you. A manager doesn't want a player who can't cope with stress in his team.

If you've seen, early on in your career, that admitting to stress is punished, you're not going to admit it. If you're not taken aside and helped, told that you are not the only one with these fears, I'm sure it can be a bit frightening, especially as everyone else seems outwardly to be coping easily. The opinion that a player 'hasn't got the bottle to cope, so I'm going to have to get rid of him' is one which managers openly espouse. It doesn't do a lot to encourage openness among players, though.

*George*: Perhaps it's not unique to football. I know people who have thrown up because they were so scared of running a difficult training-course. Apparently, Dave Allen does it all the time before coming on to perform, yet once he's sitting there on stage, he seems perfectly urbane and relaxed. He's clearly not letting on about the stress of the job either.

*Pat*: There is definitely that attitude in football. You can show no fear, no concern.

*George*: In a recent piece of psychological research carried out in Scotland, players didn't admit to suffering much stress at all – perhaps some were lying. Only the managers admitted to being under a lot of pressure.

*Pat*: You've *got* to look as though no pressure can get through to you, partly to your team-mates but especially towards your opponents. You must show no fear. Like Dave Allen, you are performing, to some extent. It's not even thought about, because it comes so naturally. That act has to be there all the time. I've seen players who have appeared the most confident people in the world and I've thought I had their personality worked out down to a 't' through playing against them and being involved in certain exchanges with them. Then I've seen them when they're among friends and they're not like that at all, and I've thought: 'Bloody hell! I blew that! If I'd known there was such a weakness of character, I could have put them under a lot more pressure!'

I'm sure that people suffer from stress in every job, but in football, the pressure not to own up to it is much stronger than in many others. There really is the feeling that if you do, you're going to lose your job and you'll never get another contract again.

*George*: The interesting thing is that you can express your emotions very obviously in football – when you score, for example – but only in certain ways.

*Pat*: And only certain emotions.

*George*: It's interesting that in research I was involved with, men and women did not show any difference in their admission of how much they expressed their emotions – they claimed to do it to an equal extent. What we didn't find out, of course, was *how* they expressed their emotions and *which* emotions. That might have shown some interesting differences. It seems players can express certain emotions to their hearts' content, and others not at all.

*Pat*:      I take it that it's a self-perpetuating thing. If you can't express the fact that you're under stress, that there is fear about your career, uncertainty over the future, then that in turn leads to even more stress.

*George*:  Definitely. In a sedentary job, this can lead to many of the physical symptoms of stress, like high blood-pressure, heart complaints, angina and so on. At least in football, there is a physical release for all that. Of course, the fact that if you give up playing and become a manager, there is no longer that sense of physical release, has had a telling effect on the health of people like Graeme Souness.

*Pat*:      People who have survived as players must have some mechanisms for dealing with that stress. The very fact that they have been able to survive in the game for so long suggests that. You don't see many players at the highest level 'losing it', because you need to be able to control 'losing it' in order to reach the highest level in the first place. Those that can't, won't have reached that level anyway. They would have cracked before getting there.

*George*:  There are exceptions. Kevin Keegan eventually left because of the pressure, and he seemed to be coping with it very well until the end of last season. There are certainly those, even among loyal Geordie supporters, who consider him a bit of a wimp for doing so.

*Pat*:      In *Viz* terms, that he's a big puff?

*George*:  Aye.

*Pat*:      It is definitely worse for the manager. I mean, I felt some of what he did at missing out on the Championship and coming so close, because that's been the story with Tranmere Rovers and the First Division play-offs for the last few years. But managers have all the additional pressure, what with the media attention and the expectations of the fans, who all, with the best will in the world, contribute to that. Managers, as you say, haven't got the same opportunities for physical release, and that exertion can be very healing. I suppose there is also the fact that a player is only one of 11 who have to share the blame usually. The manager is sitting up there on his own. Eventually, either you *can't* put up with it or you're *unwilling* to do so. I think Kevin was unwilling to do so.

*George*: What has been the single most stressful time in your career?

*Pat*: Well, we've already discussed some of my feelings recently. I think all the stress comes from wanting to do your best to support your family. Before I had children, it really was pretty free of any pressure at all. I suppose one bad time was when Howard Kendall took over at Everton. He didn't like me at all, and in the space of 12 months I went from the peak of my career to dropping down a division to make a new start at Tranmere. I think even that wouldn't have been so bad if I hadn't had small children to support, though. My son was only one at the time. That was a new situation I'd never encountered before, so that made it more stressful, too. Up until then, I could have walked away from the game. Then, for the final year of my contract at Everton, out of favour with the manager, I was stuck at the one point in my playing career when I *couldn't* walk away, though I probably wanted to for the first time. I was really hating it at that point, the unfairness of it, but I needed the money for my family. I also hated the fact that, for a short time, I was primarily doing this job for the money. Happily, it didn't last long and with the move to Tranmere, I was soon playing for pleasure again.

As soon as I started at Tranmere, the stress disappeared. I signed a longer-term contract. I had enough money to get by on, there was security in it, the joy was back and I felt very comfortable again.

*George*: And now?

*Pat*: Well, I went through a bad patch, which I told you about, but that wasn't really the stress of football – that was the stress of life. People sometimes forget that if a player is under stress, it may not come directly from the pressures of the game itself, but from outside. That's true of any job. There is, however, a certain fear around Tranmere at the moment, because everyone knows the money is really tight. There are players scared that Tranmere might get rid of them and they'll have to move to another club. There are other players scared that if Tranmere get rid of them, they'll never play football again. And there are players scared that they won't get that move to Arsenal that they wanted, and they'll have to stay at Tranmere! I've never been at a club where so many contracts were up for renewal at exactly the same time. It's an odd mood, a huge uncertainty. I've pulled myself together, though. I'm fine now! It really only existed for a very short time, but it was interesting and informative.

*George*:  I'm relieved to hear it . . .

*Pat*:  Another thing that has been occupying my mind has been the Bosman ruling. The PFA met with the Premier League, the Football League and the FA to discuss the implications. All we can really do is suggest an outline, as it's very complex territory from a legal point of view, but we have something along the lines of a Youth Training contract from 16 to 19, a 'young pro' contract from 19 to 21 and a first professional contract from 21 to 24. That will, we hope, be considered a period of training or 'research and development', to use industrial phraseology. At the end of that, the player will be literally free. At the moment, any player is literally free at any age to go to a European club, but not to a UK club. With this new system in place, at 24, a player would be completely free to move from Liverpool to Arsenal or whatever.

We have got to get all the governing bodies in football to go along with this structure. The only stumbling block may be whether the European Court of Justice accept it, which is, of course, where the Bosman case started.

*George*:  Presumably, the clubs are quaking even at the structure

you have suggested. It still means much greater free-
dom of contract for players than ever before.

Pat:     Most certainly. But it isn't recommended that it's intro-
duced at the beginning of next season, but the season
*after*. So they have a year and a half to sort it out. If they
can get a 22-year-old player to sign a six-year deal, then
they'll have him until 28, just as before. The question is
then whether the player is willing to do that. The PFA
doesn't want 19-year-olds signing 10-year contracts for
crap wages. The clubs could have a 27-year-old top
international on their books for £250 a week. As a result,
we would prefer something like five years to be the
maximum length of a contract. This way, clubs have the
security of having their young talent protected and also
valuable to them for a time, while the players are not
kept at the club on unnaturally low wages.

It might take a long time to organise this, but it's
roughly what everyone has agreed to run with at the
moment. Doubtless, it will change a number of times
before we come up with a formula that we hope will be
acceptable to everyone.

Actually, this Bosman stuff has meant that another
important matter was put to one side, which needs a lot
of discussion – but you'll hear about that later!

George:  Well, let's hope it all runs smoothly.

*But it was not to run smoothly. Vinnie Jones, keen to leave Wimbledon
when his contract was up, would make waves later in the season,
causing furrowed brows among football's governing bodies . . .*

# Power, Corruption and Lies

*Although Pat was coming to the end of his playing career, I knew he was very concerned about issues facing younger players in a game that was changing very rapidly. In our next session we were to discuss several of these issues, appropriately enough at a time when a couple of Tranmere's promising younger players were packing their bags, destined for greater things . . .*

George: I understand that the PFA are working on a new package for young players to help them cope with some of the elements that provide pressure in the game, and to stop them turning to drink and drugs for relief?

Pat: Yes. It's a very holistic approach. In the coaching area, we're looking at a lot of different elements that we think it would help young players to know about, and developing a programme accordingly. We're looking to the Dutch, who are famed for their approach to developing young players, for our inspiration, among others. In the wider programme, there will be the obvious things, such as tips on how to deal with the media, but it will go further than that – not just a preparation for professional football as a career, but directions for life itself and how to make your way through it. We'll deal with drugs in the context of many young players' spending-power and time on their hands. Some players do have addictive personalities, so we don't want them going through what Paul Merson did, if we can help it – or being banned from playing, as certain players have recently. There is drink and gambling, which are generally bigger problems for footballers with addictive personalities than drugs, although we're seeing more of the latter. This is, of course, more to do with changing youth-culture than any increased pressures or changing culture within the game. We even go to the point of offering advice about relationships.

*George*: You'll make young people who are not footballers envious! It sounds a very carefully thought-through programme. It sounds unlike any other scheme that has come before.

*Pat*: It's this idea of concentrating on the whole person, rather than just talking about things directly related to football. I've been lucky enough to be treated pretty well by the media and not to be prone to addictions, as we've already discussed, but I can think of many players today who would have appreciated something like this when they were younger.

I saw for the first time how the scheme would work last weekend, and I can't tell you how impressed I was. Our Education Society are behind it and, while I don't use the word 'revolutionary' very often, I really believe this will be a revolutionary move. There's bound to be a bit of reaction from the old school, the 'Bloody hell, lad – it weren't like this when I were a lad! What's all this foreign muck we're bringing in?' brigade, but I'm confident we'll push it through.

The chief executive of the Education Society is ex-player Micky Burns. He and his team have provided a proposal that looks at almost every area. More obvious areas include tutoring on: the laws of the game; sportsmanship; sports science; alcohol; drugs and gambling. There will also be programmes on financial planning, nutrition and diet, media training, the lifestyle of a footballer and how to behave. Some of these areas are already catered for in the current YT programme, but they will be enhanced and expanded. These young players will even be taught on the importance of being good role models, how to deal with the public (who treat them so unusually), various other social skills and even how to positively promote the good image of the game.

*George*: Interestingly, on a related matter, I was phoned up by

Radio 5 Live, who were thinking about doing a programme on psychologists in football. What they had done was to phone every club in the Premier League and First Division to ask if they ever used psychologists to help players with difficulties. Guess how many clubs owned up to doing so? One! Derby County.

*Pat*: Tranmere didn't admit it, then?

*George*: No. I think quite a lot of clubs didn't admit it. It comes back to what you were saying in our last session about the culture of never admitting that you're under pressures, you're struggling. If a club were to admit to using the services of a psychologist, it would be like an admission of vulnerability in the eyes of many in the game. When Dave Bassett employed a sports psychologist called Dr Andy Cale at Sheffield United, to start with, his title was something like 'Player Development Consultant', because it was such a taboo in football. Alex Ferguson has said that whatever happens within his club, he is adamant that no dirty linen be aired outside it. There is no doubt that if any specialists were helping Man United players with personal problems, the outside world wouldn't hear about it.

*Pat*: Well, as I said before, we had a psychologist at Tranmere in an earlier season. I think many clubs have dabbled, even if they don't retain a psychologist full-time.

*George*: I was recently phoned by a Scottish paper, asking me if I knew the name of a psychologist who had apparently gone from Man U to St Mirren. Nobody at either club would so much as acknowledge that the guy existed! I know that not everyone claiming to be a sports psychologist is really a proper psychologist, or even a proper sports scientist, but it can't do much for your self-esteem if clubs aren't even prepared to admit you exist!

*Pat*: Certainly, the PFA wouldn't be averse to putting individual players in touch with psychologists if they were experiencing difficulties.

*George*: I don't think it's all that unusual anymore, and it's not necessarily anything as extreme as drug problems or a feeling that you're cracking up. My colleague Stephen

Smith has seen, for example, players in the middle of a longer-term injury, who just appreciate talking about how they feel to a neutral party, unconnected with their club. It's by no means a surprising thing for a player to do any more – even if they don't talk about it to their team-mates.

Pat:     Football has, for a long time, been stuck in various traditions going back for generations, so any new ideas are still sometimes frowned upon by certain individuals and certain clubs. But things are changing. It's like medicine: things regarded as very cranky 20 years ago are now accepted as options a patient can try. So new ideas, even if they are only allowed to sneak in through the back door, are definitely creeping in. With some of the things being tried, you wonder whether the actual treatment is doing any good in itself, or if it's just a massive placebo effect – but if it works for that player, why not?

George:  Some argue that all that's going on in psychotherapy, despite the highfalutin theories of Freud, Jung, Rogers and so on, even some of the wackier stuff that goes on in Californ-i-a, is that you're just having a chat and getting things off your chest. The same could apply to a trip to Confession or having a chat with your mate in a pub. Social support, whoever it's from, is a great way of releasing stress. Even Alex Ferguson agrees with that.

Pat:     Actually, the West Coach approach to psychotherapy is one of the things that has stopped me moving to the States! I was approached by some American agents with a view to plying my trade in the new US league from this summer. It seems to be growing well over there. In LA, they get crowds of 60,000. The average attendance is 17,000, which is not bad at all for a newly set-up league. Last time they tried football in the States, it didn't work because they tried to build it from the top down, bringing in Pele and all that razzmatazz. Now they're trying to do it from the bottom up, and they're being quite sensible about it. They're capping the salaries, so they don't go bananas, and I think it's certain to succeed this time. I'd say that, in 10 or 15 years, they're going to be winning World Cups. That's the Americans for you!

*George*:   Mo Johnston is over there, isn't he? He's playing for a team called Kansas City Wiz, which must have sounded ideal from the word go . . .

*Pat*:     Yes, and Richard Gough is off there at the end of the season, I believe. I was a little worried that I might be turned over to the psychotherapists if I went, though! Because I'm a bit unusual – and who knows what fads they're into out there in California? – I could see the coaches bringing in all kinds of quacks to examine my eccentric approach to team involvement! There are some very strange influences in certain parts of America and I'd be very concerned who the manager was and what he might be into. Anyway, I'm staying put – for now. I did think about the possibility of Boston, though.

*George*:   Well, 'Cheers' to that.

If football is beginning to look rosy in the States, the same cannot be said for some of the smaller clubs over here. In fact, some are in serious financial difficulty, literally battling for survival. Bournemouth is one and Brighton another, the latter having had a lot of publicity over the determination of its fans – and those of other clubs, with the possible exception of Crystal Palace – that it stay in business. The club is facing relegation, Bill Archer is public enemy number one and not even demi-god Desmond Lynam can fly in like Superman and save the Seagulls. [*At the end of the season, Brighton had survived in the Third Division, playing their final match against Hereford, who were relegated instead. As my colleague Simon Halls, Brighton fan extraordinaire and former tenant of Des Lynam, pointed out, it had been nothing short of a miracle.*] What effect is this having on players at other clubs? Do they sense that this situation could happen anywhere?

*Pat*:     I remember while I was at Chelsea, there were whisperings at various points that the club was about to crash. Ken Bates had basically bought out the debt, a bit like

Terry Venables at Portsmouth recently, when he bought the club for a quid. At Chelsea, there had been this big battle going on for control of the ground between Ken and Marler Estates. There were some very complex financial dealings going on, which I followed to a degree but I eventually lost interest. It was difficult to follow precisely what the truth was, and it certainly depended on which newspaper you read. It began to filter through to the dressing-room and there were some hushed conversations among the players, but I don't think it really got to anyone.

This year at Tranmere, however, there has been an awful lot of talk about the club's financial predicament, to the extent that it is inevitably going to affect the club's ability to keep players on at the end of the season. A player may be coming to the end of his contract and they'd like to keep him on but maybe can't afford to.

This strikes at the heart of all players' fears. The papers recently quoted a figure of £2 million in debt, which for a club of Tranmere Rovers' size seems to be quite a lot. It pales slightly when compared to Bournemouth or Brighton, but we get very small gates, the players can see the club making cutbacks and it makes the players edgy to the point where they're discussing the situation among themselves quite a bit. I have yet to see it have any effect on the field. These things can have a negative effect, but of course they can also have a short-term positive effect by binding the players together, fighting for the cause.

*George*:   A good example of that is Spurs winning the FA Cup in 1991, despite all the backstage financial difficulties the club was having.

*Pat*:       Yes. That 'we're going to fight our way out of this, lads' spirit can do wonders for a team's performance on the field, but it can go the other way and make the players jittery and scared. That leads to mistakes. The real problem kicks in if the club starts having difficulties paying the players' wages on time. From my work with the union, I've become aware that that's not an uncommon thing at all, especially in the summer months when clubs traditionally have a cash-flow problem. The PFA helps out by providing loans over this period. When the players aren't there, they're none the wiser, but if it happens at the height of the season and the players see that the club is having difficulty paying their wages, it affects confidence and the team's performance can go to pieces. That hasn't happened at Tranmere and I hope it doesn't, but individual players, whose contracts are up at the end of the season, are concerned.

The other thing that's often impossible to know is what's real and what's posturing. A club could behave in a certain way because they've got a buyer, or they're trying to entice a buyer. All sorts of things go on behind the scenes. It's not unknown for a club to plead poverty when things are not actually as bad as they seem. It placates the fans and stops them from clamouring for another £2 million to be spent on players. There are a lot of politics involved. I don't know how much other players consider that aspect. Whatever the case, getting knocked out of the FA Cup by Carlisle has had a terrible effect on everyone, not just because of the disappointment of losing away to a Third Division side amid some refereeing decisions that could most charitably be described as hilarious, but because it leaves us in financial dire straits. We could definitely have done with a better Cup run. We knew that had we won, we'd have had Sheffield Wednesday at home in the next round. The income that we could have generated from that is quite extraordinary. It would have been a Sunday game on television, and we'd almost certainly have had a full house as well. That would have made a huge difference to the club's finances.

If John Aldridge hadn't been sent off, then who knows? It was a very poor refereeing decision. Most of the time, the odd bit of swearing just leads the referee to say 'Shut the fuck up!' and leave it at that. Yes, they can send you off for it according to the letter of the law, but very few will. Most realise they are dealing with adults in intense circumstances, not a bunch of naughty schoolkids in a playground. Whole teams could be sent off it they applied the law literally.

The financial implications of a refereeing decision are enormous now. I wonder how many refs actually stop and think about that. (*A refereeing decision later in the season arguably prevented Chesterfield from getting through to the final of the FA Cup.*) A very simple, everyday piece of action by a ref could have a very major impact on the finances of a club. What had us really going up the wall at Tranmere was that the following week, when we were away at Oxford United, we had another player sent off – our centre-half, Dave Higgins – for what was supposedly a professional foul. There were only two people in the ground who were of the opinion that it was a sending-off offence, but unfortunately they were the referee and linesman. Video evidence later proved them wrong and the referee admitted his mistake. The player supposedly brought down had simply fallen. Well, hindsight isn't much good to us. That sending-off turned the game and cost us another three points, even though our player was found innocent.

Then, a week later . . . *I* got sent off! But that's in the Preface. Nevertheless, if you look at it over three matches, you have one dodgy decision taking us out of the Cup and two sendings-off in the subsequent pair of matches, both later quashed. The lost points might be enough to deny us a play-off spot and possible Premier-ship football.

*George*: It's astonishing when you think about it: one non-pro-fessional's decision can have enormous financial impact on a medium-sized club, a club that's a business.

*Pat*: Everyone will tell you that professional football has evolved so much that the margin between success and failure is very narrow anyway. A point or two is all it takes to get promoted or to survive relegation. Often there are negligible differences in points separating many clubs for most of the season. In a climate like that, one refereeing decision can have tremendous weight.

While I'd hesitate to say that it could mean the difference between a club going out of business and keeping
going – though even that is possible – it can certainly
make the difference between a player having or not
having a job at the beginning of a season. This year's
exit from the FA Cup could certainly cost some of my
team-mates contracts with Tranmere next season.

George:   Refereeing errors are always in the spotlight and Danny
Baker lost his job in highlighting one of them this
season, but from what you say, unless the quality of
refereeing improves, the whims of certain individuals
are going to have some very far-reaching effects on the
lives of others.

Pat:   That is already the case. I actually hope that certain refs
are unaware of the impact they're having, because if
they have thought about it and continue to behave the
way that some of them do, they must be very sick and
twisted individuals indeed! Don't get me wrong – I
realise it's a tough job and I admire many of those who
do it, but there are a few with attitude problems. I
remember one very vividly whose trademark after
whistling for a foul was to run backwards a full 30 yards
and then call the player towards him as if to say: 'You
naughty boy. You will walk this way. Wherever I go,
you will follow.' Posing like this is the reason for all
those 'little Hitler' comments. It is totally and utterly
amazing.

George:   What planet are these people from?

Pat:   I could understand the rationale in getting a player
away from an area where there has been a scuffle, thereby defusing the situation, but players can tell when
that's the motive and when it's just being done for
show, to wield a little bit of power – and frequently, I'm
afraid, it's the latter. These people can affect the liveli-
hoods of others probably more than they realise, and
yet they're determined to bask in their moment of glory
and wield authority like some . . .

George:   Jumped-up traffic warden?

Pat:   That's not a bad comparison. I very rarely swear at refs,

but if I'm really angry over a decision one has made, I
may say: 'It's not your fault. You don't *mean* to be inadequate.' I remember listening to a referee bemoaning his
lot on the radio recently, saying what a difficult job he
had, what with 22 people trying to cheat him all the
time. Is that what some of these refs believe – that the
players are only there to cheat and get away with it,
that they are 'the enemy' and must be kept down at all
cost? It's all rather sad.

*George*:  Let's move away from further discussion of referees –
we're only drawing more attention to them! You mentioned, however, that players were worried, that some
are very likely to leave. Now, that can happen because
of a club's financial predicament, but it can happen for
all sorts of other reasons, too. You mentioned already
that sometimes a player largely unnoticed by the fans
leaves a club, and because he's been the 'glue' holding
the side together, the team dynamic deteriorates almost
immediately. What can be the psychological effects of
other kinds of players leaving clubs?

*Pat*:  Things are different at Tranmere from the way they
were at Everton or at Chelsea. There, players would be
sold because the manager didn't rate them or it was
'time to go', but not because they were poached by
bigger clubs and the club could do little about it if they
wanted to keep their heads above water, financially.
That's the position at Tranmere. We have had to sell
players we would rather, if our hearts ruled our heads,
have held onto. Previously, we had lost Ian Nolan, who
has gone on to do very well for Sheffield Wednesday, a
player with whom I had a particularly good understanding on the field, and we had also lost Steve
Vickers, who went to Middlesbrough and has kept his
place in the side. When those two left we had the
strength-in-depth in our squad to deal with it, but now
we have just lost another two players within a couple
of days of one another: Ian Moore, an up-and-coming
centre-forward, and Ged Brannan, a midfielder who
has probably been our strongest player this season. This

time there's no hiding it – the club is weakened by their departure.

George: And how likely is it that more will follow?

Pat:      At the end of the season, it's inevitable. We're not in a position where we want to sell any more, but we have to and that's causing concern to both the players and our manager. It would be particularly crippling for the club if some were to move abroad, because as a result of the Bosman ruling, once they are out of contract with us, the club wouldn't get a bean for them. With players being sold, there is the feeling among some fans that Tranmere's appetite for success might not be as strong as that of some other clubs, despite the reassurances of the manager and chairman. That can get to players, too.

I have to say, the manager handled the two latest departures well. He took the whole side into a room together and explained very fully his decision to allow them to leave. If that's not done, the rumours flow like rivers. Players can be like gossiping fishwives when it comes to rumours about why players leave clubs. You've heard many of them yourself, no doubt.

Well, John Aldridge has enough insight to know how easily rumours can start and he was determined to deal with it honestly. He wouldn't have risked giving us a load of bullshit – we'd have seen through that. He told us that we still had one of the strongest reserve teams around, better than many Premiership ones. They beat Liverpool's and Everton's reserves this year.

George: It certainly sounds better than Newcastle's reserve side, which is nonexistent due to a strange experiment by Kevin Keegan.

Pat:      I'm sure Kenny will restore it. But our manager's point was that we still have strength in depth – he had just dropped me back into the reserves after 10 games to prove it! Shaun Teale is a Premiership-standard defender who can't get a game; Gary Stevens, a 46-game England international, is out of the first team at the moment with injury. Also unable to break into the first team side are John Morrissey, one of the best wingers in the league; Danny Coyne, the Welsh international goalkeeper; and so on. By going through the names, he gave us a boost and reminded us of what talent we had to spare, and it didn't sound calculated – it came from the heart.

I have to say that this is the first time I have been at any club and the manager has made this kind of move to reassure the players about their colleagues leaving. It's very unusual. I suppose that's because at a club like Everton you were never *forced* to lose players – you got rid of them! There's more of a necessity for it at Tranmere, but the manager was certainly sussed enough to spot that necessity. It helped relieve some of the tension. It took delicacy and it was well-handled – probably a key moment for a young player-manager like John Aldridge.

We knew that the crowd would feel their departure, too, and by the next game at home, against Barnsley, you could feel the uncertainty in the crowd, the inkling that it might be the start of the slippery slope. The manager had communicated his views to the fans, too, and I think they were able to tell from our performance that day that there was no loss of passion on our part. If a team is demoralised, the fans can smell it and I think they realised that as far as the players were concerned, it was 'business as usual'. Some fans were angry, there's no doubt about that. But when they saw our commitment in tackling and running ourselves into the ground, I think there was a certain amount of reassurance.

*George*:  I encountered a very similar atmosphere at Brentford, whom I went to see against Watford this season with my friend Matt Goff, who is also very much into the psychology of the game. Brentford had just sold one of the fans' favourites, Nicky Forster, to hated rivals Birmingham City. Manager Dave Webb certainly had some explaining to do, but he managed this quite well through the programme notes – the fans didn't riot. There was still a lot of hostility from the fans, though.

[*Brentford's early form was to nosedive after this, and the club missed out on promotion, losing to Crewe Alexandra in the play-off final.*] Of course, Kevin Keegan took it one step further a couple of seasons ago when he faced the fans on the steps of St James' Park to explain why the club had sold Andy Cole to even-more-hated rivals Man U.

*Pat*: Different managers handle it in different ways, but accountability has increased a lot. People expect information from the club, they feel entitled to it.

In the past, managers wouldn't feel the need to explain their actions. 'Like it or lump it!' was Bill Shankly's view! They'd just say, 'Trust me!' In a sense, that's what Keegan was doing, albeit very publicly. I think that managers have to do even more than that now. People want explanations, they want answers. Fanzines and fan power mean that fans no longer expect to be treated in a childlike manner, but as intelligent adults. I fully agree that fans have a *right* to know what's happening at their club. There's no doubt that fans will get more information. Some of it may be *mis*information – the club may not want them knowing the full truth – but it'll be information of one sort or another.

It was interesting to see the manager giving out information about the Ged Brannan transfer, because it was actually rather delicate and, towards the end of it, had got rather ugly. So he gave the fans a very full picture, but he left certain details out! They didn't get the whole story. But the fact that we wanted him to stay, he was offered a good contract and the club was 'being held to ransom' over the timing of his move all came out. Sometimes it's good that fans don't know everything. 'We have to sell players because we haven't got two pennies to rub together' is not necessarily the message a lot of clubs want to give out, though it's frequently the truth.

*George*: What about players being sold for 'personal reasons': trouble with local gangsters over gambling debts; messy sex-lives; drug problems . . .

Pat:      It does go on. Generally rumours get out, often accurate
          ones, particularly if the club represents a small, close-
          knit community. On the other hand, some are patent
          nonsense. Who *hasn't*, for example, heard a story about
          the circumstances surrounding Peter Beardsley and
          Kenny Dalglish's relationship at Liverpool? I think it's
          widely believed that there wasn't a lot of love lost
          between Peter and Kenny when Kenny resigned as
          Liverpool manager, but some of the reasons that have
          been suggested for it are miles from the truth. I *believe*
          they are, anyway. If people don't get information, then
          the rumours start. They start in the dressing-room. Then
          one player tells one journalist, he tells another, he tells a
          friend and it's in the pubs and clubs by the end of the
          week! There are those in the game – no names! – who
          are a bit facetious and like to start the odd rumour just
          for a bit of a giggle, to see how far it gets. With that kind
          of misinformation floating about, *not* keeping the fans
          informed is just about the most dangerous thing a club
          can do!

George:   But not all the rumours you hear are nonsense?

Pat:      No. But ones I've heard about Beardsley and Dalglish
          almost certainly are. Many of the others have a ring of
          truth about them!

George:   Even if any coldness between Kenny and Pedro existed
          purely for professional reasons – the fact that Kenny
          didn't give him sufficient opportunity to display his
          craft at Liverpool – it surely couldn't have been great
          news for Beardsley when Dalglish was announced at
          Newcastle's new manager?

Pat:      That kind of thing happens a lot in the game. When I
          was leaving Everton, there was a possibility I would go
          to Galatasaray in Turkey. I couldn't get away from
          Howard Kendall quickly enough. At that point, it was
          very much a toss-up between playing in Turkey and
          staying in Britain. I remember the club chairman trying
          to convince me. 'Look over the Bosporus and you know
          you will want to play here!' he said. Well, I replied that
          when I looked over the Clyde, it convinced me that I'd

rather stay in Britain! I should really have said 'Mersey' rather than 'Clyde', given that I went to Tranmere Rovers instead. Still, it's easy to be more clever with hindsight.

Well, within four months, Kendall was being linked with Galatasaray! I remember sweating blood, thinking: 'My God! I came so close to reliving the nightmare of my final year at Everton for a second time!' Poor Andy Hinchcliffe had to face that nightmare for real. He left Man City while Kendall was manager and there was little love lost between them. I'm pretty sure that 'words were exchanged' between the two as Andy left Man City. Well, he went to Everton and then – horror of horrors! – so did Howard Kendall. Naturally, Andy was dropped, but he had the last laugh because he's now an England international, demonstrating beyond reasonable doubt that he *can* play.

I've probably gone on a bit about old Howard. In reality, the bad feeling has gone now and we've had a few chats and even the odd laugh. I realise now that my feelings about him are the same feelings that every player has about at least one manager during his career. It's very normal. It is important to get over it, dispel the bitterness and realise that some managers just aren't going to take to you. The anger probably helped at the time, because it was channelled in the right way, towards showing him I was 'a player'. I didn't want to leave this job holding any bitterness towards it – there have been too many positive things happen in my career to allow any disappointments to leave a sour taste.

George:  Despite the comforting words of managers, how much does it dent confidence, deep down, when a club's best players start leaving?

Pat:  It's another of the oldest clichés in the book that 'the confidence has gone' at a club, because it's so imperative to a side's success. If the manager sees that it has been dented, it's time to press the panic button and try to sort it out. But it's an inevitability. In a club of

Tranmere's size, good players *have* to leave. The same applies to Brentford, to any club outside the Premiership.

The other effect you can spot is when a very gregarious player leaves. I've already spoken about the likes of Gazza and Billy McKinlay and the effect they can have on morale in the dressing-room, even if they're injured themselves. Well, I've come across several others. There was Shaun Garnett at Tranmere, who left for Swansea City, and among the most gregarious of all, a player whose company I really loved, was Peter Beagrie at Everton.

*George*: He of the back-somersault goal celebration?

*Pat*: That's the one. Hilariously funny – most of the time! – and ideal for perking everyone up. It was the same with Shaun Garnett. When he left, you just heard the same phrase over and over again: 'Bloody hell! It's *quiet* around here!' Another player in the same mould was Gary Bennett, who we bought from Wrexham and sold on almost immediately to Preston North End. Again, it went quiet when he left. Players sometimes grow to fill that role when there's no one else to do it – you need it that much. At the moment, I don't think there is a *natural* clown at Tranmere. I mean clown in the likeable sense, the Gazza sense. These players are sometimes unaware of their own importance – sometimes, being aware of their impact would spoil it – and how much they lift the spirit. But dressing-rooms are poorer for their absence. Strangely, there wasn't anyone like that at Chelsea when I was there. We were a fairly serious bunch of chaps. I didn't realise it at the time, because it was my first major club. There wasn't that madness.

*George*: This was pre-Dennis Wise?

*Pat*: Of course. I think when there isn't a player there to create the madness, alcohol might have to be the substitute. We've definitely used that at Tranmere this season when the madness was needed.

*George*: What about individual players' feelings towards colleagues leaving? There must be some ambivalence,

I'd have thought: happiness and excitement for the player about to embark on a new adventure, but sadness that he's off. Some players might even experience jealousy . . .

Pat:  Feelings are strongest if it's a player who has been with the club for years, has come up from the youth side and has a special bond with other players in the same position. There is no doubt that these players look after one another, on the pitch and off, so one of their group leaving is a wrench. That was certainly true of Ged Brannan, who had been with the club for nine years. Not having been at the club that long myself, it was interesting to look round at the faces of the players when they discovered he was going, and see what the reactions were.

The vast majority were really pleased for him, very happy that he was making that step in his career. But I've seen the jealousy over the years, too, and it can be nauseating jealousy. It tends to come from players who feel that they have 'missed the boat', maybe with some justification – maybe they were unfairly overlooked by the scouts from the bigger clubs, or were injured at their peak or whatever; maybe they just weren't good enough, or as good as they thought they were. They hold that jealousy in and find it very difficult to conceal.

In Ged's case, I was probably the first player to voice my feelings about it to him. We were in the coach, heading back from the Wolves game, and it was announced that he could be leaving us for Man City. I told him I was very disappointed that he was going because he was such an important part of the team, a very good player. But saying it was actually unnecessary from one point of view: everyone was thinking it and I think Ged knew it. I thought it was right to voice it, though, and I think players like to hear it said. They don't have to wonder whether they were respected and valued when someone comes out with it. The first things players tend to think of are the readies and the new house and so on, but I think that when Ged looks back in a few weeks' time, he'll appreciate how much we valued him at Tranmere.

You sometimes get another reaction when a player goes – again, typically from the old school – which is: 'Right! Bugger him! He's not one of my mates any more!' I'd suggest there's something of that in the old Liverpool way: there's no room for emotion over this, let's just get on with it. That definitely still exists at a lot of clubs and with a lot of individuals. At Tranmere, though, elation for the departing player was the pre-dominant emotion, which may surprise people outside the game, but there is very little sadness at the depart-ure. In the end, we're all going the same way, we all want to make it to the top, and if one of us gets a step nearer, that's a cause for celebration.

Having said that, if another couple of Ged's con-temporaries were to leave, you really would find the rest of that 'nucleus' who grew up in the game together, the couple that were left, who hadn't moved onwards and upwards, feeling a little bit naked. Then they can go one of two ways: curl up within themselves, becom-ing less of a person and certainly less of a player, or grow more independent and stronger as a result, which is what you'd hope.

George:   Are there any other issues that affect young players today that you think we should talk about?

Pat:   Well, there is all the business about managers accepting bungs. I had just agreed to take on the role of PFA chairman when these bung allegations first exploded, in what the press dubbed 'The Season of Sleaze', i.e. 1994–95. It's certainly not the case that those in the modern game accept that bunging goes on and turn a blind eye to it. I can understand fans feeling angry about it, as it's ultimately their money that clubs are wasting, but it angers players, too, and especially young ones. If a British manager gives a large oiling-fee to a middleman or – perish the thought – accepts a huge 'gift' from an agent as part of a deal, suggesting that he might have paid over the odds for certain players, then young British players are entitled to feel angry about it and many do. It usually means that an East European player or a Scandinavian player ends up at a club which could have bought a British player or developed one for the same money or less. So the clubs lose money which originally came from the pockets of the fans, and players in this country end up getting overlooked simply because certain agents and managers have got a bit greedy.

Imagine having a team-mate who has cost your club a lot of money and, at the back of your mind, you're asking whether he was really bought because he is an outstanding player, or if it was just to line the pockets of certain individuals. It's not fair on that player's team-mates, let alone on the player himself. I've had several players tell me what an infuriating and sickening feeling it is to have worked for 20 years and done your best to succeed in the game, and end up losing your place in a team to a player who is inferior to you and has been bought to swell the bank-balance of the manager. Very few bungs have been proved, others will probably go unproved for ever, but quite a few players have a right to feel aggrieved. Certainly, where an individual has been shown to be involved with bungs, his reputation among players in the game can turn to mud overnight. A player would even be within his rights morally to sue a manager in those circumstances. After all, his livelihood might have been affected, he might have been forced to move house, uproot his whole family, all because a manager wanted to make a few bob – a few hundred thousand bob, in fact.

It is even worse when the work-permit system is considered. Foreign imports have to play two-thirds of all games. The rule exists to provide a check against the import of cheap foreign labour. It works well usually, but occasionally it backfires because it means that even if the foreign players are playing dreadfully, they get a game. The situation arises because, if you are a manager and you have spent a fortune on a player, then decided that he's rubbish and that you're going to drop him after five or six games, you can't because the club's directors are going to say: 'Hey! Steady on! We paid a mint for this player! We must give him the opportunity to perform – even if it's only to fulfil the criteria of the work-permit.' Thus, even if the player is crap and the British footballer battling for his place is playing like Maradona, it is: 'Hard cheese, local lad!'

Some have suggested that those within the game have been soft on those who have admitted accepting bungs. All I can say is that in my experience, the anger towards them within the game has been incredible. As for Grobbelaar, Fashanu and Segers, we've had a hung jury and their case is going to retrial. Most players I know are accepting a 'wait and see' position, though they might harbour their own private thoughts. If they get off, their fellow professionals will stand by them. If it turns out that they really threw matches for personal profit, or even conspired to do so, people will be fuming, as it would have struck at the whole ethos of the game. It would reflect very badly on other players, as people assume guilt by association – everyone tends to be tarred with the same brush.

*George*:  If they're found guilty, it looks like they'll be tarred and feathered by their fellow pros! But, being honest, did you ever hear rumours of match-rigging during your time as a player?

*Pat*:  No, never once. I was as shocked as many fans when the *Sun* first made its allegations about Bruce Grobbelaar. As I've said, footballers can be like fish-wives when it comes to gossip. I felt sure that if any of this had been going on, I'd have got to hear about it. Word gets through. People talk. Even someone who's a bit of an outsider like me would have known. So all the surprise within the game is not some kind of PR job – it really has surprised people. I was actually commentating on the game between Wimbledon and Everton when Segers let that dodgy goal in, keeping Everton up and relegating Sheffield United. At the time,

I remember saying, 'He's really blown that! That was *hopeless.*' It never crossed anyone's mind that it might have been deliberate.

These allegations have been hanging over these players – and over football as a whole – for a very long time, and continue to do so, given that the jury couldn't agree at the trial. Every single national newspaper and TV station had phoned me on the day when the verdict was due to be announced, because they wanted me, as chairman of the PFA, to comment on the outcome. When it was announced that it was a hung jury, the phone remained quiet, which I was actually quite relieved about.

We might have to tighten up the rules about players gambling on matches in which they themselves play. A lot of people perhaps don't realise that that gambling actually goes on a great deal. Players might have 'inside information', too. They might have agreed that their goalie is going to take the first penalty in the game – but the bookies don't know that! You can get fairly long odds on the keeper scoring the first goal! It is suggested that players do not bet on matches at all.

*George*: My mate James Terrill, who works at William Hill, will be sweating as he reads this bit. For what it's worth, he's never heard of any allegations of deliberate match-rigging, either.

*Pat*: I think the law has to be more stringent on that side of things. At the PFA and in the other organisations, we have taken it very seriously and have done as much as possible to stop the practice of any players betting on any matches at all.

*George*: It's interesting that snooker players regularly bet against themselves as a form of insurance policy, apparently. It makes you wonder why Lou Macari never took up the game! In the States, betting on sports events is completely illegal, isn't it? I think it all goes back to when certain players in the Chicago White Sox, including the legendary 'Shoeless Joe' Jackson, were accused of throwing the world baseball series for money.

*Pat*:     That's true. It's not unheard of in football that clubs facing relegation will bet on themselves getting relegated as a form of insurance cover. That certainly goes on in the game, too.

*George*:  Well, let's just hope that, however it's resolved, the image of football is unscathed by all these allegations. I wouldn't bet on it, though.

# Great Expectations

---

*Injuries continued to dog Pat's game. As the final month of the season dawned, it had been a far from fulfilling year . . .*

Pat: Looking back on it, this has been one of the two least satisfying seasons of my career, the other having been my final one at Everton when I wasn't getting on with Howard Kendall. The main reason this season has been a disappointment is all the injuries I've sustained. I hope it won't sound like I'm bleating on about this too much, but for the first time in my career, injuries have been the dominant theme of the season, so they've been cropping up a lot in the book as well.

My position in the first team took a knock when we played against Oldham. My place in the first team had been looking quite secure for a couple of months until then. I'd had 12 or so games and things weren't going badly, but in that match I did something I don't normally do. After making a goal in the first minute, I had a quiet 45 minutes, because it was one of those very tight games where the ball hardly touched the ground. The atmosphere was very frenetic and I made a conscious decision to play something of a 'percentage game', keeping up a defensive grind but deciding to save my really sharp, energetic play until later in the game, when I thought things would open out. I felt that Oldham would tire and spaces would open up. This was a bad mistake – it got me substituted! Of course, the game *did* open out afterwards! The player who came on in my place had huge amounts of space and scored within a minute, making me look even worse! Tranmere played well and won, and I was pleased about that, but unfortunately I wasn't on the pitch to be part of it.

The manager didn't say another word to me but by the next game, which was against Wolves, I wasn't even on the bench. He had seen that I had had a quiet game and punished me for it. That's what happens when you try to play 'intelligently' – it wasn't all that intelligent a tactic for me after all! Two days afterwards, on Monday, my family were ill. I didn't attend training, but being a nice and – I hope – caring, dedicated chap, I made sure that my family were resting comfortably and went out on a run. Another bad idea. I pulled my calf muscle. Sometimes I wonder if I'm just being stupid with this dedication lark.

Anyway, I was out for four weeks with that. I did come on briefly in one game, but then pulled it again within five minutes and had to go off. And that's been the end of my season, really. The odd game here or there, interspersed with injuries. I suppose it happens when you get to my age. But that doesn't make it any less infuriating.

To rub salt into the wound – metaphorically – Tranmere then took Lee Jones on loan from Liverpool., who not only plays in my position but played wonderfully from the moment he joined us. He has made a big difference to the team and I wish him well. For me, however, it was like stepping on a snake when playing Snakes and Ladders. I'd had some very good games this season, scoring a few goals, getting a few Man of the Match awards, but here I was, back at square one.

George:  What are the emotions you experience when a player who plays in your position is bought by the club you play for?

Pat:  It's happened to me at Chelsea, Everton and now Tranmere. At Chelsea it was Roy Wegerle and at Everton it was a Polish international called Robert Warzycha. It's definitely a strange feeling, and one I've talked to lots of players about. Obviously, they get paranoid. There's the feeling that 'the manager can't rate me because he's buying someone to replace me'. It's a natural fear and, most of the time, probably well-founded. Naturally, having bought a new man, the manager is under pressure to play him. The strange thing is, though, I've always enjoyed the challenge. I know it sounds a very peculiar reaction, but it's true.

These purchases have helped me crystallise where it is I'm going and, if needed, reintroduced a bit of fighting spirit. The first was Roy Wegerle, who is one of the most exceptionally talented players I've ever known in my life, and has also been a good mate over the years. The first day he trained, he ran down the line and did this brilliant turn, something I could never do. As well as demonstrating that, when it came to speed he was like lightning. He was just *obnoxiously* talented: he was like a rocket, brimming with skill and possessing a thunderous shot – and the bugger was good-looking too.

For about two days, I remember thinking he was so good that he put me to shame, that I'd better get a transfer straight away. I'd always prided myself on my skill, but he had much more of it. Then it occurred to me that I had other things that contributed to my game which helped me, too – my physical fitness, strength and stamina, and also my mental strength. At the same time, I began to notice one or two weaknesses in his game. Admittedly, in Roy's case, there were only one or two, but not having played at the highest level before, there was a bit of naïveté about his game and one or two other little chinks in his armour. As soon as I'd spotted them, the attacking spirit possessed me and although we were friends, the competition between us was very intense. It teaches you to play to your strengths. If others can do certain things better than you, you end up determined to capitalise on the things that you do better than *them*. In the end, Roy didn't get my place at Chelsea – I was able to hang onto it. I did, however, enjoy playing in the same team with Roy. We actually built up a bit of an understanding on the field.

*George*:  Psychologists talk about 'halo effects', which are part-

icularly evident in a lot of job interviews. The interviewer likes certain things about a candidate and these
things take on a disproportionate significance, allowing
the interviewer to think that the candidate is wonderful,
and hiding any faults he or she may have. Perhaps the
same thing is going on here: you only see the good
things at first, such as the speed and the skill in turning.

Pat:     You're perfectly right. Absolutely spot on! I hadn't come
across the phrase 'halo effect' at the time, but I had
definitely allowed myself to be blinded by certain
shining aspects of his make-up, and it definitely took
me a while longer to find the weaknesses. Since then, at
the various clubs I've been, there have been dozens of
players brought in whose position approximates to my
own, but I haven't panicked since Roy at Chelsea. They
always start well, usually scoring in the first couple of
games – that's practically tradition – but you soon start
to spot the faults, the little chinks. They have talents
that you may not possess, but that cuts both ways.

With Robert at Everton, which was in my fourth year
with the club, he was like the Bionic Man in his first
game – his pace was breathtaking. I remember a couple
of journalists telling me that I'd better pack my bags,
the writing was on the wall for me. But by that time, I
wasn't fazed. I was quietly confident that I was a better
player. Sadly, Robert didn't survive in the British game.
I think his strength was almost entirely pace, and that
wasn't enough. If players dropped five or ten yards off
him, he was much less effective. Adapting to the culture
might have had an effect, too.

Now, Lee Jones at Tranmere looks *brilliant*. Really
brilliant. There is no other word. As with Roy, in the
end my biggest ambition would be not to wrestle my
place back off him but to play *alongside* him. Because
I'm versatile enough to play in a number of positions,
that may become possible and I think it would be a
wonderful experience. I think we'd complement one
another really well and it would really bring out the
best in both of us. That's happened with Ivano Bonetti

to some extent, who, again, plays in a very similar position to my own. He hasn't had many games this season, but I don't think it's always been his fault. There has been a bit of a personality clash with the manager. Or more precisely a culture clash that just couldn't be patched up.

Eventually, you have to give in to it. Eventually, I'll be so old that someone will come in and they really will be a better player – and it'll be time to call it a day and ride off into the sunset. Next year, probably!

George: What about the manager's season?

Pat: I think John Aldridge would tell you himself that he's learned a lot this season, and that next season will really be the one that will test his mettle. After stepping back from the players a bit and not going to the races with them, he's recently taken a bit of a step forward to be more part of the group again. In fact, he went to the Grand National with them, but he didn't see much racing because of the bomb scare. I think you do have to distance yourself from the game a bit, though, and he might do that by playing less – there have been some indications of that this season – or just by enjoying a long holiday to take stock. Being such a legend on Merseyside, I think he's got a longer period of grace than most managers, but he knows that in the next season or two, his performance will be under great scrutiny.

After all, look at Everton. Whoever thought that they'd sack Joe Royle? He's won an FA Cup and a Charity Shield with them, but that's not enough for the board nowadays. Look at Tommy Burns at Celtic, sacked at a time when the club was still in with a mathematical chance of beating Rangers to the Championship. He was arguably too nice to be a manager. Boards have no patience at all any more. If Alex Ferguson had gone to Manchester United today and had had the results he did when he first started there, he would have been sacked within two years. Now he's one of the most successful managers in the game. It makes you think. If most clubs had the conviction to stick by their original decisions and give their managers a reasonable amount of time to turn around what is, in effect, a fairly large organisation, they would have progressed further, quicker.

*George*:  Have expectations in the game today just totally lost touch with reality?

*Pat*:  There are several sets of people whose expectations you have to consider. At the base of it all, there are the fans, and here a club like Everton illustrates very well how high the expectations have become. They won the FA Cup not long ago and yet their supporters consider them to be very unsuccessful at the moment – in fact, they are fuming. I went there in 1989 when we were beaten 3–2 in the FA Cup final – in extra-time by a great Liverpool team – and it was made clear to us in no uncertain terms that we should consider ourselves failures. That came as a shock to me. There are very few clubs in the land that would have that attitude, that reaching the FA Cup final and finishing fifth or sixth in the league was a failed season.

In the mid-eighties, they had a fantastic run, they're considered one of the original 'Big Five' football clubs, though that's clearly an anachronistic label these days, but even so . . . I was taken aback that anyone should assume that an FA Cup final place for their team is bordering on a right. There is the fact that they can see Liverpool's ground just by looking across the park. Because of its proximity, Anfield has become the benchmark for what they feel should be achieved at Goodison Park.

All these expectations come from the fans in the first place, but these are then transferred to the management and coaches and, of course, to the players, so all these groups of people end up infecting each other with inflated expectations. On top of that, of course, are the expectations of impatient chairmen and, increasingly these days, shareholders. However, the chairman and shareholders rarely have any direct effect on the players.

*George*: And being infected with inflated expectations can be very painful! Living up to them can be little short of impossible.

*Pat*: At Everton, the *players* expected to win the FA Cup! Can you believe that? *Anything* can happen in the FA Cup: look at Chesterfield! Who would have predicted a Chelsea v Middlesbrough final this year – or any final, any year? Yet that was the expectation. If Everton enter a competition, they really think they are going to win it from day one. Just getting to the final isn't nearly good enough.

I've played in teams that were no worse than that Everton side – but they certainly didn't carry that weight of expectation around with them, and that may well have been the biggest reason why they didn't get there. But the Everton players had real self-belief. While they were winning, that expectation worked for them, rather than making them nervous. It was only after they failed to meet up to that expectation that things got bitter. If delusions of your own invincibility can get you into extra-time in the FA Cup final, who's to knock them? I realised that what I had taken to be empty boxing clichés, along the lines of 'If you don't think you're gonna win, you won't,' actually had a lot in them. The club's most recent FA Cup win wasn't down to being the best side in the land – I don't believe they were at the time. It was all down to that expectation. If being unrealistic helps you, then roll with it!

It wouldn't be true to say I hadn't encountered that attitude before. As I was growing up, it existed at Celtic Boys' Club. It was very much a case of: 'You won every match this season and won the Cup for the Under-Whatever. Next season, you're going to do exactly the same!' And again, it generally happened, so it was ingrained in me. I remember at times, early in my professional career, finding it difficult playing with players who didn't share this attitude. They accepted defeat slightly more easily, more rationally than I did. By then, it was alien to me to accept defeat.

I was up in Glasgow talking to Celtic fans recently, and although I'm very passionate myself, I've not been as close to it as I would like for a while. I couldn't believe how hostile they were towards Tommy Burns. He had to go in the end because the fans demanded it. Tommy will handle it, though, because he was brought through the same Celtic Boys' Club tradition that I was. Though disappointed, he will understand that not winning the league was not good enough. Even though there were some powerful external, extenuating circumstances – such as David Murray's massive bank-balance being at the disposal of Walter Smith. Does that sound bitter?

*George*:   Not at all! Tommy actually spoke to me for my previous book and I have to say that compared to his predecessors, Lou Macari, Liam Brady, and even Billy McNeill in his second spell as manager, Celtic had much more success under him. Not so long ago, in the club's 1993 annual, they were celebrating having won the Tennents Sixes. That's what the club had fallen to! At least they won the Scottish Cup under Tommy. Not enough, though, as you say. They had to prevent Rangers from getting their nine Championships in a row and they failed. It's the same with Everton – before Joe Royle took over, Mike Walker had nearly taken them to relegation. It was only Hans Segers' dismal goal-keeping that saved them. Fans should judge on the baseline at which a manager started. That would be the rational thing to do. Mind you, whoever said we fans were rational?

*Pat*:        I feel very sorry for Tommy, because I like him very much. Fans' views are now so incredibly short-termist that they seemed to forget how far he had taken the club – with a little help from Fergus McCann's investment. They are now right up to Rangers' coat-tails. In the early nineties, as you say, they were nowhere near them.

It was drummed into me at Celtic Boys' Club that you have to put *yourself* under pressure to win. You expect to win yourself, making losing unacceptable. As I have said, I'm not sure whether all the players at Chelsea and Clyde shared that view. In fact, the person who carries that view most strongly at Tranmere is our player-manager, John Aldridge, because I'm sure that the old Liverpool way was very much the old Celtic way. The most important years of his playing career were those at Liverpool, without a doubt, and the club's traditions have affected him in quite a short space of time, given that he played for other, smaller clubs before and since.

Now, the problem for those of us who think that way is that we won't allow ourselves to accept defeat. We're only tuned to expect victory after victory. So if we are playing and are 1–0 down in the 89th minute, we still can't accept that we're going to lose. There's nothing contrived about that – it's deep in our hearts. Thus, when the whistle blows and it's still 1–0 and we've lost, my maturity and my sense of balance have to kick in very quickly if they are to override my sense that we shouldn't or cannot lose.

It's an extraordinary dilemma, and it's why you see so many players and managers getting angry and 'losing it' after a match – even attacking their team-mates in the tunnel sometimes. To tune your mind to one attitude for the whole week and then to have to accept what has been unacceptable, in the time it takes to blow a whistle, is almost impossible. The frustration after putting so much into it physically and emotionally is hard to control. Any loss is an injustice – and if there were one or two questionable refereeing decisions, as there always are these days, it makes it even worse.

Players go home and have a rotten evening, week-end, week . . . So do the fans.

*George*: One very clear illustration of that was the Newcastle fans in tears after missing out so narrowly on the Championship last season. You have to have been in that position to empathise, really. Some of my mates bottled it up, but it was still affecting them well into the summer holiday.

Pat:     I know what you're saying. It's an issue for the fans, too. You have these two competing stresses. On the one hand, you *have* to win, you need to win, it's imperative. It's more important than life and death, as Bill Shankly suggested. But on the other hand, it *is* only a game. There will always be losers. Far worse things happen than missing out on the Championship. The Hillsborough disaster really brought that home.

So there are these two conflicting pressures, attitudes, drives – and both, in their own way, are right. It's what makes managers scrunch up on the bench in an almost foetal posture, it's what makes fans cry, it's what causes players to kick lumps out of one another in the tunnel on the way back to the dressing-room. It's very hard to reconcile these two forces. You are like Jekyll and Hyde. It's certainly not a good idea to be interviewed when you're trying to bridge that gulf in your mind between having had to win and not having won, but life going on. I think Kevin Keegan was captured just at that moment in the famous interview when he blew his top with Alex Ferguson.

George:  At a club level, it's been terrible from that point of view for Wimbledon. They came so close to glory this season in both cups and even stood a chance of getting a European place from their league position, but they missed out narrowly on everything. That must be crushing.

Pat:     It is. A number of managers have been in that position. It's a consequence of having too many irons in the fire. Look at Alex Ferguson, asking to have the season extended because it looked as though Man U would be snowed under with playing commitments. Well, they lost to Borussia Dortmund, so that was either the problem out of the way or else it was the effect of the problem. But did you notice Alex's expression when Wimbledon put them out of the FA Cup? I watched him carefully at the interview afterwards, and I wouldn't say that he didn't care about the result but it certainly wasn't the end of the world for him. I believe that, as far as he's concerned, the Championship and Champions League – the European Cup – are the big ones for a club like Manchester United. It's clear he doesn't care much about the League Cup and I think, increasingly, the FA Cup is perhaps being seen as a little less important. It was the same for Walter Smith when Celtic knocked Rangers out of the Scottish Cup. He didn't seem particularly upset.

I know the fans expect to win everything, but I think these managers are letting their heads guide their hearts here. They are focusing on what's important and it wouldn't surprise me if a few years down the line, the bigger clubs are increasingly looking upon the FA Cup almost as a bit of a distraction from the main chance.

*George*: So the fans may still have totally unrealistic expectations, but the managers are no longer listening?

*Pat*: To an extent that's true. Financial success for the big clubs comes from the Championship and the Champions League, but for smaller clubs like Wimbledon, it makes sense to go for any trophy you can – you can't afford to be as focused. And that tires the team and can mean that you finish with nothing. In Jock Stein's day, the philosophy was to win everything – and in 1967, Celtic *did* win everything they entered, including Quizball! – but football has become more complicated and more wearing, and I think that at the very top, managers, who have themselves been through the pain that Joe Kinnear must have experienced at Wimbledon, are prioritising a bit more carefully.

*George*: But that doesn't stop the fans wanting more and more. The shift in expectation is phenomenal. Five years ago, Geordie fans were happy to stay in the Second Division, as it then was. Now they want to win the Championship every year. It's a staggering shift in aspiration.

*Pat*: I think that's what finished off Kevin Keegan. I'll always remember one quote which summed it up for me and made me think he wouldn't stick it that much longer: he said the personal lows after losing were too low compared to the highs after winning. That's a feature of the modern game.

*George*: It's the price of fame. There's another lyric in *Evita* (I must start finding some trendier lyrics – the trouble is, Oasis's stuff never seems to mean anything!) which goes: 'You don't care if they love you, it's been done before. You'll despair if they hate you, you'll be drained of all energy.' I think that's Keegan all over. I saw *Evita* the day before he resigned and the two are now incontrovertibly linked in my mind. 'Oh What a Circus' could have summed up the reaction to his departure on Tyneside, too! I suppose that was the greatest paradox: Keegan was revered to such an extent in Newcastle that the pressure for him to deliver became too much. In a sense, the love of the fans and their belief that he was superhuman was what finished him off, when he found himself, at the end of last season, all too human.

*Pat*: But again, it wasn't just the fans. I mean, the fans started the ball rolling, but I think he was putting most of that colossal pressure on *himself*. He's one of a breed of managers so totally committed that second-best is failure.

*George*: It's a bit different this year, though. If Newcastle finish second this year, which seems their best hope, then they get a qualifying place for the Champions League. They finish *pseudo*-champions!

*Pat*: Well, they have stiff competition for that place from Arsenal and Liverpool. That will probably go right to the wire. But I empathise with Kevin in many ways. Second-best is not enough for me, either. As I mentioned earlier, a journalist once asked me after a game how happy I was with the way I had played, and in a moment of total honesty, I told him that in all the time I've been playing, I've only really been satisfied with about half a dozen of my performances. I tend to remember my bad games much more clearly than my good games.

*George*: They say that's the mark of a pessimist. Psychologists studying the links between personality and memory suggest that optimists tend to be quite selective in what they remember: they only recall the good times. Pessimists tend to dredge up the bad times.

Pat:    I'm not sure that I'd like to think of myself as a pessimist. Wouldn't that also be the mark of a perfectionist?

George: Certainly. In fact, when you completed the personality questionnaire, you emerged as no more and no less optimistic than the average person, so perhaps you look on the bright side of certain aspects of your game and your career, and on the darker side of others.

Pat:    There's definitely a gloomy side to aiming that high. I suppose the optimism comes from believing that you can achieve it, but the pessimism comes from missing the ideal so often, from the fact that you know, deep down, that you're *not* going to achieve it. It's the dichotomy that we've been talking about. But certain players and managers after a defeat are a million times worse than me. The pain, the despair they clearly go through is so enormous that you wonder why they put themselves through it. You can hear it in their voices. They sound like yours did when you heard that Terry Venables had sold Scribes.

George: Well, come on! That *is* a tragedy! First Keegan and now Scribes . . .

Pat:    I was dying to work that line in! I think I understand how you felt – I was feeling the same way when the cook left my favourite curry-house in Liverpool at around the same time.

George: Craig Brown is very interesting. I met him before the Scotland v Estonia replay in Monaco, which wasn't a good performance by the Scottish team, and he's a brilliant bloke with a great sense of humour. I remember him in one interview with *90 Minutes* saying that as a player at Rangers, he was third choice to play in his position – behind a Catholic and an amputee! What interests me about him is that I don't know how optimistic or pessimistic he is underneath it all, but he's always very guarded when it comes to the weight of expectation. The fans in Monte Carlo thought we'd hammer Estonia 7–0 (or *at least* 3–0, which is what we would have been awarded but for the spinelessness of UEFA, due to the Estonians failing to turn up last time – an action which looks set to get Middlesbrough relegated this season). Craig never seems to get carried away, though. He always stresses that there are no easy games and that the fans shouldn't get too carried away. He keeps a lid on the sort of euphoria that accompanied Ally's Tartan Army to Argentina in '78.

*Pat*:     I think the debacle in Argentina is imprinted – it's *burnt* – into the consciousness of every Scottish football fan the world over. That was the ultimate illustration of the unrealistic expectations of fans. We were going to *win* the World Cup. I mean, *come on!* Even Ally McLeod himself now admits that he allowed himself to be swept up in it all. Craig has learned from that, but from a lot of other people as well, one of them being Jock Stein. It was Jock who immediately took that expectation out of Scottish football. It took someone like Jock, who was revered by Scottish fans – Celtic ones, in particular – to say: 'Hey! Wait a minute! We're only a wee nation. Let's not go bananas. Any success we get should be regarded as a bonus.' The fans wouldn't have accepted that off anyone else at the time, but they listened to Jock. It's amazing to think that Stein dampened expectations, when it was he who had promoted the Celtic ethos of not accepting defeat, which led to what seemed ridiculous levels of expectation. Of course, in the end they were realised at Celtic.

Craig worked with Jock a bit in his early days as Scotland boss – in fact, he was offered the job of Jock's assistant, which he didn't accept at the time. I don't think a lot of fans realise that. So he learned a lot from him and now he doesn't allow himself to get carried away – witness his calm dignity during Euro 96.

I was commentating for Radio 5 Live on a brilliant Scotland performance against Austria recently and it's so easy to start going over the top, but working in football is a great humbling influence. For every win over Holland or Russia there is a defeat by Peru or Costa Rica. It isn't being over-sophisticated – it's just having a memory! If you ever start getting too big for your boots, the game will cut you back down to size. The Scottish fans are so passionate and veer from the lows to the highs and back so uncontrollably that it's like a roller-coaster, one I've enjoyed riding myself. One thing Craig has done is impose a bit of control over it.

George: The managerial equivalent of the safety standards officer at Blackpool Pleasure Beach?

Pat: If you like. Maybe the roller-coaster isn't as thrilling any more, but while there may no longer be the 4–1 victories, there aren't the 4–1 drubbings, either. I mean, by today's standards, that was a *hammering* we gave Austria! 2–0! We *annihilated* them! Funnily enough, commentating on that game was the first time I'd met Craig since he dropped me from the Scotland squad, which I had been so upset about. I was standing there as the squad walked in, waiting for my press ticket. It was a strange moment, obviously, because many of them had been my team-mates and they had been as close as any team-mates I'd ever played with, so wonderful was the feeling in the group.

Craig was physically trying to drag me into the dressing-room so that I could be with the lads again, but I thought it would be better to stand back a bit and acknowledge that I was no longer in the side. Like all Scottish footballers, as soon as you stop playing, you want to be back in the stands with your scarf out, cheering the boys on. I thought that was the place for me to be that night.

But talking to Craig, it was absolutely apparent that there was no ill-feeling, no atmosphere between us. In fact, he was kind enough to give me a few hints about what his game-plan was going to be, which helped my radio broadcast considerably!

George: It's because I warned him we were doing a book!

Pat: I was really happy for him and for the lads. It was strange being out of it, but in a sense I still felt part of it.

Funnily enough, my Dad taped the match commentary and although I had been completely unaware of it at the time, I kept referring to the team as 'we'! I feel very good about that sense of belonging. Earlier on in my career, I never felt that need to be part of a group, but now my association with the Scotland team is something that I look back on with great affection. Although I've never really been one for gangs, I felt that the Scotland team had been a gang I was proud to join.

George:   To change the subject a bit, although the end of the season is almost upon us, it's interesting to see that sportsmanship is not dead and bitter feuding hasn't stood in the way of gallantry. What did you make of Robbie Fowler's gentlemanly conduct when he fell in the penalty area during the Arsenal game and then was awarded a penalty – and the *intent* to bring him down was written all over Seaman's face, even if he didn't succeed in doing so – but tried to convince the ref that it shouldn't have been a penalty at all! This is a bit of a change from the Liverpool of old – diving and being awarded penalties was always something of a Scouse speciality.

Pat:    Oh, that's certainly true. Before furious fans start writing in, I have to say that I was having a conversation recently with a former Liverpool player who admitted that he'd fall over as soon as he got in the Kop End penalty area, so it isn't just a myth put about by rival fans. But Fowler's gesture came in an incredible week. He had stood up for the striking dockers, wearing a T-shirt pledging his support under his Liverpool shirt, and then there was this very gentlemanly action. I thought it was wonderful.

There is a bit of a 'diving' culture creeping back into the game – *galloping* back in, in fact – and without being xenophobic about it, the influx of foreign players have contributed to it a bit ... no names! It's a shame, because it was one problem we really didn't have in Britain compared to the rest of the world. But whether it should have been a penalty or not is really by the by.

What struck me was the honesty of it.

Let's face it, you have to be Robbie Fowler to hope to get away with it – to be brutally frank, a more average player would have been slaughtered by his team-mates and manager. Many players would be fuming if one of their number exhibited that level of fair play in that situation. That's what makes it all the more remarkable. I'm very glad he did it, particularly just before the annual PFA dinner. It shows that sportsmanship is not dead in the game. Gordon Taylor and I have applauded it publicly and UEFA made a big thing about it too, but deep down, if it hadn't been Robbie and if Liverpool hadn't won that match anyway, I think a player acting like that would have been tarred and feathered in the dressing-room afterwards. I've occasionally told a referee that something wasn't really a foul or that he shouldn't book an opponent for something he's done to me, but even when I think of myself, with my lofty sense of fair play, to my shame I would think twice about arguing with a referee to deny my team a penalty.

The other incredible thing is that when his protestations were ignored, Robbie actually took the penalty. Again, had it not been him, I think one of his team-mates would have physically wrestled the ball off him and taken it himself. To show that level of indifference to it being awarded, then to take it in such an apologetic way so as to have it parried by the keeper, then for missing it to be generally accepted speaks volumes about Robbie's stature as a player. I hope also that the media coming out in praise of what he did might stop a few managers or captains giving their players stick for behaving in the same way in the future. [*Alas, it was not all good news. Shortly afterwards, Robbie Fowler was sent off and missed three crucial games for Liverpool at the end of the season.*]

George:  What about the way certain Liverpool fans must have felt at the time? The fans can sometimes be a bit intimidating, can't they, whether it's opposition fans or, in this case, your own?

*Pat:*    It helps if you're not easily intimidated, and I don't
          think Robbie is. I don't think I am, either. When
          Manchester United played Galatasaray, there was a lot
          in the papers at the time about what an intimidating
          atmosphere it was, banners proclaiming 'Welcome to
          Hell' and so on. Well, I played there with Everton – in
          fact, I nearly signed for them, as I mentioned – and we
          won 3–1. I scored a couple of the goals. Well, it might
          have been a friendly but the fans rioted anyway, burn-
          ing Union Jacks and running on the field with those
          intense, staring eyes. But I remember thinking at the
          time that there was nothing to worry about, it was all
          just posturing. It probably springs from being brought
          up in the East End of Glasgow, which can be quite
          rough, but I'd seen it all before. It was all pure front.
          There was no real danger whatsoever. Some of the other
          lads ran off, but others noticed what I did: that there
          was no genuine threat there at all.

          So we just walked through them. They ran about a
          bit, shouted a little and then went away. There must
          have been five or six hundred of them on the pitch, but
          I felt no danger. There were flags everywhere and flares
          all over the place – not the trousers, the fireworks – and
          it sounded very intimidating, but it really wasn't. We
          all had a bit of a giggle about it in the dressing-room
          afterwards.

          When Manchester United played there, the same sort
          of thing went on. I think Eric Cantona was a little
          sucked into it – he has a habit of allowing himself to be
          intimidated and somewhat over-reacting – but Alex
          Ferguson made a brilliant comment afterwards to the
          tabloid press, who had naturally been blowing things
          out of all proportion. What he said rang so true and I
          understood what he meant so well: 'You think that's
          bad? You've obviously never been to a Glasgow
          wedding!'

*George:* But you have encountered more serious intimidation?
*Pat:*    The worst was for Scotland when we made the mistake
          of beating Mexico in the Under-19s Junior World Cup

quarter-finals in the Aztec stadium – 110,000 fans rioted and they *weren't* kidding on. The stadium is like a sheer cliff-face when you're on the pitch, and there were glass bottles, seats and small animals raining down, not to mention fireworks. I was quite nifty in those days – that had been my nickname at school, Nifty Nevin – and I ran off at the end of the game, looking out for these projectiles and dodging them. Paul McStay opted for the alternative tactic of sprinting for the tunnel and hoping for the best. As he did so, a five-litre glass bottle, thrown from about a hundred feet above, missed him by inches, exploding right behind him. He knew nothing about it, but he was nearly killed that night. Had it hit him, it would have left him brain-damaged at the very least. Well, when that kind of experience happens to you at quite a young age, you tend to brush it off and not think too deeply about just how serious it was. But I know I have never been intimidated by a crowd since then. When you've seen the real thing and got through it, you can recognise front a mile off.

In fact, we'd played the Mexicans a year earlier in Motherwell, again in a so-called friendly. My shirt was wet from the amount of spit that flew my way, and at one point, one of their players just punched me uncon-scious off the ball! I came to shortly afterwards. The referee hadn't seen it, I hadn't seen it, but a policeman who had been watching *had* seen it and he nabbed the boy. The referee didn't know what to do, so the police-man told him, in no uncertain terms, that the lad was being sent off. I remember that game best for that head-line, 'Nevin and Dick Shine'. I still fish that headline out sometimes, and show it to my wife. It makes me feel good about myself.

But to get back to the point, those sorts of experiences meant that I was never concerned when taking corners at St James' Park, as thousands of Geordie fans shouted what they'd do to me if they got hold of me, let alone fallen for more subtle kinds of intimidation such as the 'This is Anfield' sign which greets visiting players as they step out of the tunnel at Liverpool – that's the only reason it's there. I've seen it affect other players, but never me. Wimbledon were wonderful at it, of course, with the ghetto-blaster blaring from their dressing-room, the door wedged firmly open – I'm sure they brought their own wedge.

*George*:  They were also very good at resisting intimidation from other teams. I heard a story that they used blu-tac to put up an addendum to the 'This is Anfield' sign that said: 'Yeah? We're *really* scared!'

*Pat*:  The Dons' managers have been great amateur psychologists. I think Dave Bassett is still the king of all that. And they were successful. Whole teams were actually knocked back that a team could be so brash as to fail to be intimidated by much bigger sides with a much grander tradition. Although it wasn't fashionable to say it during my Everton days, I really admired them. They were like a breath of fresh air.

It's caught on, too. Crystal Palace were soon up to speed for on- and off-field intimidation and even at Tranmere now we have a boogie-box blasting out our favourite tunes. If clubs were completely honest, they'd admit that we've all learned a great deal from Wimbledon.

But it *is* all front. It's all a game. The same is true of what Alex Ferguson does when he makes sly comments about other teams and their managers. Kevin Keegan and Arsene Wenger took it very seriously, but I'm sure it was just part of the game to Ferguson. He'll use anything to give his side an edge, including gamesmanship.

One of my worries for the modern game is that young players are less likely to go through experiences of the sort I had against the Mexicans at such a young age. They have less chance to play first-team football at the moment because of the influx of foreign players. This means that younger British players often only get the chance to play on the big stage later on, at, say, 23 or 24. At that age, where there is an intimidating atmosphere, you tend to take it all more seriously if you haven't come across it before – it's easier to cope with some things when you're a teenager, or maybe it's because you have a steeper learning-curve at that age. The dearth of that type of experience leaves our players mentally weaker and it is a real concern of mine.

George: What advice would you give to a nervous young player about to play in an intimidating atmosphere?

Pat: The trick is sometimes to switch off. For a long time, there has been a pre-match management cliché which is: 'Get your mind in the game. Concentrate on the game' – and I'm not convinced that that's right at all. I think it helps a lot of players to clear their mind before a game, not to let their worries get to them. I find that relaxing and not worrying about the game to come can leave you very well-prepared, particularly if the match is being played in an intimidating atmosphere. I realised this even at Chelsea, where I would often be listening to music on my headphones at five to three.

I've even seen a player recently *be relieved that he wasn't playing because it was too big a game!* I'd never seen that before. It was the lack of 'big time', high-pressure experience early in his career that was the root cause of his weakness. But those are the pressures of the modern game. If intimidation or anxiety about the outcome can sap your confidence, it's perhaps better not to 'get your mind on the game' at all, but to keep relaxed and just take it as it comes.

George: You'd make a wonderful cognitive-behavioural therapist.

Pat: Thank you. I'll assume that's intended as a compliment.

# Should I Stay or Should I Go?

*Before the very end of the season, there was still unfinished business for Pat in his capacity as chairman of the PFA. While Rick Parry proved no hassle, Vinnie Jones was causing grief – and not because of his disciplinary record. There was also the eagerly-awaited annual PFA Awards dinner, awaited particularly eagerly by me because Pat had secured me a ticket. At Tranmere, however, Pat's predictions were to prove correct. The club, in its financial struggle, was forced to release a number of its players . . .*

George: So, after all the headaches involved in negotiating with the Football League over the benefits to players in the First, Second and Third Divisions of increased TV coverage, which nearly led to a players' strike, I gather you were expecting even more grief from the Premier League over the same issue – and were pleasantly surprised?

Pat: Yes. It came as something of a shock, in fact. At the PFA, we've essentially tried to negotiate over TV money with each body separately: the FA, the Football League and the Premier League. It's not quite 'divide and conquer', but it certainly makes it easier than being up against all three of them combined. Obviously, the Premier League is where there is most money at stake, so, after all the aggro we had with the Football League, we were expecting the worst. The FA deal, for what it's worth, breezed through very easily.

Rick Parry is the chief executive at the Premier League and after chatting to him, I realised that he wanted this sorted out as effortlessly as possible, prior to his leaving the Premier League to seek pastures new at Liverpool. He was just incredibly sensible about the

whole thing. He didn't go for the hard-headed
posturing that you often get in employer-employee
negotiations, which we'd had plenty of from the Football League. He was very fair with Gordon Taylor from
the PFA. Gordon reciprocated the approach, feeling that
he could work well with Rick, and simply talked
through what he felt was a sensible deal. Rick agreed
with him and went back to his management committee,
Gordon reported back to us, both committees nodded
and, other than some legal i-dotting and t-crossing, that
was that!

Previously, I'd had visions of all sorts of difficulties –
Premier League players out on strike and all of that –
but none of it happened. Everything was pretty much
finalised and in the bag before anyone even spoke to
the papers. At our management committee meeting, we
were all quite taken aback at the simplicity of it all – but
also, after what had come before, it was a huge relief for
me, especially as I was expecting it to ruin a large
section of my summer. Generally, the bigger the body
you're pitting your wits against, the dirtier and nastier
the fight gets, but not a bit of it this time.

I will only remain chairman of the PFA while I'm still
a player, which may only be until the end of next
season, when my Tranmere contract runs out. I'm glad
the TV contracts are settled, because whoever takes
over from me would have been thrown straight into the
lions' den on the matter of negotiations over TV money.
As it is, they'll have five-year deals with all the three
bodies concerned, the FA, Football League and Premier
League, well and truly in the bag and fully sorted out.

George:  But to make up for this, I gather Vinnie Jones has been
rattling his chains. It was interesting to see Alex
Ferguson refer to Vinnie Jones diplomatically at the PFA
dinner. What Vinnie is doing has certainly set tongues
wagging within the game. As I understand it, because
of the Bosman ruling, once a player is out of contract
with his club, he can go where he likes abroad within
Europe and pick up whatever the club have paid for

him personally, less the fees of any agents or solicitors he may employ. Certain players have already done this. John Collins went from Celtic to Monaco when he was out of contract, for example. Now, obviously this is very annoying to clubs and very lucrative for players and their agents.

Vinnie, however, clearly doesn't like foreign food because when his contract is up at Wimbledon, which has presumably just happened or is about to happen, he doesn't want to go abroad but to go to another *British* club. At the moment, the Bosman ruling does not affect transfers from one British club to another, so Wimbledon clearly feel that, unless he goes abroad, he's still their player – but he's got a bunch of legal people challenging that.

Now, from the PFA's point of view, you have these guidelines which you'd like to implement which would mean that players are free to move between British clubs if they are out of contract, but only after a certain age. Vinnie is obviously over that, but by making his move now, before the recommended code is accepted, he might prevent it *ever* being accepted. Have I got the gist?

Pat:  Yes, that's about it. But it's the *implications* of his actions, if he gets away with what he is trying to do, that would cause the real damage. It's really quite upsetting what Vinnie is up to. The union has had the trust of its members for many years. Most PFA members appreciate that we try to serve their interests and are right behind us. No other players' union in the world has got its members the benefits that we have in England – and I say that as a Scotsman. Now we've told our members: 'Trust us on this one. We know what we're doing. It might have a short-term effect on one or two people who could make millions, but we're trying to save the longer-term lifeblood of the game, so please bear with us.'

We have upwards of 3,000 members and all of them have toed the line, knowing that we're trying to intro-

duce the guidelines I have spoken about, which represent a mature attitude to dealing with the Bosman
ruling . . . all of them, so far, except Vinnie.

Vinnie is determined to push the system and it could
spell the ruination of half the leagues. I think that's no
exaggeration. Vinnie is trying to make out that he has a
moral argument, but others are seeing it as a desire for
self-publicity with an element of personal greed. He
may not earn what Ravanelli does, but he's not on bad
money at Wimbledon. He knows he can get a very, very
worthwhile contract under the existing system, there or
at another club that might want him. There are plenty
of players who have it tougher than him. I really do
hope that his motivation is more to do with self-
publicity than with greed.

The agents will benefit if he succeeds. If transfer fees
to clubs are abolished for all out-of-contract players, the
players themselves will make a fortune and their agents
will cop 10 or 20 per cent of it. I know Vinnie is getting
some help from a law firm, so he has sought legal
advice on this. It's difficult to know who else may be
behind him, though, although it's obvious who stands
to benefit if he gets his way.

The point of the code that we are agreeing with the
FA, the Football League and the Premier League is that
it will safeguard the interests of the smaller clubs. It
will also safeguard the interests of young domestic
players currently threatened by the influx of foreign
players. If the equivalent of the Bosman ruling were to
take over completely in this country for domestic transfers, as Vinnie would like, then the smaller clubs would
almost certainly scrap their youth policies overnight.
There would be no point in having any. Why develop a
player for five years only to have Manchester United or
some similar huge club turn up, pick the player up and
walk away with them?

Now, if Vinnie understands the full implications of
the argument that he's put forward, and I'll give him
the benefit of the doubt and say that he probably does,

then it follows that he's prepared to kill off half the smaller clubs in this country in pursuit of his own personal gain. Considering where he learned his trade, it is doubly distressing. We hope he has second thoughts.

George: Well, let's hope that Vinnie *doesn't* understand the implications of what he's doing. I guess time will tell. [*Time* did *tell and Vinnie saw the light. See Pat's 'Dream Team'.*]

Do you think you will remain PFA chairman until the end of next season?

Pat: I've hinted to Gordon Taylor that I wouldn't mind someone else coming along to take up the reins, but frankly, there hasn't exactly been a stampede caused by people clamouring to take over. I think the job is perceived as a bit of a poisoned chalice. I didn't realise how poisonous it could be until I had agreed to do it! The talks over the TV money were very stressful, and, of course, it can affect your game. I hope it hasn't had too detrimental an effect. I can handle the meetings, studying and travelling. It is also an honour to do it. It is challenging, enjoyable at times, and very, very interesting. The constant need to deal with the press is the biggest strain.

It can affect you in other ways, too. In my capacity as PFA chairman, I met Tony Blair to talk about Labour's support for using cash from the National Lottery to help lower-division clubs struggling to meet the recommendations of the Taylor Report. This was before the election, you understand, and I was well aware that whatever my personal politics may be – and I suspect readers will have figured out that I'm not a *huge* fan of the Tories – I was determined to be very apolitical about it and not make it look like it was a gesture of personal support of the Labour party from me, purely official PFA business. You can't afford to be party political when you represent players from all shades of the political spectrum, many of whom, of course, have traditionally voted Conservative to keep their tax down.

Well, you can imagine what happened. There were Tranmere shirts popping up out of nowhere and by the time it appeared in the Merseyside papers, it looked as though I was speaking at a Labour rally. Say what you like about them, they know how to turn things to their advantage. The Tranmere chairman didn't see the funny side, however, and neither did various directors and supporters whose politics may be a little to the right of mine. They all wrote in to complain. I had to defend my position, explaining what had happened, and, of course, the other players gave me an enormous amount of stick over it.

*George*:  Though now, of course, you can take credit for Labour's landslide. The Tranmere Rovers vote obviously made all the difference!

*Pat*:  Don't tell our chairman that! Actually, I'm not sure what his politics are.

*George*:  As for the PFA Awards dinner, I was very pleased to see Alan Shearer and Peter Beardsley honoured, especially as Peter may not remain at Newcastle much longer. David Beckham's Young Player of the Year Award was also richly deserved (he came second to Shearer in the Player of the Year Award, simultaneously). It's a huge occasion, isn't it? Some 1200 people! And you have to introduce it all. Plus you had the joy of sitting between Alex Ferguson and Howard Wilkinson all evening, which must have been wonderful.

*Pat*:  The sheer scale of it can be daunting. When I first took it over, the guest of honour was your friend Terry Venables, whose last Saturday at Scribes you had been sadly celebrating the night before. It was my first speech to the assembled masses and I did not enjoy it, especially as Terry does that kind of thing so well. The following year was easier. I sat between Kenny Dalglish and Denis Law, in addition to which we gave the Merit Award to Gordon Strachan, so I made a comment about the Scots taking over which went down well.

*George*:  Yes, I notice that although the managers of Wales and both Northern Ireland and the Republic of Ireland were present this year, there was no sign of Craig Brown representing Scotland ...

*Pat*: Well, that's what happens when you don't pick me! Actually, he was unavailable. But the following year, it was Pele. He was wonderful. To sit next to and talk to such a hero for three or four hours was the experience of a lifetime. He is a very intelligent man, but also a very wise man. He understood every word I said, despite my Glasgow accent, but he also understood so much about the workings of the PFA. He really grilled Gordon and I about it, because he is trying to do similar things for the players in Brazil. At the end of the evening, I asked for his autograph. I think I've only ever done that twice before.

*George*: Who were the others?

*Pat*: David Hay at Celtic, funnily enough, and Holly Johnson of Frankie Goes to Hollywood, but that was only because my wife hated their music, so I got him to write: *To Annabel – Relax! Holly Johnson*. She groaned when I gave it to her!

Anyway, Pele gave me his autograph. He wrote: *To P. Neven* – he spelt it incorrectly, but that didn't matter – *Thanks very much* and he signed it *Edson = Pele*. Then he uttered a line which I've been eating and drinking off ever since: 'My friends call me Edson. Please don't call me Pele. Call me Edson.' Well, that's stuck with me, but it was a marvellous evening all round. Pele is like royalty to the football fraternity.

Anyway, it was impossible to top that this year. The Pope turned us down, so we got Alex Ferguson.

*George*: Who is still worshipped as a god all over the world wherever two or three Manchester United supporters gather in his name.

*Pat*: Actually, I asked him and Howard Wilkinson all evening about their views on the game. Howard has some quite surprising views. Not being an ex-footballer – he was a schoolteacher – his opinions are very refreshing. Some of them are probably a bit abstract, while others may be echoed by other managers, albeit in more simplistic, earthy language. He certainly seems to be enjoying his new job with the FA and has some very strong views on the place of psychology in the game, for example. You'd enjoy talking to him. There are certainly a few thoughts I might use for future articles. Crossfertilisation – that's a good word! Then again, theft and plagiarism are good words, too.

*George*:  I was actually surprisingly impressed by Alex Ferguson. Not only did he tell a joke about wanting an extension for his speech – which I'm sure would have had Arsene Wenger rolling in the aisles – but I actually took a snap of him *laughing*, which is every bit as rare as a Van Gogh original to collectors of football ephemera! Most funny of all, however, was him having to hand over the Player of the Year Award to Alan Shearer after failing to sign him at the end of last season! That gave me a warm glow all over.

I noticed that there were not that many players from the Premier League there, but loads of ex-players.

*Pat*:  It's actually harder for players to make it now. There were quite a few fixtures being played that Sunday, which didn't used to happen – including two FA Cup semi-finals. If there are games on Monday or Tuesday, managers would not be over-pleased with their players swanning off to the 'PFA party' all night. For people not actively involved in the game at the moment, like, say, Joe Royle, it's an informal opportunity to talk with like-minded people and maybe see if there might be any jobs going. Picking the date is very hard nowadays. Finding one towards the end of the season when there's nothing going on is simply impossible.

Actually, mention of Joe brings me onto a totally different theme, which is how traumatic the end of the season can be. One of the worst things that managers have to do is to tell players that a club no longer requires their services. Some may then go onto other clubs on a free transfer, some go into non-league football and others never play again. It's a very, very sad time. I remember Joe was telling me about breaking the news to one young player and the boy started crying. Well, in no time at all, Joe was crying along with him. They say that some people are too nice to be managers, and that particular task is probably the most heart-breaking that a manager faces. Often, it's not because the players are not good enough to make it – a smaller club just can't afford to keep them all. It's a gut-wrenching time all round. I hate it.

I've seen it handled in the most insensitive way – perhaps because a manager didn't want to face that player and explain it in person: the player has simply come in and been handed a brown envelope containing a P45. I think that's devastating. There was one player who had been 18 years in the game and who had come in that day expecting his contract to be renewed, or at least to be released with some respect. You can imagine how it must have felt, having spent all those years in the game at the highest level – all that effort, playing through pain, taking chances with his future health for the club and showing an impeccable attitude all those years. Then, for the final act to take place in a darkened hallway, where a club minion thrusts a cheap brown envelope, in an even cheaper way, into his hand . . .

As a union, we've done everything we can to help players get a job after their football days are over, and many young players have taken advantage of the schemes we have set in place. Some go on to coach and many have completed their coaching badges. But, in a similar way to the fact that you don't really invite the possibility of defeat until after it has happened, you never think it's going to be you whose career will end that season.

It's a very melancholy time. You're surrounded by young players with shattered dreams, some trying to put a brave face on it, some I've come across weeping openly. As PFA chairman, I get to see the list of all the players released from their clubs at this time of year. It's a list of some 400 or so names, hoping against hope that some other club will pick them up, even though they have been branded rejects by their own. Occasionally it does happen and clubs have occasionally snapped up some real surprises through that route, players whose own clubs had somehow missed their potential. But it's the exception rather than the rule.

In the end, of all the youth trainees that come to a club at 17, maybe one each year will make it all the way. People always see the glamour in the game and think of the successes and the phenomenal earnings of the Shearers and Gascoignes, but sometimes they forget about those left behind, those that didn't quite make it and all the grief wrapped up in that. Outsiders only ever see the glorious, shimmering tip of the iceberg.

*George*:  I remember talking to Lee Akers, a player at Dulwich Hamlet, on the way back from Scribes once. We'd all had a few drinks and the conversation got a bit poignant. He said that if anyone wrote a book about non-league football, it should be called *The Nearly Men*, because so many of those who inhabit the non-league world came so close to making it at one of the top clubs. They all have their memories of when they were 'let go', and that stays with them forever, along with the dreams of what might have been.

*Pat*:  Yes, I think that memory always survives. But it's at its worst at the time. Even if you're still safe for another year, you see your friends being released and it preys on your mind. It's a little bit like surviving a fire when your friends didn't. However much you try to rationalise it, you end up blaming yourself, or at least feeling very sad and guilty.

It always makes you question the fact that you're staying in the game, especially when you reach my age. If I felt that I was past my sell-by date, that the younger players had overtaken me, I'd walk away from it. I've been reassessing my position ever since I started in the game. The question I used to ask myself was always: 'Am I enjoying this?' That has changed, over the years, to: 'Am I getting *any* enjoyment out of this?' It's a subtle shift in emphasis. It may seem selfish, when other players end up on the scrapheap, but why else does anyone carry on doing a job? It's because I enjoy it and I'm fairly good at it sometimes, as well as for the money. If I was no longer good at it, I'd give up because I'd feel a fraud. And I certainly still enjoy it, or parts of it. I like training and I love to play, to make goals and to score. You do end up holding onto the enjoyment you derive from that for as long as you can.

George: With John Aldridge being new to management, how did he deal with the difficult business of releasing players?

Pat: I was quite impressed with how he did it. He did it in the way you should deal with it: no handing players brown envelopes in passing, he had each player come in and talk to him and discussed things with them individually. He gave them the reasons behind his decision, the decision itself and a slight pep-talk. As far as I was concerned, it was very much a case of, 'See you next year.'

George: Did that surprise you, what with rumours that Tranmere wanted to lose you circulating in the middle of the season, and never really being sure whether you were part of the manager's plans or not?

Pat: I suppose it reassured me a bit. It was a vote of confidence. I was also flattered to hear, through the grapevine, that there was interest in me from another club and also, as I think I've mentioned, from the States. It's good to know that someone still thinks you've got it.

So I'm definitely set to play another year. At the end of that, I'll take stock and probably retire – but who knows? If I'm still playing well and still enjoying it . . . I'll be out of contract with Tranmere then.

George: But you won't be 'doing a Vinnie'?

Pat: Certainly not! At my age, the rules are that I'll be on a free transfer anyway.

George: Is it harder to surprise defenders as you get older? Have they worked your game out and can predict exactly what you're going to do once you reach a certain age?

Pat: I think the learning curve for most players really slows

down when they get to about 21. The really great
players keep learning and keep adapting after that time.
But it gets harder and harder to teach an old dog new
tricks.

I mentioned early on that one of the most refreshing
things about the international stage is that even the
world's best defenders won't know all your tricks when
they meet you for the first time. With players who you
meet again and again, year after year, it becomes more
difficult to surprise one another and can also make your
game less exciting, because your little repertoire of
tricks has been discovered and discarded.

I used to do this dummy that is one of my specialities
and it used to fool the likes of Stuart Pearce in the old
days. Ten years on, however, he's no longer fooled – I'd
end up in Row Z of the stand if I tried that on him now!
When I was younger, I had an image as a bit of a
dribbler, someone who was great at close control of the
ball, but I've had to drop a lot of that over the years
because once people are aware of it, it no longer works.
Three opponents would just come in very quickly, close
down the space and hoof me all over the place. What I
then tended to do – this was after just three or four years
in the game – was draw people towards me and slip
balls through them. Once people knew that I was going
to do that, I adapted it, dragging players as far from
their area as possible. It was no longer necessarily with
a view to beating them, it was just to get them out of
position, allowing the overlapping full-back lots of
space. So I was using what they thought I was going to
do against them!

You have to keep 're-inventing' different parts of
your game. If you can't adapt, you tend not to last long
in the game. That's particularly true if all you've got
going for yourself at an early age is pace. You can have
two or three brilliant seasons and then, five years down
the line, you're finished.

*George*:  Whole club systems and styles can be 'found out', can't
they?

Pat:    Yes. I think Everton stuck by the system that had served them so well in the mid-eighties for just slightly too long. That was then their downfall for quite a few years. The game had moved on, and they'd been left behind a bit from a technical point of view.

George: Have there been any players, though, who have steadfastly stuck to the same style, the same box of tricks, and have got away with it successfully for years and years?

Pat:    There *are* one or two, and though they stick out a mile and they've become a standing joke, they *have* survived. They do it so well that you know that they're going to do something and they then do it, but it doesn't matter. You fall for it and there's nothing you can do about it.

My friend Peter Beagrie is a fantastic example. He's got one trick and he does it superbly: he goes to cross the ball, the defender has to lunge slightly and he pulls it back. It's the oldest and simplest trick in the book, but he *elongates* it, making the defender really stretch. Now, the defender *knows* he's going to do it, but if he makes no attempt to stop him, Peter will just put the cross in, so he has to lunge and he's caught like a rat in a trap.

I'm not saying that's all Peter does, but that's what his whole play is built around. There are one or two others, too. Everyone in the game knows what a 'Glenn Roeder' is: it's a step over the ball with your left foot, taking it away with the outside of your right foot and a shimmy. You know he's going to do it, but you still fall for it. There's a horrifying inevitability to it all. It's like a film where you can predict exactly what's going to happen, but you're still compelled to keep watching it. It was sickening the way he'd always get away with it at Newcastle – you'd almost laugh as he went by you, thinking: 'I *knew* that was coming!'

There are one or two little tricks that I've got which, if I do them well, are almost impossible to guard against. One is a little back-flip scoop that I do when players are running in towards me. I hope I've got others! So have Peter and Glenn, of course, but what

I've described has been their speciality and has taken them a long way.

George: Another aspect of getting older is being more prone to injuries. It was injuries this season that really threw a spanner in the works and, despite splendid perform-ances in some of your games, really conspired to make it a disappointing season. You started with injuries and finished with injuries. What is the way forward?

Pat: I went to see a specialist about my foot. He suggested an operation now, and I agreed. Then, half an hour later, we changed our minds.

George: It's called a second opinion.

Pat: Indeed. There were two possible courses of action. If I had been a younger player, he probably would have operated on it. But if, as planned, I only have one or two more years in the game, he felt that I could probably get by on injections.

George: So that might see you through till the end of your career as a player?

Pat: I hope so. It will definitely have a bearing on my pre-season training regime. I have discussed it with John Aldridge and he seems very understanding. There will be much less running on hard surfaces and much more on sand-dunes. I think I'll be doing a lot of cycling as well.

George: But no running down the sides of mountains just before you're all due back?

Pat: Not this time. Once bitten, twice shy!

# Fame

*In our final session, I was keen to expand on a theme central to the changing world of football today. What does Pat make of his image? And what is his attitude to fame? Bringing out a book is likely to affect the former and – who knows? – perhaps even the latter . . .*

George:   With the season over, it's time to reflect. It was a better season to be a Newcastle fan than to be a Tranmere player this year. Tranmere didn't quite make the play-offs and Newcastle, to the surprise of many, finished second in the Premier League, beating Liverpool and Arsenal on goal difference and giving themselves the chance to play in what we used to call the European Cup but is now, increasingly, the Champions League . . .

Pat:   Are you saying all that about Newcastle just to see it in print?

George:   Yes. Not that Newcastle's players need it. Certain clubs are so much in the spotlight that all of their players – even the more occasional contributors like the Steve Watsons and the Robbie Elliotts – become written about and their faces are soon well-known. Fans might struggle to name the entire Leicester or Wimbledon teams, but they tend to know all the Man U and Liverpool players whether they like those clubs or not.

   Chelsea was always a high-profile club from the glamour and fame point of view. They might not always have had Gullit and Zola, but their players were always among the better-known. How did it feel to be in the spotlight from an early age?

Pat:   For my part, I've never really wanted fame. I was scared stiff of it, to be honest. If people treat me as a famous person, I find it quite painful and downright embarrassing. At Chelsea there would be certain people fawning all over me and it got on my wick! I used to go quite over the top in my efforts to avoid fame and idolisation, taking tremendous steps to try and reassure people that I was perfectly normal and interested in normal things.

That, of course, backfired because not being interested in fame and in doing things that footballers are supposed to do seemed to many a weird way for a footballer to behave, leading to more intrigue and more scrutiny.

The reason that fame scares me so much is that I've seen from an early age how ephemeral it is in sport, and particularly in football. It passes very quickly indeed. If you live that life, wallowing in the recognition, loving to be spotted, adoring the adulation, then it becomes very hard to cope when all that is suddenly taken away from you, which definitely happens at the end of many playing careers.

I had a chance to live that life at Chelsea in particular, but I gave it away – I *threw* it away, in fact. I kicked it into touch. For other people, it gets *taken* away and if you have grown to love the roar of the crowd, the silence that follows is very painful. I have observed a lot of people in the game and their attitude to all the recognition. If you let yourself get sucked into it, it's very easy to get carried away with the illusion that it's actually *you* that people love, as opposed to your talent. This is especially true if you've been living that life for 15 years.

George:　I suppose it's a bit like stars of soap operas whose fans – and the tabloids help this confusion – actually believe that they are more or less the character that they play. The fans may have very little interest in them as human beings or actors – they just like the people they portray on their screens, people who are fictional.

Pat:　Yes. In the case of football, what they love is your goal-scoring or your aggressive defending or whatever. That's why people are often disappointed with football biographies and finding out that the player concerned is not quite what they imagined him to be. It's not *you* that people generally love, it's what you can *do*.

George:   I remember a documentary about Robert Maxwell, a man who courted fame shamelessly, in which they interviewed a Russian lover from late on in his life. She said that he once complained that no-one loved him. She tried to reassure him, citing all the people who regularly came to his sumptuous parties. 'They don't love *me*,' he said, 'they love my *money*.'

Pat:   That's exactly what I'm talking about, except that in the case of a footballer, it would be: 'They don't love me, they love my talent, image, fame, friends and the attention I get.' They might love the money as well, of course, if he's a generous player!

But certain players try not to court fame, and I think that has become more acceptable now. In my Chelsea days, you were considered mad not to do so if you had the chance to, but Jurgen Klinsmann is a good example of a player for whom it was never an item on his agenda. I saw him on *Football Focus* driving into White Hart Lane in a little VW Beetle and it brought back memories of the little, battered old MGB-GT I used to own at Chelsea. I had always intended it to be a dressed-down vehicle, the antithesis of flash. Jurgen was talking about how much he loved London because you could be totally inconspicuous. If you wandered around, the odd person might recognise you, but you certainly weren't followed everywhere.

It was a joy to hear him saying those things, because no-one would have dreamed of voicing such opinions five years earlier. I wasn't jealous that that attitude was not acceptable when I was at Chelsea, just happy that it's now beginning to creep in a bit.

Another person who is very obviously taken with London in the same way is Gianluca Vialli at Chelsea. My friend and team-mate Ivano Bonetti knows him quite well and told me Vialli would quite fancy meeting up for a chat and a coffee. I asked Ivano how Luca, as he calls him, coped with all the publicity in London and he said that Vialli couldn't believe how easy it was. When he had been in Italy, he had disguised himself before going out, putting on false beards and things. If he walked about as normal, people would recognise him and follow him everywhere he went.

His girlfriend had sent him out to get some bread and milk somewhere fairly central – I think it was Kensington High Street – and he dived into the shop and dived out again. Then he noticed that no-one really paid much attention to him. Even if he was recognised, people just shrugged their shoulders and got on with their lives. I think we're more reserved about these things than they are in Italy. He eventually got back to his flat with two cratefuls of food, because he was so excited that he could walk about without being bothered that he went back into the shop to buy some more!

He has obviously seen the downside of fame, even before it is taken away from him – the hassle and the irritation that you can get with constant recognition. But he also knows that once he stops playing, that will evaporate and the fans will find someone else.

George: Fans can be very fickle from that point of view, can't they? Hell really hath no fury like a fan scorned. If you go off to another club, you're sometimes vilified for the rest of your life – especially if you do a Denis Law and relegate your previous club!

Pat: That's part of the ultra short-termism that exists in the modern game, which we've already discussed at length. The Denis Law example is an extreme one: relegating Man United clearly gave him little pleasure – you could see that on his face. But it does demonstrate that it's not you they love. It's you *in their colours*, scoring for them. And if it wasn't you, it would be someone else.

I have some tips on avoiding the drawbacks of fame for any players that are interested. Of course, a lot of the people who complain about the pressures of fame are the ones who jog around Hyde Park in fluorescent lurex body-suits, accompanied by three bodyguards – so it's not going to work for them. It won't work for those who complain about having no privacy, conducting the interview from Stringfellow's.

George:    No use to Charlie Nicholas, then?

Pat:    None whatsoever. Well, Charlie has matured since then, if we are to be honest. A lot of it is down to how you walk: you don't hide or cower exactly, but you kind of . . . *crouch* slightly. Long overcoats are always a good idea and, instead of the trendy nightclubs around Covent Garden, try the South Bank or Ronnie Scott's at the back – you're much less likely to be hassled in those locations. I'm not sure Charlie Nicholas would have enjoyed that, though.

Now I think of it, all these digs at Charlie Nicholas arise because you were a Spurs fan when he was at the Arsenal. Charlie is actually a good lad, y'know!

I do know certain players who are very likeable people, but who have really revelled in the fame that they received when playing, then looking really quite lost at the end of their careers, wondering why no-one wants to know them any more, and that has really terrified me. I don't want to fool myself into thinking that I'm loved by thousands, only to find that I'm not.

When I first started playing for Chelsea, I had a favourite song called 'This is the Day' by The The, and there's a lyric in it by Matt Johnson which goes:

*All your friends and family – think that you're lucky*
*But the side that they'll never see*
*Is when you're left alone with your memories*
*That hold your life together like . . . Glue.*

That's a wonderful lyric. The writer has seen how famous people are seen by others but knows the pain that can follow it if you live it too much. It was a song – and indeed an album – which I lived on for a long time during my Chelsea days.

George:    Has increased TV coverage increased the glamorous

*Pat*:       Definitely. People like Ryan Giggs get it more than ever
             before, but I don't think you need to have suffered the
             worst of it yourself to appreciate what some of these
             people must go through.

*George*:    There are some players now who are known univer-
             sally, even by those who take no interest in football
             whatsoever. Eric Cantona is a good example. It's hard
             to imagine him once his playing days are over – yet he's
             certainly not been a patch on some of his earlier per-
             formances this year.

*Pat*:       Cantona has surprised me with some of the things he
             has said, because I consider him to be quite an intelli-
             gent man, yet he has come out with statements suggest-
             ing that once he's finished playing football, he is not
             sure that he'll take any further interest in it. That's a
             very odd thing for a player to say. It makes you think
             that perhaps he is only interested in his own position
             within the game, that he doesn't care for the fans he has
             such a rapport with, and that doesn't gel with some of
             the other things he has said. But he does have a complex
             personality and the rest of his life should be very inter-
             esting. [*To everyone's surprise, Eric Cantona announced his
             retirement from professional football at the end of the season.
             Few players have such a capacity to startle.*]
                 I think players with huge fame will have major
             problems ahead of them as that fame begins to trickle
             away. Some players deal with it very well, others very
             badly. Some deal with it very well *and* very badly at the
             same time, George Best springing to mind. The media-
             training package that the PFA has set up will, I hope,
             give players a little insight into how to deal with fame,
             but there's no way that you can really teach someone
             about the incredible effects that hyper-stardom when
             you're young can have on your later life.

*George*:    Except by showing them a photograph of Michael
             Jackson, perhaps?

*Pat*:       Yes. There but for the grace of God and all that. But

The image that players have and the reverence in which they're held – or *appear* to be held?

there are few easy answers you can offer people. The holistic approach to youth training which I talked about in an earlier session should help, but it won't provide all the solutions.

You have to bring people down to earth sometimes and remind them that, in the end, it's only kicking a ball. There are jobs that are more vital, more honourable, more honest, though less well-paid and less acknowledged.

Every now and again, I listen to Cliff Morgan on Radio 4. He's got a very old-fashioned, Corinthian view of sport, he's a great defender of amateur sport. When things are becoming too businesslike around me, when the 'professional' bit of my job title seems to outweigh the 'footballer' part, I like to listen to his show. Some of the people he has on are greats from the past and others are incredibly dedicated amateurs who are incredibly skilled but take part in sports that are seen as less glamorous, or don't get so much TV coverage. Sometimes he talks to those who, although very keen, haven't necessarily won gold medals, but have come close and their enthusiasm has remained. All of them, though, share this Corinthian spirit, which many would love to see back in football. It is still there *somewhere* and you occasionally see flashes of it back again, but it really isn't seen that often. If you're a little caught-up with your own self-importance in football, you should listen to some of those interviews.

I remember an interview recently with a rugby player – amateurism there is dying out too, of course – which finished with Cliff Morgan's comment: 'Isn't it great to have a job where all you do is play games?' I remember thinking at the time: 'Find me a footballer who really feels that way!' I know I argue that football has to be run like a business nowadays, that there is no alternative to that approach, but it's worth hearing sentiments like that sometimes to get your feet back on the ground. Deep down, I do feel that way about my job. It is a wonderful job, but, as in life, it is easy to get side-

|          | tracked from your original ideals if you are not careful. |
|----------|-----------------------------------------------------------|
| *George*: | Has being recognised ever landed you in trouble? |
| *Pat*: | Definitely! But only on a couple of occasions, I'm glad to say. I'd joined Chelsea and had been living in London for about a year. I was sharing a flat with a friend called Adrian Thrills, the guy who initially dubbed me 'The first post-punk footballer', a label that has rather stuck and which, considering it came from my flatmate, might possibly be accused of being a bit of a con. He was a mad-keen Tottenham fan and I went along with him to see some of the great European nights they enjoyed, quite unaware of the animosity that has traditionally existed between Spurs and Chelsea. We stood on The Shelf, which you'll remember as an ex-Spurs fan yourself. |
| *George*: | Yes. That's mainly executive boxes now. |
| *Pat*: | Anyway, I didn't drive at the time, so we just came back on the tube as we normally would. I wasn't wearing a Tottenham scarf, I should stress – I do draw the line somewhere! My mate got out, but I stayed on for another couple of stops, by which time I was beginning to feel a little uncomfortable, to say the least. There was a skinhead in the same carriage, his forehead slightly below his nose, his knuckles dragging behind him on the ground – by no means a typical Spurs fan, but every club seems to be stuck with a few – and he pulled a knife on me. |

He asked me who my favourite player was and, in my best Dick Van Dyke Mockney, I said: 'Micky 'Azard.' 'Nah!' says the chap. 'You're Nevin! You're Chelsea!' It's some indication of his IQ that he clearly thought that if I played for Chelsea, I wouldn't know the names of any Tottenham players – hence his opening gambit! Despite an accent even less convincing than Ben Elton's, I think I half-fooled him. Unfortunately, you can always rely on the tube to stop in the middle of a tunnel during these situations. I looked around at the other passengers and, naturally enough, there were a hundred *Evening Standard*s raised, hiding their owners.

Then the train jolted and he fell, so I caught him and said: 'You awlwight?' – which confused him briefly. The train pulled into the next stop, whereupon I summoned up every iota of my East End *Glasgow* accent and enquired: 'Whit the fuck's that up there?' He turned around, I smacked him in the face with the bag I was carrying and legged it! He came sprinting down the platform after me, but I had a good 20 yards on him and I was a bit nippy in those days. At the end of the tube station were two policemen, so I was saved. By the Thursday afternoon of that week, I had a car.

So that was one incident, and it was a shame because up until then, I had merrily travelled on public transport and had encountered no trouble at all. There was another incident when I was accosted by an extreme right-winger in a hairdresser's. I've no idea what he was doing there, because he was another skinhead and about six-foot-nine. To make it worse, he was a Chelsea supporter and started lecturing me that 'we don't need those darkies in our team'. I raised myself to my full five-foot-six and replied that I thought we did. Well, we had a bit of an argument and ended up agreeing to differ. There was no violence threatened, but if I hadn't been a Chelsea player, the situation would never have arisen.

There was also one occasion up at Newcastle after Chelsea had just played at St James' Park. My pals had come down from Scotland and we decided to have a night out on the 'Toon'. Incorrect play! I was followed and eventually chased down the street by a bunch of Newcastle fans.

George:    Surely not!

Pat:       Split up from my mates, I thought I was in for a hiding, so I remembered another Glasgow lesson: 'If you're going to go, take a few with you.' I ran into a restaurant so that I could pick up a chair to fight them with. Sadly, it was a Wimpy and all the tables and chairs were nailed to the floor. Luckily, they didn't come in – they just stood outside and banged on the glass for a while.

The only other thing which has happened, which I do find very offensive, is when I'm out with my wife and someone comes up to talk to me and stands in her line of view, as though she doesn't exist.

I suppose that in all the time I've been in football, that's not too bad a record. I've certainly never had to face being mobbed or followed around like Vialli has. At the same time, I've never courted fame or pulled it towards me, so that might have helped. I'd imagine that some of today's younger players in the full glare of the spotlight have rather more people trying to pick fights with them. In Europe, it can be even worse. The passion in places like Spain and Italy is so intense that you can kiss your privacy goodbye.

That's one of the reasons that I decided not to play in Turkey. I had flown across to Istanbul with my wife and son to talk to Galatasaray's owner. At the airport, there were two television crews waiting and 300 fans chanting, 'Nevin! Nevin!' It was supposed to make me feel welcome. In reality, they could have done little more to put me off! My family couldn't have lived a normal life there. Having touched that kind of fame a couple of times, I know I don't want it.

*George*: Yes, it seemed to prove too much even for Graeme Souness, which is certainly saying something.

*Pat*: How very true.

*George*: One of the things our conversations over the course of the year has given me is more insight as to what goes on behind the scenes in the game. It is increasingly more difficult to fathom because, as football has got glossier, I suspect some of the honesty of it has been a little compromised. All the big players now have an image. We got used to the fact that, in the general election, spin-doctors played as big a part as some of the politicians. We expect stories of pop stars and actors to be the product of their publicity departments, fed to the papers to promote records and films. But what about footballers? Just mixing with them suggests that the bad boys may not be as bad as certain people would have us believe, and by the same token, the 'Mr Cleans' are seldom whiter-than-white either. With agents peddling stories to the papers or constructing personas for players to boost their bankability, what we are, the fans, to make of it all?

*Pat*:  I don't think it is just created by those behind the star. The tabloids make their own contribution. They like a player to have an image. They like to pigeon-hole. In the world of the popular press, Gary Lineker is Mr Goody Two-Shoes and Gazza is a beer-swilling yob. They like simple, two-dimensional caricatures.

*George*:  Meeting Gazza for the first time was an education for me. He was so self-effacing and had such a gift for story-telling and humour.

*Pat*:  His humour doesn't translate well to soundbites or to the screen in people's living-rooms. It hinges on having a small audience. There are a lot of in-jokes involved. That can crack team-mates up, but can be totally lost on a more general audience who aren't aware that it is mostly a complex self-parody. Not that television necessarily wants to portray him as anything other than a yob for the most part. But he is very sharp and very creative, and people tend never to see that side of him. He's a great person to have in a club.

*George*:  But not in the house?

*Pat*:  It's very easy for journalists to build a story around a stereotype. It's much easier than probing further.

*George*:  And they've got a few stock 'types', haven't they? There's the violent nutter; the cheeky, chirpy chappie; the clean-cut hero; the troubled gambler/drinker/snorter... and, of course, the tortured intellectual, a category reserved for you along with Iain Dowie, Brian McClair, Gary Mabbutt...

*Pat*:  Yeah, the whole PFA management committee! It's an image I was stuck with early on and I've always laughed at it. I just saw it as me being normal. There's no reason why a player shouldn't see a play by Shakespeare or Chekhov at night. It astonished me that everyone found it so unusual.

*George*:   It tells you something about their own prejudices, doesn't it?

*Pat*:       In some cases. It's true that not many footballers go to the theatre regularly, but then what percentage of the population as a whole does so? I doubt the percentages would be very different. There are simply very few professional footballers. Footballers represent a wide cross-section of the population. Early in my career, instead of self-promotion, I was able to use my image quite successfully to give me a platform on various political issues at the time – the condemnation of apartheid in South Africa, for example.

What annoys me intensely, though, are the manufactured images and as you say, these are creeping into the world of football now as never before.

*George*:   The thing that gets me is that you just don't know the reality anymore. I mean, is Cantona this *Rive Gauche* philosopher-poet that the people behind him would have us believe? Is he just an aggressive battler whose image is wholly fabricated? Unless you have met him, there's really no way to tell. You end up so cynical that the image is entirely manufactured that you ignore the elements of it which may be true.

*Pat*:       It's harder to appreciate for me, being on the inside and having talked to most of these players at close quarters, but I agree. It must be nearly impossible to tell which players are peddling an image and which ones you're seeing as they really are.

To take it away from football, I've got to know Gary Rhodes quite well in the last year or two. Now there, a lot of people would probably think: 'That is a manufactured image. He's too lively, too bouncy, too in love with what he does. He's too good to be true.' But that is absolutely 100 per cent what he's like off-screen, too. I really like him for that. The BBC didn't have to adapt him or turn him into something he wasn't. That is exactly the way he is.

By the same token, you can look at Julian Dicks and ask whether he's really that hard, or if there's an element of that American All-in Wrestling hype to his personality. I have to say I think he probably *is* pretty hard. I wouldn't like to pick a fight with him!

Image can hide a lot of unseen sides of you, though. What is your image of, say, taking a player off the top of my head, Norman Whiteside?

George: I was on a radio show with Jim White, the *Guardian* writer and rabid Man United fan, and he said that Norman was the best player he'd interviewed, because he was a 'top lad and he drank for United'. I guess that's my image of him, too, although I know that he's now a qualified chiropodist. He's incredibly popular in Northern Ireland, where I work a lot – not surprisingly, considering that it was in a Northern Ireland shirt that he became the youngest player ever to play in the World Cup. I'd also add the 'hard man' thing. That was definitely part of the package.

Pat: I'm not surprised he's still popular in Northern Ireland, because he was absolutely and utterly brilliant. This image of the drunken, good-time party lad that he's got would drive any man to drink. I know Norman very well from our Everton days and he's a very, very Christian chap. I've never, ever heard him swear. He has that hard-man tag, but if it wasn't for the injuries he sustained, I'd say he would have been the best all-round player I've ever played with. At Everton, he scored 16 goals in one season from midfield! At that stage, he was 25 and already running out of time due to his injuries. In the two seasons I played with him, I can't remember him losing the ball or giving away possession once – and that includes in training.

I got on very well with him. He's a very intelligent and strong-willed man, and very fair to everyone he deals with. Alright, he *was* a hard player and he *did* like a drink, but it's such a shame that everything else about him is lost in this image that people carry of him as a hard-drinking bruiser. The drinking and any aggression on the pitch were two very small parts of his personality, and they have been blown out of all proportion. I've also heard some people describe him as a 'thick Irishman'. I really would like to take these people to one side and tell them that they've got his image all wrong.

If you're as good as Norman at 17, you must know how brilliant you are – people have criticised his pace, but in his teens he was one of the fastest 100-metre runners in Northern Ireland. If you then sustain injuries in your teens as terrible as those experienced by Norman, before you have reached the peak for which you know you were destined, I think there's a pretty good chance that you'd be driven to the odd drink, too. So I can understand that side, but it is a negligible aspect of what he is like overall.

When things are getting on top of me, it only takes seeing a disabled child or an item about some tragedy on the news to bring me back down to earth and remind me of how lucky I am. One of the things I always remember is doing some shooting practice with my brother-in-law Liam during my spell with Everton. It was lashing with rain, we were ankle-deep in mud and we spent all afternoon firing shots at one another, laughing and joking. It was brilliant fun.

The score was 39–38 or something when I saw someone from the corner of my eye, where there shouldn't have been anyone – I mean, it was a *deluge*. It was Norman with a big coat on, totally soaked through. He had been told by this time that he was finished, that he would never play again. I was 28 or so, but he was only 25.

There was no need to say anything, and words wouldn't have been enough. Our little game just died. That guy would have given anything to join in. He was born with such talent. And he couldn't. That thought always puts my problems in perspective. You can't complain that training is dragging on a bit today when there are people like Norman who would give anything just to be able to kick a ball again. A terrible, terrible waste. If he had reached his true potential, if he'd had a couple more years free of injury, he would have been one of the greatest players these islands have ever produced. I would love to have seen him playing at 32.

It must be heart-breaking for Norman to know that people have the image of him that they have, when he knows how good he was. The vast majority of football supporters haven't seen him at his best – some Man United players and fans have – and I think that's where an unfair image is an awful thing.

*George*: What about your own image?

*Pat*: Well, perhaps I could ask you what image you had of me before we met? It's always difficult for anyone in my position to know what people really make of me. I think I've mentioned this before. Rabbie Burns: *O wad some Pow'r the giftie gie us To see oursels as others see us* . . .

*George*: I guess it was just the image of the consummate articulate player. The image was probably one of the reasons we approached you in the first place. There is no disguising the fact that it was specifically you we wanted for the book. It wouldn't have been quite the same with, say, Duncan Ferguson! Everyone I've mentioned your name to always says: 'Oh, yes! He's very clever, that Pat Nevin.' Joe Kinnear's wife, Bonnie, also said that she admired you for your knowledge of the history of art, which is one of her own interests – I'm not sure whether it's one of Joe's.

There was also the fact that you had been in the game a long time. A player like Gareth Southgate or Noel Whelan, while very articulate, is unlikely to have had the same wealth of experience. There was the 'post-punk footballer' label, as you say, which I've encountered several times. I think the only thing I wasn't sure about was what kind of sense of humour you'd have. But as soon as we met, I knew we were on a similar wavelength. That helped drive the sense that we could do something a little bit different with this book.

*Pat*: You weren't under the impression that I was deeply into Russian literature?

*George*: Not particularly, but I suppose I wouldn't have been greatly surprised to find out that you were . . .

Pat:    All I used to read about myself was the really heavy stuff: that my bedtime reading was Tolstoy and Dostoevsky and that all I ever saw at the cinema were epics by Kurusawa or Jean-Luc Godard retrospectives! I was very concerned that people must have this seriously highbrow image of me. I think that must have made me seem a bit unapproachable and when I *was* approached, people would expect me to talk at great length about the relationship between Raskolnikov and Marmeladov in *Crime and Punishment* or whatever! I'm glad if I've killed that image off a bit in recent years.

George:    I remember the Scottish radio show *Only an Excuse,* which is now on TV every Hogmanay having a laugh at the year's football, and they had the titles of various football autobiographies that people were reading: *Mo – The Mo Johnston Story* by Maurice Johnston, Ally McCoist's *My Story* and *Existentialism My Way* by Pat Nevin.

Pat:    Yes. I enjoyed that, I have to say.

George:    Well, this book may not have been *Existentialism My Way* but I hope it has provided some insights into your mind, and indeed into what it's really like to be a player at a more general level. I hope the readers will have found something new in it.

Pat:    Of course, if this was a traditional footballer's autobiography, we'd have some intensely predictable 'Dream Team' at the end.

George:    We would never stoop to that, though.

# Pat's Dream Team

1  *Albert Camus* (Algeria)

He has been my literary hero these past 18 years and, of course, he played in goal for Algeria.

2  *Stuart Pearce* (Newcastle United and England)

He has been my favourite opponent. Psychologically, he is world-class, never showing emotion and always totally honest. I always had to make sure I was on top of my game when I played against him.

3  *Tony McAndrew* (Chelsea)

When I needed to know how a player should behave and how a team should work, he provided the answer.

4  *Annabel Nevin* (Scotland)

Basically because I think she would look great in a football strip.

5  *John Peel* (Radio One)

Another person I would like to see in a football kit, though for totally different reasons. Also, if he was in the team, the music on the team coach would be unsurpassable.

6  *Vinnie Jones* (Wimbledon and Wales)

For seeing sense and having some compassion by dropping his 'domestic Bosman' case. I absolve thee from all thy sins, my son.

7   *Eric Cantona* (France. Used to play for some side in the North West)

For coming to this country and relieving me of the title 'Number One Arty-Farty Footballer'.

8   *Tommy O'Neil* (Clyde)

A fine player and much like Tony McAndrew. When I needed someone to learn a few things from, he never once gave anything other than a perfect team-orientated example.

9   *Football journalists* (On a free and you're welcome to them)

In particular, all those I stumbled across playing at Chelsea Barracks in 1986. They were absolutely awful to a man, and made me realise that I needn't take a blind bit of notice of anything any of them ever said about me.

10   *Edson = Pele* (Brazil)

Well, you've got to make room for your mates.

11   *Gordon Taylor* (PFA)

The single most important, visionary, skilful, dedicated and honest man involved in English football today.

And as a sub . . .

12   *Jean-Marc Bosman*

He would be on the bench so I could be manager and make him warm up for 89¾ minutes every week before bringing him on, because he has caused me and everyone else so much trouble over the last few years. Maybe it should be his Belgian club that deserves to languish on my bench – but he'll have to do!